THE ACCIDENTS OF STYLE

ALSO BY CHARLES HARRINGTON ELSTER

What in the Word?

The Big Book of Beastly Mispronunciations

Test of Time

Verbal Advantage

There's a Word for It

Tooth and Nail

THE ACCIDENTS OF STYLE

Good Advice on How Not to Write Badly

CHARLES HARRINGTON ELSTER

St. Martin's Griffin ⚏ New York

www.stmartins.com

Library of Congress Cataloging-in-Publication Data

Elster, Charles Harrington.
    The accidents of style : good advice on how not to write badly / Charles Harrington Elster.—1st ed.
        p. cm.
    Includes bibliographical references and index.
    ISBN 978-0-312-61300-6 (alk. paper)
    1. English language—Errors of usage.   2. English language—Usage—Problems, exercises, etc.   3. English language—Style—Problems, exercises, etc.   4. English language—Grammar—Problems, exercises, etc.   I. Title.
    PE1460.E37 2010
    428—dc22

                                                                    2010012012

First Edition: August 2010

10 9 8 7 6 5 4 3 2 1

For Myrna,
con abrazos y besos

The ability to use language is like the ability to drive a car. You can be an excellent driver without knowing the difference between a carburetor and a distributor, but you'd better be able to distinguish the brake from the gas pedal.

—Mark Davidson, *Right, Wrong, and Risky*

It seems astonishing that so much bad writing should find its way into print when so much good advice is to be had.

—Robertson Davies, *The Enthusiasms of Robertson Davies*

It is not, of course, any single violation of meaning or idiom, however frequent, that harms the common property of language. If frequent, the error becomes general—becomes the language—in the traditional way of change. What does harm, now and hereafter, is the loss of the feeling for words, the disappearance of any instinct and any preferences about their formation and combination.

—Jacques Barzun, *A Word or Two Before You Go*

Without minute neatness of execution the sublime cannot exist.

—William Blake, English poet and artist (1757–1827)

Abusus non tollit usum.
"Misuse does not nullify proper use."

CONTENTS

Introduction   1

A Note to the Reader   5

How Accident-Prone Are You?   7

The Accidents of Style   11

Are You Roadworthy?   257

Bibliography   271

Index   275

THE ACCIDENTS OF STYLE

Introduction

In what some have called the greatest match in tennis history, Rafael Nadal defeated Roger Federer to win the 2008 Wimbledon championship. When Federer's final shot failed to clear the net, the elated but exhausted Nadal collapsed on the court.

"The conquering Spanish hero" was "lying prone on the grass," wrote Charles Bricker of the *South Florida Sun Sentinel* in a syndicated report that appeared—its glaring error intact—in scores of other newspapers across America, including my local fishwrap, *The San Diego Union-Tribune*, which ran a photo of Nadal lying flat on his back with his arms stretched out.

What was the error that slipped by all those yawning copyeditors? The misuse of *prone* to mean "lying on one's back." *Prone* means "lying facedown, on one's belly." The word *supine* means "lying on one's back." Rafael Nadal was lying supine on the grass of Wimbledon's center court, but nobody seemed to know it.

You could call this confusion of *prone* with *supine* a slip, a blunder, or, if you want to be fancy, a solecism. If you want to be fancier still, you could use the precise rhetorical term for it: *catachresis*.* Whatever you want to call it, when a sentence hits an icy patch and skids off the road into a tree, I call it an accident of style.

Just like automobile accidents, accidents of style occur all over the English-speaking world, in print and on the Internet, thousands of times every day—not *everyday*, which is an adjective meaning "daily" or "ordinary" and always modifies a noun, as in *everyday life*

---

*Misuse of one word for another, or using the wrong word for the context (pronounced kat-uh-KREE-sis).

or *everyday problems*. (Even the illustrious *New York Times Magazine* is guilty of this blunder. See Accident 1.)

Accidents of style happen when people are merrily writing along and, for one reason or another, fail to observe the rules of the road. Maybe they get distracted and make a wrong turn. Maybe they get too cavalier and lose control. Maybe they've forgotten what the operator's manual says to do, or they never bothered to read it.

As the misuse of *prone* I cited illustrates, accidents of style are not restricted to writing that is hasty or unpolished. They occur in all avenues of communication, from the unsupervised byways of e-mail and blogs to the edited superhighways of newspapers, magazines, and books. Even in the most reputable publications, accidents of style are surprisingly common incidents—not *incidences*, an erroneous plural of *incident* and *instance* that repeatedly runs sentences off the road and into trees.

Accidents of style can happen anywhere, anytime (not *any time*). They can be minor, a fender bender that makes the reader wince for a moment but soldier on, and they can be fatal, a fiery wreck of mangled prose that destroys the writer's credibility and kills the reader's patience. Finally, accidents of style happen to everyone, to the amateur and professional alike—although, as with driving, the experienced writer will have *fewer* accidents while the apprentice writer will, sadly, have *less*.

So what can you do to insure yourself against these accidents of style and ensure that you are a wreckless—not a reckless—writer?

You can learn how not to write badly.

But, you may ask, shouldn't I aspire to write well rather than worry about making mistakes? Shouldn't I study good writing rather than bad? Of course you should, but if you don't know enough about what constitutes bad writing, how can you fully appreciate, much less emulate, what is good?

Anyone who puts words together for any serious purpose wants to make a favorable impression. And the best way to make a favorable impression, in life as well as in writing, is to know first what makes an unfavorable one.

The road to writing well begins with learning how to recognize and correct faulty composition. This book shows you how to steer around the ruts and potholes in that road and safely navigate its hairpin turns. It's a crash course in careful usage. Whether you write for work, for school, for pleasure, or for publication, *The Accidents of Style* will help you avoid hundreds of common word hazards and get the most mileage out of your efforts to drive home what you want to say.

A Note to the Reader

Most books of this kind are arranged either alphabetically, as dictionaries of usage, or in chapters covering various categories—word choice, grammar, spelling, punctuation, and so on. This book takes a different approach.

The Accidents of Style is a meandering road trip along the hazardous highways of English usage, a peripatetic trek for writers of all levels. Your affable tour bus driver (a seasoned cicerone) will cover some rugged linguistic terrain, discussing 350 perilous points of interest along the way. The itinerary proceeds in order of increasing complexity from the rudiments to the punctilios. We will begin with the everyday blunders that trip up inexperienced writers and end with the niceties that nettle the most practiced ones. In short, the road gets trickier to navigate as you go along.

You can use *The Accidents of Style* as a reference, looking up specific topics in the index. Or you can read it linearly as a primer designed to teach you, step by step, how to become a wreckless writer, one who is not prone to accidents of style. For your enjoyment, and perhaps also exasperation, I have included a pretest ("How Accident-Prone Are You?") and a posttest ("Are You Roadworthy?") so you can assess your progress toward wrecklessness, if you are so inclined.

I suggest taking the whole tour first and then using this book as you would a photo album, consulting particular snapshots whenever you need to refresh your memory. But you are the accidental tourist and I am merely the guide. Whether you open *The Accidents of Style* for an excursion or an expedition, a sojourn or an extended stay, I am confident that your journey will be enlightening.

How Accident-Prone Are You?

The following twenty sentences contain 101 common accidents of style. See how many of them you can find—and how many you miss. A score of 90 or better qualifies you as a wreckless writer. The number in parentheses after each sentence shows the number of errors in that sentence. Answers follow the test.

1. Because I can not afford a car, I ride two busses to work every-day. (3)
2. Due to the fact that our hot water heater is broken, we won't be able to run the dishwasher or take showers for awhile. (3)
3. Up until now we didn't know that this bacteria causes the illness, so if people don't want to get sick they better wash there hands. (4)
4. There's a couple things I always think to myself whenever I get bored of a job or disinterested in what I'm doing. (5)
5. Since every one of you are in favor of the proposal, we have a completely unanimous concensus of opinion. (4)
6. Noone informed us that the headaches would re-occur until he felt nauseous. (4)
7. After graduating Yale, a doctorate degree at Harvard became her next goal because she wanted to be an alumni of two of the best schools in the nation. (4)
8. He's one of the only restauranteurs I know who meets that criteria because he has a variety of different skills. (5)
9. Just between you and I, its one of the things that has been both-ering me alot, and I'm not sure how to diffuse the situation. (5)
10. Having said that, at this point in time we will utilize the staff we presently have and we don't anticipate any major restructuring. (6)

11. If your looking for the penultimate summer beach novel, this thrilling story set in ancient Rome in 40 A.D. during the cruel reign of Caligula, offers non-stop entertainment that will keep you laying on that warm sand for hours. (6)

12. If I would've known they would play the exact same background music ad nauseum and make us eat stuff from the kid's menu, I would've worked at the pizzaria instead. (5)

13. He found her infinitesimal energy totally enervating, working in close proximity to her had an incredible affect on him. (7)

14. Today, only one in forty-five Americans routinely bring a reusable bag to the grocery store, but some food industry experts predict that within five years between 20 to 25 percent of all grocery shoppers will emulate these eco-conscious trendsetters. (4)

15. We are a non-profit organization who is dedicated to servicing, as best as we can, indigent and homeless individuals who have fallen between the cracks of society. (6)

16. As the number of divorces continue to soar, it begs the question why so many young women like Sarah and myself are still so anxious to say " 'til death do us part". (6)

17. When mother said, "I don't like that restaurant," my Aunt Dorothy was surprised and said, "But they have a prix fixe menu that includes: soup, salad, entrée, and dessert—and it only costs twenty dollars." (4)

18. After the judges verdict, they were neither reticent to discuss the financial debacle at CoproCorp or loathe to accept responsibility for the havoc they'd wrought. (6)

19. At the risk of repeating myself again, the reason I don't feel badly is because compared to most people I have less problems to keep me awake at night. (5)

20. What it is, basically, is an *homage* to naive youth, a heartwrenching story that hearkens back to that sweet, innocent, childish, moment in each and every one of our lives when we first fell utterly and unequivocably in love. (9)

Answers to "How Accident-Prone Are You?"

1. Three accidents: *can not* should be *cannot; busses* should be *buses; everyday* should be *every day*.

2. Three accidents: *Due to the fact that* is wordy; *hot water heater* should be *water heater; for awhile* should be *for a while*.

3. Four accidents: *Up until now* should be *Until now; bacteria* should be *bacterium; they better* should be *they had better; there* should be *their*.

4. Five accidents: *There's* should be *There are; a couple things* should be *a couple of things; think to myself* should be *think; bored of* should be *bored with; disinterested* should be *uninterested*.

5. Four accidents: *are* should be *is; completely unanimous* is redundant; *consensus* is misspelled; *consensus of opinion* is redundant.

6. Four accidents: *noone* should be *no one; reoccur* is not hyphenated and it is misused for *recur; nauseous* should be *nauseated*.

7. Four accidents: *After graduating Yale* is a dangler; it should be *graduating from Yale; doctorate degree* should be *doctoral degree* or *doctorate; alumni* should be *alumna* or *graduate*.

8. Five accidents: *one of the only* should be *one of the few; restaurateur* is misspelled; *meets* should be *meet; criteria* should be *criterion; variety of different* is redundant.

9. Five accidents: *I* should be *me; its* should be *it's; has* should be *have; alot* should be *a lot; diffuse* should be *defuse*.

10. Six accidents: *Having said that* is misused; *at this point in time* is redundant; *utilize* should be *use; presently* is misused; *anticipate* is misused; *major* is a vogue word.

11. Six accidents: *your* should be *you're; penultimate* is misused; *40 A.D.* should be *A.D. 40;* the comma after *Caligula* is incorrect without an additional comma after *story* to set off the phrase; *nonstop* is not hyphenated; *laying* should be *lying*.

12. Five accidents: *would've known* should be *had known; exact same* should be *same* or *exactly the same; ad nauseam* is misspelled; *kid's menu* should be *kids' menu; pizzeria* is misspelled.

13. Seven accidents: *infinitesimal* is misused; *totally* is adverbiage; *enervating* is misused; the comma should be a period; *close proximity* is redundant; *incredible* is a vogue word; *affect* should be *effect*.

14. Four accidents: Grammatically speaking, *bring* should be *brings*, but using *brings* here instead of *takes* is also a usage error; it should be *between . . . and; emulate* should be *imitate, mimic,* or *follow.*

15. Six accidents: *nonprofit* is not hyphenated; *who* should be *that; servicing* should be *serving; as best as* should be *as best; individuals* should be *people* or *men and women; fallen between the cracks* should be *fallen through the cracks.*

16. Six accidents: *continue* should be *continues; begs the question* is misused; *myself* should be *me; anxious* should be *eager; 'til* should be *till;* the period should be inside the closing quotation marks.

17. Four accidents: *Mother* should be capitalized and it should be *my aunt Dorothy;* there should not be a colon after *includes; only* belongs after *costs,* not before.

18. Six accidents: *judges* should be *judge's* or *judges'; verdict* should be *ruling* or *decision; reticent* is misused for *reluctant;* it should be *neither . . . nor,* not *or; loathe* should be *loath;* havoc is *wreaked,* not *wrought.*

19. Five accidents: *repeat again* is redundant; *the reason . . . is because* is redundant; *feel badly* should be *feel bad; compared to* should be *compared with; less* should be *fewer.*

20. Nine accidents: *What it is . . . is* is an ungainly vogue phrase; *basically* is a vogue filler word; *"an* homage" should be *"a* homage"; *heartwrenching* should be *heartrending; hearkens back* should be *harks back;* there should not be a comma after *childish; childish* is misused for *childlike; each and every* is redundant; it should be *unequivocally,* not *unequivocably.*

THE ACCIDENTS OF STYLE

Every day or *everyday*?

The confusion between *every day* and *everyday* occurs multiple times *every day;* it's an *everyday* accident. Even *The New York Times Magazine* is not immune to it: "As a kid, I had a sailor shirt and the same old corduroy pants, and that's what I wanted to wear everyday." Make that *every day.*

What's the difference? *Every day* is a stand-alone phrase that can fit almost anywhere in a sentence, while *everyday* is an adjective meaning "daily" or "ordinary" that always modifies a noun, as in *everyday life, everyday clothes,* and *everyday problems.*

The trick to getting it right lies in determining whether the phrase can stand by itself ("I think of you *every day*") or whether it is tied to a following noun. If something can be used *every day,* it is suitable for *everyday* use. Some chores must be done *every day,* which makes them *everyday chores.* What's the first line of the song "Everyday Blues"? It's "*Every day* I have the blues," of course.

AMAZING GAFFE

"We see them everyday, animatedly carrying on conversations within visible companions."   —*The San Diego Union-Tribune*

Note how the typographical error *within visible* for *with invisible* turns a logical sentence into a ludicrous one, making it appear that someone is speaking from within the body of someone else. That's certainly not something you're likely to see *every day* (not *everyday*).

ACCIDENT 2

Reckless or *wreckless*?

The proper spelling is *reckless*, with no *w*.

Reckless means "without caution, not caring about consequences, thoughtless, rash." *Wreckless* means you haven't been in a wreck; you have a clean driving record. Wreckless writers obey the rules of the road. Reckless writers have accidents of style.

This rudimentary mistake is surprisingly common: "Moore is also charged with *wreckless* driving" (WVNS-TV, West Virginia). "A petition . . . to end the *wreckless* and inhumane killing of dogs by law enforcement" (*Georgetown News Democrat*, Ohio). "If we were *wreckless*, thoughtless, or disrespectful" (*Glasgow Evening Times*).

ACCIDENT 3

Misuse of *can not* for *cannot*

"*Cannot* should not appear as two words," decrees *Garner's Modern American Usage*, and Mark Davidson, in *Right, Wrong, and Risky*, says, "Depending on which dictionary or usage book you consult, *cannot* is the *only* acceptable form, the *preferred* form, or the form that is by far the more common."

The style manual of *The New York Times* mysteriously does not have an entry for *cannot*. It should, because the first instance of *can not* that I found among more than thirteen thousand hits on Google News was from that newspaper. Other offending sources included *Rolling Stone, Entertainment Weekly*, FOXNews, *The Boston Globe*, and msnbc.com. Too bad the editors there failed to consult the style manual of The Associated Press, which has this terse comment on the matter: "cannot."

So be sure to write *cannot*, not *can not*. The only exception to this dictum, says Garner, is rare: when *can* is part of another construction, such as *not only . . . but also*. Here's an accident-free example from *The Baltimore Sun:* "By improving the way we confirm cases of the H1N1 flu, we can not only reduce public panic but also minimize the number of cases and more efficiently use our limited health resources."

ACCIDENT 4

It's *a lot*, not *alot*—and don't ever write *alittle*

If *alot* were simply a typo, there wouldn't be more than twenty-four hundred hits for it on Google News. Why do so many of us seem to think, in all earnestness, that *a lot* is one word instead of two? Clearly, a lot of people out there are typing *alot* on purpose, and some of them are even typing *alittle* too: "*Alittle* more than a quarter-century ago, the West Pasco Historical Society turned what is now a nearly 100-year-old building into its museum in Sims Park" (tampabay.com, the online edition of the *St. Petersburg Times*). It makes you wonder how long it will be before we start writing like the ancient Romans, withthewordsalltogetherlikethis. Until that woeful day, *a lot* is still two words in standard English, *alot* is an atrocious accident of style, and *alittle* is gibberish.

ACCIDENT 5

It's *no one*, not *noone*

Most of us learned a long time ago that *no one* is not one word. But believe it or not, this basic boo-boo sometimes appears in edited, or at least professionally written, English. For example, an article on the website of a Philadephia TV station reports that "noone is going to be displaced," and the *updated* version of a breaking news brief at the website of a TV station in the San Francisco Bay Area informs us that "police said noone was hurt."

This mistake is distressingly common in postings at newsblogs, where Mr. and Ms. Noone don't seem to care about the poor impression they make when their hastily composed comments contain this and other fourth-grade gaffes.

ACCIDENT 6

Anyway and *any way* are okay, but not *anyways*

You may do something *any way* you want, meaning that you do it in any manner you see fit, or you may do it *anyway*, meaning that you do it regardless or nevertheless. But it's incorrect to do something *anyways* or to begin a statement with *anyways*. Bloggers who write *Anyways, as I was saying, ya just gotta love him anyways* may have readers who love them anyway, but they're not likely to get a lucrative offer from a New York publisher anytime soon.

Misuse of *it's* and *its*

Of the distinction between *it's* and *its*, Constance Hale in *Sin and Syntax* writes, "Learn this or die." You may laugh, but she's not kidding. Confusing *it's* and *its* is a fatal accident of style, the grammatical equivalent of a head-on collision with a Hummer at sixty-five miles an hour.

Thankfully this accident occurs mostly in informal, unedited writing, whose readers may be more forgiving of such glaring mistakes. But it does occasionally happen in reputable media outlets, and when it does you can almost hear the earsplitting screech of brakes followed by the horrible crunch of metal: "Its [*It's*] a tool that doesn't cost billions of dollars" (*Los Angeles Times*); "Harrigan said he expects big car companies to bring battery tech in-house within the next few years, as GM wants to do for it's [*its*] Chevy Volt" (*BusinessWeek*); "The 100-year-old theatre is a beauty too with it's [*its*] elegant creamy gold colouring" (*New Zealand Herald*); "Its [*It's*] a shame it has to be that way" (KOMU-TV, Missouri).

Yes, it's a shame indeed when people write *Its a shame. It's* with an apostrophe is a contraction and means "it is" (or "it has")—that's what *it's* all about. *Its* without an apostrophe is the possessive form of *it*, and mastering *its* proper use is *its* own reward.

If you're still feeling an itsy bit ditzy about this distinction, here's a mnemonic sentence for you: If a Hummer is heading toward you, *it's* wise not to get in *its* way.

Misspelling of *accidentally, incidentally,* and *coincidentally*

We rarely misspell *fundamentally, departmentally, supplementally, monumentally,* and *temperamentally,* so why do we so often misspell *accidentally, incidentally,* and *coincidentally* with *-ly* at the end instead of *-ally*? It could be the lure of false analogy with words like *evidently,*

eminently, and *intently,* but more likely it's a case of spelling following pronunciation.

Many speakers condense the -*ally* at the end of these words
into a single syllable. Instead of saying *uh-lee,* as they would with
fundamentally (fun-duh-MENT-uh-lee) or *monumentally* (mahn-
yuh-MENT-uh-lee), they say *lee:* ak-suh-DENT-lee; in-suh-DENT-
lee; koh-in-suh-DENT-lee.

There is nothing wrong with this condensed pronunciation; it's
an example of *syncope* (SING-kuh-pee), the loss or omission of a
syllable in the middle of a word, as when we say *chocolate, grocery,*
and *family* in two syllables instead of three. Just be careful not to let
the syncopated pronunciation become the model for your spelling.
Remember, there's an *ally* (uh-lee) at the end of *accidentally, incidentally,* and *coincidentally.*

ACCIDENT 9
Gasses or gases?
From the *Chicago Tribune:* "Research balloons chase volcanic gasses." From the online *National Geographic News:* "A composite im-
age of Messier 83 reveals the shining stars and red hydrogen gasses
of the 'Thousand-Ruby Galaxy.'" Did these estimable sources get
the spelling of the plural of *gas* right or wrong?

Wrong. Though some dictionaries recognize *gasses* (dictionaries
will list anything if people use it enough), *Garner's Modern American
Usage,* perhaps the most respected style guide in print, is unequivocal: "*gases,* not *gasses,* is the plural form of the noun *gas.*" The variant
with two *s*'s is probably a mistaken analogy with the plural of words
that end in double *s: pass(es), miss(es), mass(es), lass(es),* etc.

Watch out for *busses* in Accident 25.

ACCIDENT 10
Confusion between *your* and *you're*
It happens to all of us at some point. Even the least accident-prone
among us will get blindsided by this blunder. You're typing away
furiously on your keyboard when suddenly *you're* (*your!*) fingers are
not quite sure what *your* (*you're!*) doing and they rebel. And despite

you're (*your!*) best efforts, those mutinous fingers start typing *your* for *you're* and *you're* for *your,* and soon *your* at *you're* wit's end. And of course the stupid spell-checker is no help because it was created by a software programmer that Bill Gates managed to clone from a piece of bellybutton lint.

There are two ways to handle this crisis. You can dismiss it like the cavalier contributor to the *Hartford Courant* blogs who wrote, "When your a 'genious' like me, you can spell it any way you want." Or you can stop texting and tweeting for ten seconds and wrap your recalcitrant thumbs around these two words: *spelling matters.*

Yes, believe it or not, people judge you by the words you misuse— even in the casual atmosphere of e-mail and the blogosphere. If you want to be taken seriously by anyone who takes verbal expression seriously—especially teachers, employers, clients, and customers— you must never let anything you write be seen by others until you have purged it of your missteps, particularly any confusion between *your* and *you're.*

If you sometimes have trouble remembering that *your* is the possessive form of *you* and *you're* is a contraction of *you are,* try to memorize this: *It's* your *life, and* you're *the master of it.* You're *in control, so do* your *best.*

ACCIDENT 11
Confusion of *there, their,* and *they're*
"There is no there there," wrote Gertrude Stein in a rare moment of lucidity at the end of one of her notoriously incoherent sentences. At least she didn't write *There is no their they're* and cause a three-car accident of style.

There refers to place or position (*over there*); *their* refers to possession (*their house*); and *they're* is a contraction of *they are* (*they're going over there to their house*). Reckless writers, especially Internet journalists and bloggers, sometimes dreadfully confuse these three homophones: "People need to have there [*their*] own plan in place" (communitycommon.com); "Whether those young adults view what their [*they're*] doing as 'banking' remains to be seen" (Information week.com); "Sci-fi fans will feel right at home with the classic plot involving man's desire to exploit the aliens for they're [*their*] own selfish goals" (*Firefox News*).

ACCIDENT 12

There's does not mean "there are"

There's is a contraction of the words *there is* (or *there has*). Although in casual speech it's not unusual to hear people use *there's* to mean *there are*—"Hey, *there's*, like, only two doughnuts left in the box"—in any writing meant for public consumption this usage is a sign of slovenliness, or perhaps evidence of a perverse belief that, good grammar be damned, we should write in the same lazy way we talk.

"*There's* many good things about No Child Left Behind," writes a candidate for city council in an interview at DesMoinesRegister .com. "*There's* a few local places they still want to play," writes Andrew Cothern in the online edition of the *Richmond Times-Dispatch*. "*There's* only about three mentions of me from a total of over a million results," writes Gregory Bergman in his book *BizzWords*. And a pullout in an op-ed piece in *The New York Times* proclaims, "*There's* enough lousy drivers already."

As these quotations illustrate, there are enough careless wordslingers out there already. *There's* is not "more natural" than *there are*. It's just sloppy. There are no good excuses for it, and there's nothing to be gained by it. When you mean *there are*, write *there are*.

And while we're at it, the same advice goes for *here's*, which is sometimes paired with a plural noun: "Here's two stories you'll never forget!" (real-estate ad headline); "Need to replace Manny? Here's some suggestions" (headline at newsday.com). Make that *Here are two stories* and *Here are some suggestions*.

ACCIDENT 13

The pandemic confusion between *lay* and *lie*, yet again exposed and denounced

Most people today, including many professional writers and editors, simply have no idea how to conjugate these everyday verbs properly.

Misusing *lay* for *lie* is surely the most prevalent accident of style in the English language, and despite the preventive measures proffered by scores of style guides, the collision rate continues to rise.

To use *lay* and *lie* wrecklessly, the first thing you must do is memorize these two sentences: *To **lay** is to put or place. To **lie** is to come to rest, recline.*

If you are not putting or placing something, you cannot use *lay.* That's why *I laid in bed, I laid down for a nap, I was just laying there,* and *I have laid in that bed before* are all wrong and make you out to be a chicken who deposits fat, fresh eggs in your bed.

Here's how the verbs are conjugated:

*To **lay** is to put or place:*
You lay *the book on the table.*
You are laying *the book on the table.*
You laid *the book on the table.*
You have laid *the book on the table.*

*To **lie** is to come to rest, recline:*
You lie *on the bed.*
You are lying *on the bed.*
You lay *on the bed.*
You have lain *on the bed.*

You see how the present tense of *lay* is the same as the past tense of *lie?* That's where all the trouble starts. You can't tell a dog to *lay down* (that means *put down*), but you can say you *lay* in bed (you reclined there in the past). Confused by this, people compound the problem by misusing the past tense of *lay* (which is *laid*) for the past tense of *lie* (which is *lay*); for example, *I laid in bed last night.* There's that chicken again.

I know it may be tough for you to keep these two verbs straight, especially when so many educated people around you are confounding them. But I exhort you not to chicken out. It's worth the effort. Properly distinguishing *lay* and *lie* will distinguish you as a careful user of the language, a cultivated person just a cut above the rest.

ACCIDENT 14

It's spelled *ecstasy*, not *ecstacy*

There is no *Stacy* in *ecstasy*. The misspelling with two *c*'s is common, but even your spell-checker can catch it.

ACCIDENT 15

Misuse of *imply* for *infer*

To *imply* is to hint or suggest rather than say something outright: *Her statement implies support for his proposal.* To *infer* is to use one's power of reasoning to come to a conclusion based on evidence: *He inferred from her statement that she supported his proposal.*

You may *infer* (come to a conclusion, derive a meaning) from something *implied* (hinted at, suggested, stated indirectly). But don't use *infer* when you mean *imply:* "Overnight, the McCain campaign created a new TV ad that puts Obama's remark next to one of Palin's comments, inferring [*implying*] that Obama was responding to her with a sexist barb" (voanews.com). This is the stylistic equivalent of driving through a stop sign while talking on your cellphone.

Here are (not *here's*) three more examples of the reckless (not *wreckless*) use of *infer* to mean "suggest" or "hint": "In recounting the inning, Lugo seemed to infer [*imply*] that the balls weren't playable" (*Boston Herald*); "Listing on this publication does not infer [*imply*] an endorsement by Hot Springs National Park" (National Park Service flier); "Charter claims the DirecTV ads infer [*imply*] that Charter's recent bankruptcy filing means Charter will soon go under" (BroadbandReports.com).

Thankfully, most writers, like most drivers, follow the rules of the road and use *infer* to mean "to come to a conclusion based on evidence," thus avoiding the verbal equivalent of a head-on collision. For your own safety you are hereby advised to heed the example of Paul Snyder, who, in reviewing the 2009 movie *Star Trek* for the *Huffington Post*, both correctly and perspicaciously writes, "We can *infer* that Spock gets laid."

ACCIDENT 16

There is no *ex-* in *espresso*

Did you know that if people misuse a word often enough, the mistake will eventually find its way into the dictionaries? That's because lexicographers (otherwise known as dictionary editors) are a curious bunch, not so different from the folks who slow down to gawk at a gruesome accident on the highway. When our words hit the guardrail or rear-end each other, the lexicographic paparazzi are always there to record it for their grisly files. And if enough of us run the same red light, you can bet your BMW they will feature the infraction in the next lurid edition of their dictionary.

That's the bad news. The good news is that some lexicographers, like the more civilized drivers on the road, will politely avert their gaze from all the twisted metal and gore, and every once in a while you'll find a dictionary coming to the rescue after an accident of style. In its entry for *espresso*, *The New Oxford American Dictionary* courageously flips on the Mars light and siren and calls the spelling *expresso* and the pronunciation ik-SPRES-oh "incorrect," a label that dictionary editors who are still willing to issue citations reserve for the most heinous linguistic crimes.

Any experienced usage cop will tell you what these namby-pamby dictionaries won't: If you misspell it *expresso* and pronounce it with an *x*, you're a drunk driver going the wrong way down a one-way street. If you spell it *espresso* and pronounce it es-PRES-oh, you'll never get pulled over or pay higher premiums.

ACCIDENT 17

Misuse of an objective pronoun as the subject of a sentence

I gasped when I came across this semiliterate sentence in the *Washington City Paper:* "Her and her child both die from the illness." The objective pronouns *her, him,* and *me* cannot function as the subject of a sentence. It's terribly, terribly wrong to say or write *Me and my friend are going out, Him and his wife are coming over,* or *Her and her child both died.* Those sentences need a pronoun in the nominative case: *my friend and I; he and his wife; she and her child.*

ACCIDENT 18
It's that big *a* problem, not that big *of a* problem
"California wouldn't have this problem (or at least this big of a
problem) . . . if it hadn't increased its spending by forty percent
since 2003" (*The Atlantic* online). And that sentence wouldn't be an
accident of style if the writer hadn't inserted *of* after *big*, turning the
idiomatic phrase *this big a problem* into the nonstandard *this big of a
problem*.

This superfluous *of*, writes Mark Davidson in *Right, Wrong, and
Risky*, occurs "in phrases beginning with *how, that*, or *too* followed
by an adjective." So remember, no matter *how* smart *of* a person or
how nice *of* a person you are, you won't be considered *that* good *of* a
writer as long as you think the intrusive *of* is not *too* big *of* a deal.

ACCIDENT 19
Write *off*, not *off of*
"There have been Russian submarines patrolling off of the U.S. east
coast" (bestsyndication.news). *Of* is unnecessary in that sentence.
In polished writing, a cat gets *off* the couch, not *off of* it; people live *off*
the land, not *off of* it; and you take a ring *off* your finger, not *off of* it.

ACCIDENT 20
Avoid *please be advised that*
Unless you want to sound like a stuffy lawyer or self-important
bureaucrat, do not use the phrase *please be advised that*, especially at
the beginning of a letter. It adds nothing but useless words to your
sentence, and it puts the reader on alert that what follows may also
be wordy and pretentious. Deleting *please be advised that* from a sentence takes two seconds, eliminates twenty pounds of dead weight,
and causes no syntactical harm: "~~Please be advised that~~ failure to get
either of these in by this date will result in an automatic disqualifica-
tion for the season." "Should you not hear from us within 7 days, then
~~please be advised that~~ your application has not been successful."

Also avoid the similarly stiff and stuffy *This is to inform you that*
as an opener. Usually it needs no substitute wording and can simply
be deleted: "~~This is to inform you that~~ after 10 years of running the

Club the time has come for me to stand down as Chief Executive" (Grays Athletic press release).

It's spelled *all right*, not *alright*

"A sound case could be made for shortening *all right* to *alright*, as many informal users of English do already," says *Bryson's Dictionary of Troublesome Words*. "English, however, is a slow and fickle tongue, and *alright* continues to be looked on as illiterate and unacceptable, and consequently it ought never to appear in serious writing."

I hasten to add that *alright* should also never appear in less serious writing, the kind that tries to be serious while affecting a breezy, informal tone—which is to say, much of what passes for online journalism and commentary these days. Yet, judging by the deluge of hits on Google News, *alright* does appear with alarming frequency in writing that doesn't take itself seriously enough. It is often used in headlines and titles—"Wednesday night is alright [*all right*] for fighting" (*Los Angeles Times* blogs); "Are the Kids Alright [*All Right*]?" (*People* magazine)—and in quotations, perhaps to make them seem more casual: "I'm pretty sure by the time we get to training camp we'll be alright [*all right*]" (newsday.com).

As if that weren't bad enough, some writers toss a gratuitous *alright* into an otherwise law-abiding sentence to make it sound more relaxed and colloquial. The result is never good: "*Alright*, I'm all for taking precautions and being hyper-vigilant whenever a potentially dangerous situation arises" (*Huffington Post*); "Amazon's new Kindle DX is bigger, *alright*, but is it better?" (*Chicago Sun-Times* online). In these examples, even if the writers had spelled the word properly it wouldn't have been all right.

It's *intact*, not *in tack*

Yes, this accident of style actually occurs in edited writing: "Keeping the fan folds *in tack*, place medium to large rubber bands every 1 to 2 inches apart" (*Detroit Free Press*); "Hanna Seifert then kept her unbeaten record *in tack*" (*Waikato Times*, New Zealand). The misrendering of *intact* in print may be a by-product of the mispronunciation in-TAK, which omits the final *t*.

ACCIDENT 23
It's *have run* and *have gone*, not *have ran* and *have went*

The erroneous *have ran* and *have went* are rare in edited writing. But they are rife just about everywhere else. I have heard native English speakers of all backgrounds and levels of education say *should have ran* and *could have went*. I have heard this solecism spill from the lips of broadcasters, high-level administrators, and executives, and even from some teachers, lawyers, and a few of my fellow writers. Search *have ran* and *have went* on the Internet and you will get well more than half a million hits for these illiteracies, most of them linking to extemporaneous posts and amateur, unsponsored blogs. "Where have all the flowers gone?" sang Pete Seeger back in the sixties. In 2010 I'm wondering, "Where has our good grammar gone?" I'm afraid it appears to *have went*.

The *have ran* and *have went* blunders stem from a misunderstanding of how to conjugate the irregular verbs *run* and *go*. Regular verbs are generally easy to conjugate because they change their form—from present to past to past participle—according to a predictable pattern: *you walk, you walked, you have walked; you love, you loved, you have loved; you study, you studied, you have studied*. But irregular verbs in English can have unusual patterns: *I sing, I sang, I have sung; I sleep, I slept, I have slept; I write, I wrote, I have written; I grow, I grew, I have grown*. And sometimes they have entirely unpredictable patterns: *we eat, we ate, we have eaten; we read, we read, we have read; we slay, we slew, we have slain*. The irregular verbs *run* and *go* fall into the unpredictable category: *they run, they ran, they have run; they go, they went, they have gone*.

Blunders occur when people try to make these unpredictably conjugated verbs follow more predictable patterns. So they say *I run, I ran,* and *I have ran* instead of *I have run*, and *I go, I went,* and *I have went* instead of *I have gone*. The human impulse to make things more orderly is natural and commendable, but in this case the result is a grammatical disaster. *Have ran* and *have went* are lethal accidents of style, tantamount to parking your car on the tracks ahead of an on-coming train. The only way to avoid them is to memorize the proper conjugations: *run, ran, have run; go, went, have gone.*

ACCIDENT 24
It's *have drunk,* not *have drank*

"Obama's Beer Summit: What Kind of Beer Would You Have Drank?" asks the headline at AssociatedContent.com. As the search engine at Google News likes to say when your fingers stumble over the keys like besotted sailors on shore leave, "Did you mean 'What kind of beer would you have *drunk?*'"

When you've had something to drink—whether it's plain water or whiskey neat—you *have drunk* it. To say or write *have drank* is a clear signal to the language police that you've exceeded the legal limits of the English language and your grammar needs to sober up. These woozy sentences should never have seen print: "According to reports, Toyota is working on a way to lock your ignition if the driver has drank [*drunk*] too much" (*The Post Chronicle,* New Jersey); "Normally, Steve doesn't care for coffee, but in this case he probably would have drank [*drunk*] an entire pot" (*The Post-Journal,* New York); "The Auld Dubliner has doormen who will assist in walking out clientele who have drank [*drunk*] too much" (*Arizona Daily Wildcat*).

ACCIDENT 25
It's spelled *buses,* not *busses*

Buses, with one *s* in the middle, are large motor vehicles. *Busses,* with two *s*'s in the middle, are kisses. That's all there is to it, despite what you might see in your dictionary—which, no doubt, unhelpfully lists both *buses* and *busses* as acceptable plurals of *bus.* Why do dictionaries sanction both forms? Because, as any dictionary editor will tell you, *busses* appears frequently in edited prose, including badly edited prose (a distinction dictionary editors refuse to make).

What your dictionary and its editors won't tell you is what you most need to know and what you can easily find out with a quick search on Google News: *buses,* the proper plural, is almost thirty times more common in edited prose than *busses*. Style-guide prescriptions aside, that's reason enough to prefer *buses* for the vehicles and reserve *busses* for osculation.

AMAZING GAFFE

"It's a battle that may never have a clear winner, but for the residents who live there, it's one worth fighting." —Angela Lau, *The San Diego Union-Tribune*

Perhaps the residents who *don't* live there pick their battles more carefully. The writer apparently forgot that a resident is a person who lives in a particular place.

ACCIDENT 26
It's *by accident*, not *on accident*
Using *on* with *accident* is a fourth-grade accident of style that is starting to creep into adult writing. Things don't happen *on chance* or *on accident*; they happen *by chance* and *by accident*.

ACCIDENT 27
Confusion between *whose* and *who's*
Who's is a contraction of *who is: Guess who's coming to dinner? Who's the fairest of them all? Whose* is possessive, indicating ownership or connection: "A guy whose muscle is for hire" (*Detroit Free Press*); "Whose art is Katrina art? (*Christian Science Monitor*).

The reckless writer, *whose* sense of grammar and spelling may be shaky and *who's* writing with little regard for typos and brain cramps, will sometimes bungle this elementary distinction: "Whose [*who's*] holding their hands?" (voicesnewspaper.com); "Carlson, who's [*whose*] father Tom played golf at Viator" (*Chicago Daily Herald*).

ACCIDENT 28
It's *for a while,* not *for awhile*

Miswriting *for a while* as two words (*for awhile*) rather than three is one of the most common accidents of style. A search on Google News yielded more than thirty-five hundred hits for the erroneous two-word version in *The Washington Post, Dallas Morning News, San Francisco Chronicle, San Jose Mercury News, Boston Globe,* and other respected publications.

In *for a while, while* is a noun meaning "a period of time." *Awhile* is an adverb meaning "for a while, for a brief period of time." You can *stay for a while* or *stay awhile, rest for a while* or *rest awhile,* but it is redundant and ungrammatical to *stay for awhile* or *rest for awhile* because *awhile* means "for a time."

ACCIDENT 29
Don't *think to yourself*—just *think*

Unless you're thinking out loud in the presence of others—in which case you are technically speaking your thoughts, not thinking them—you always think *to yourself.* There is no other way to think. But, perhaps because of the lyric that Louis Armstrong popularized ("And I think to myself, what a wonderful world"), writers are often tempted by this pleonasm:* " 'Maybe they're actually ahead by now,' I think to myself" (*New York Daily News*). Delete *to myself* and just *think.* The same goes for the pleonastic variations *think in my head* and *wonder to myself:* "It did get hot out and I couldn't help but wonder to myself [*wonder*] why there were no vendors" (*Arizona Silver Belt*).

ACCIDENT 30
Misuse of *amount* for *number*

Would you say *the amount of people at the party* or *the number of people at the party?* Would you say *the amount of things I have to do* or

---

*Every writer should know the word *pleonasm* (PLEE-uh-naz'm). It means "the use of words whose omission would leave one's meaning intact" (*Webster's New International Dictionary,* 2nd ed.).

the number of things I have to do? If you chose *number,* then you've called the right number. If you chose *amount,* you won't amount to much unless you follow my advice about this common accident of style.

Number refers to things that can be counted, itemized, or enumerated—in other words, considered separately or individually. We speak of the *number* of people at an event, a *number* of things to do, a *number* of problems to solve, the *number* of items in a bag, the *number* of papers on your desk, the *number* of dollars in your wallet, the *number* of volts in an electric current, and the *number* of errors in a book (not this one, please!).

Amount refers to things that are considered collectively—in other words, as a mass or whole. We speak of the *amount* of sugar in a recipe, the *amount* of trouble we are having, the *amount* of time something takes, the *amount* of money or cash you have, the *amount* of food we buy, and the *amount* of paper on your desk.

In short, if you can count it or if it's composed of separate items, use *number: the number of letters we received; the number of words she wrote.* If you consider it as a whole—even if it's composed of separate items, such as letters or words—use *amount: the amount of mail we received; the amount of text she has to edit.*

Writers and editors continually have trouble with this basic distinction, misusing the noncountable *amount* for the countable *number:* "That was the lowest number of firms in 15 years and the smallest amount [*number*] of dollars since the first quarter of 2003" (*Denver Business Journal*); " 'This is the best budget that I've had the opportunity to vote on,' Slossberg said, adding that the package included the highest amount [*number*] of spending cuts and the lowest amount [*number*] of tax increases among the various Democratic budgets" (*Hartford Courant*).

ACCIDENT 31
Misuse of *loose* for *lose*
The verb to *lose* rhymes with *booze* and the adjective *loose* rhymes with *goose,* and I've never heard a native speaker of English mispronounce these words. But I've seen lots of loose sentences, not a few

composed by college-educated professionals, lose control and crash horribly because *loose* was miswritten for *lose*.

You don't have to look hard to find this accident of style; I got 91,000 hits on Google Web for *loose everything* and 303,000 for *nothing to loose*. I also found this blunderful sentence posted at politico .com, in which the writer managed to commit four errors (not counting writing in capital letters): "YES SENATOR'S YOU CAN LOOSE YOUR SEATS IN THE USCONGRESS."* (It's a wonder he didn't also write *you're* for *your* and *seat's* for *seats*.)

But *loose*-for-*lose* is hardly confined to semiliterate or unedited writing. The mistake often wrecks a sentence that someone was paid to write: "People who were more conscious about their size were more likely to loose [*lose*] weight than those who did not. Nevertheless, the research also discovered that happier people were less likely to succeed at loosing [*losing*] weight" (topnews.us); "Tweets are stored on the device so you can keep reading even if you loose [*lose*] your phone signal" (independent.co.uk).

Spell-checkers won't catch this error, so you must be a vigilant proofreader. And it may help to remember that when you lose something, it is *lost*—with one *o*, not two.

ACCIDENT 32
Confusion between *affect* and *effect*

Because the words *affect* and *effect* are pronounced alike—with a schwa, or indistinct vowel, in the first, unstressed syllable—they are frequently confused in print. If you have trouble keeping these words straight, you must begin by remembering that *affect* is a verb meaning "to influence" while *effect* is usually a noun meaning "a result." Memorize this sentence, keeping in mind that *a* comes before *e:* "If you *a*ffect something, there will be an *e*ffect."

The most common mistake is using *effect* to mean "to influence": "It's going to effect [*affect*] businesses, it's going to effect [*affect*]

---

* (1) *Senator's* should be *senators;* (2) *senators* should be set off with commas: *Yes, senators, you;* (3) *loose* should be *lose;* and (4) *USCONGRESS* should be *U.S. Congress.*

schools, and we're going to have a much higher rate in the community" (WCBG-TV, South Carolina); "It is too early to tell how the scandal will effect [*affect*] Huron as an ongoing business" (*Chicago Tribune*); "He says the papers must discuss how gay and heterosexual couples are effected [*affected*] by California's ban" (*San Jose Mercury News*).

So to *affect* is to influence and an *effect* is a result. That's simple enough. But things get trickier when *effect* is used as a verb meaning "to bring about, accomplish, produce a specific result." This use of *effect* as a verb is correct: "But he is not seen as someone who will *effect* change" (*The New York Times*). In this example, *affect* ("to influence") is misused for *effect* ("bring about"): "Rep. Bob Filner . . . said he expects San Diegans will have a chance to see 'some of the polarization that this process has affected [*effected*]'" (*The San Diego Union-Tribune*). When something is *effected*, brought about, accomplished, people are *affected*, influenced, by it.

The verb to *affect* is also sometimes used to mean "to make a pretense of, pretend to be or have": "In her bright orange tube top, denim mini and towering stilettos, Lucretia Williams was doing her best to *affect* a steely urban chic" (*The New York Times*). The corresponding adjective is *affected*, "artificial, fake, pretentious," as *an affected accent*, and the corresponding noun is *affectation*, "a false or pretentious display."

To sum up: One thing can *affect* (influence) another, and when it does there is an *effect* (result) that has been *effected* (brought about). If something you *effect* (accomplish) is *affected* (fake, artificial), you may find that how you *affected* (influenced) others did not produce the desired *effect* (result).

ACCIDENT 33

Be careful with *very*

Isn't *be careful* a firmer admonition without *very* wedged in the middle? Use *very* sparingly, says *The Elements of Style*. "Where emphasis is necessary, use words strong in themselves." That's ~~very~~ good advice.

ACCIDENT 34
Avoid the lazy, mechanical use of *basically*

Columnist David Lazarus of the *Los Angeles Times* writes, "Here's the deal: Banks are basically saying that because they're going to have to change some lending practices to comply with the bill, they'll be facing greater risk."

And here's my deal: What purpose does *basically* serve in that sentence? What meaning does it convey? Is there a difference between *basically* doing something and just doing it?

"The trouble with this word, basically, is that it is almost always unnecessary," says *Bryson's Dictionary of Troublesome Words.* In speech, *basically* is annoying—especially when used as a sentence-opener—but forgivable; after all, to err is basically human. In writing, however, *basically* is sentence padding, a vague and useless filler word, a red flag that says the writer can't be bothered to remove extraneous matter. Basically, *basically* is really pretty much like *really* and *pretty much:* superfluous and inappropriate in polished prose.

Ask yourself if the following sentences would in any way be harmed by the deletion of *basically:* "He'll raise gas-mileage standards by 40 percent, *basically* accelerating new rules put in place during the Bush administration" (*U.S. News & World Report*); "That *basically* means smaller cars with very expensive new technology" (RealClearPolitics.com); "Kobe Doin' Work is *basically* an infomercial disguised as a movie" (CBSSports.com); "Nobody can provide the consistency that Buehrle provides, something Ozzie Guillen *basically* admitted after the game" (ESPN.com). I suppose you could substitute *essentially* for *basically* in these examples, but why?

Sometimes a lazy writer tries to make *basically* stand in for *almost, nearly,* or *practically,* a usage that is also inept: "Diagnosed with MS in 1981, she had tried *basically* every medication designed to treat the disease" (*Chicago Tribune*); "Before 1987, such complaints were *basically* unheard of" (*Seattle Post-Intelligencer*). *Basically* may stand in for *fundamentally* (as in *human nature is basically good* or *the process is basically sound*), but you are usually better off using the more precise *fundamentally* when that is what you mean.

Thoughtless use of *basically* is like a fender bender caused by gross inattention—as when the driver is text-messaging, fiddling with the CD player, or trying to retrieve a french fry that has fallen to the floor. It is surely one of the most easily avoidable accidents of style. To paraphrase Mark Twain, when you see a *basically,* kill it.

WHEN YOU SEE AN ADVERB, KILL IT

Mark Twain once wrote, "When you see an adjective, kill it." I confess I like adjectives, and capital punishment for this part of speech strikes me as a draconian editorial sentence. Adjectival overindulgence is but a misdemeanor meriting a few sound thwacks with a blue pencil. But adverbs—now there's another matter. Adverbs on the loose can be downright dangerous. Whenever you consort with adverbs, take my advice and carry a loaded firearm.

Adverbiage is the word I have used (since about 1990) for the overuse or awkward use of adverbs, words that modify verbs and tell you how an action is performed. Most, though not all, adverbs end in *-ly.* For example, in *they listened carefully, carefully* is the adverb modifying the verb to *listen.* In *he used the word properly, properly* is the adverb modifying the verb to *use.*

There is nothing inherently wrong with adverbs—as you can see from my pointed use of *inherently* in that statement. Adverbs can perform a useful service in expressing nuances of quality or manner. But adverbiage occurs when the adverb is part of a cliché or hackneyed phrase; when it is an awkward creation, such as *friendlily, sillily, consideredly,* and *opinionatedly;* or when adverbs are overused, as in this sentence: "The report *clearly* states that the *only thoroughly* and *completely* effective method for increasing sales *rapidly* is to *competitively* engineer and *efficiently* market our products." That horrendous utterance commits all three errors—hackneyed use, awkward use, and overuse. One *totally* has to wonder how anyone can write so *uglily.*

In *Simple and Direct,* Jacques Barzun offers these examples of adverbial clichés: *to seriously consider, to utterly reject, to thoroughly examine, to be absolutely right, to make perfectly clear,* and *to sound definitely interested.* In each case the adverb is superfluous; nothing is lost by removing it. In fact, each phrase is strengthened as a result. *I will consider it* conveys more promise of serious attention than *I will seriously consider it. I reject the allegation* is firmer and more confident than *I utterly reject the allegation. To be right* is unimpeachable compared with *to be absolutely right,* which suggests that there are degrees of rightness. And *let me make one thing clear* is a stronger statement than *let me make one thing perfectly clear* because inserting the adverb *perfectly* makes you sound either condescending or defensive.

Good, tight writing has no unnecessary words. The aspiring stylist ~~quickly~~ learns to ~~mercilessly~~ cut them out, and the first ones to go are adverbs.

ACCIDENT 35

There is no e between *g* and *m* in *judgment*, *acknowledgment*, and *abridgment*

In British English there's an *e* between the *g* and *m* in these words: *judgement, acknowledgement, abridgement.* But in American English we shorten things to *gm: judgment, acknowledgment, abridgment.*

ACCIDENT 36

Write *could have, should have, would have,* not *could of, should of, would of*

Say *could have, should have, would have* aloud quickly, as you would in conversation, and you will hear *could of, should of, would of.* You can faithfully and acceptably represent this pronunciation by writing the contractions *could've, should've, would've.* But if you write what you have spoken as it sounds, with *of* instead of the abbreviated *'ve* for *have,* you will have committed an inexcusable accident of style.

Using the semiliterate *of* after *could, should,* and *would* is unforgivable in any kind of writing—including blogs, posts, and e-mail, where it commonly appears. And to those journalists who are infatuated with all things colloquial and think it's jocular and endearing to use the spellings *coulda, shoulda, woulda,* I issue this caveat: An exceptional stylist can make lowbrow writing work, but if you're not an exceptional stylist, don't experiment with colloquialized spellings. It annoys editors and it can strike readers as either ignorant or condescending.

For example, consider this sentence written by a theater critic for the *Cleveland Plain Dealer:* "But if it's drama you crave, you shoulda [*should've*] been at the Palace Theatre in PlayhouseSquare on Tuesday when the tour of the Mel Brooks schlocker almost didn't open a two-week Cleveland run." The only thing this deliberate use of the nonstandard *shoulda* tells readers is that they are in the hands of an incompetent or patronizing writer. What readers crave is writing that respects their intelligence, not writing that mimics their vulgarisms.

ACCIDENT 37
Pair is not a proper plural
We often hear and read *pair* used as a plural: *three pair of socks.* This usage is no longer standard, and in careful writing *pairs* is the preferred plural.

ACCIDENT 38
Don't grow *grow*
A transitive verb directs its action on an object. An intransitive verb just acts, without affecting anything directly. We live, work, and play intransitively, but we cook food, do chores, and make money transitively.

The verb to *grow* can be intransitive (*a child grows*) or transitive (*they grow tomatoes*). Traditionally, the transitive *grow* has been used only of plants and of things (such as hair and nails) that grow on people or animals. In recent years, however, *grow* has been applied to abstract things that increase their size figuratively rather than literally. For example, we now hear of people *growing* their businesses, *growing* their assets, and even *growing* their vocabularies. This trendy use of *grow* is eccentric and smacks of business jargon. Careful writers should avoid it.

ACCIDENT 39

Misspelling and misuse of *forward* and *foreword*

In my years of service as an ELP (English Language Patrol) officer, I have seen so many wrecked sentences and mangled words that even the most grisly accident of style no longer shocks me. But when my editor at St. Martin's Press, Daniela Rapp, told me that she frequently sees the words *forward* and *foreword* confused in book proposals submitted to her by published authors, it took me the rest of the day to reattach my jaw.

It strains credibility that professional writers could make such an elementary mistake, but, sadly, they do. It's not that they don't know that *forward* means "ahead, onward" or "toward the front" and that a *foreword* is "a brief introductory statement in a book, especially one written by someone besides the author." It's that they heedlessly type *forward* when they mean *foreword*, or vice versa, and don't bother to check what they've written: "Mrs. Myrick, a founder of the House Anti-Terrorism Caucus, wrote a forward [*foreword*] for the book" (*Washington Times*); "Though plans are only in the early stages things are moving foreword [*forward*]" (KTVA-TV, Alaska).

Some writers even manage to add misspelling to misuse. Here, for example, is the sportswriter Michael Grange in the online edition of Canada's *Globe and Mail:* "Jay Triano has published a book called *Basketball Basics, How to Play Like the Pros.* Steve Nash is on the cover and wrote a very nice foreward [*foreword*]." The first comment on Grange's article was from an exasperated reader who admonished him for the error and added, "Sorry Michael, but it's the second time I've seen this on a respectable website in the last day or so, and as a book writer myself, it bugs me."

The hybrid spelling *foreward* for *forward* also appears in reckless writing: "Gardenhire said he is looking foreward [*forward*] to having a stadium the Twins don't have to share with the Vikings and the University of Minnesota" (*Hartford Courant* blogs). And sometimes reckless writers put a *word* in *forward*: "It gives us something to look forword [*forward*] to, an escape from reality, and a goal to reach" (vaildaily.com).

If you ever find it challenging to keep *forward* and *foreword* straight, it may help to memorize this: "*For* there is no *word* in *forward*, and a *foreword* is a *word* before."

Proper use of *shrink, shrank, shrunk*

"I think these jeans shrinked in the dryer," said my daughter Judith, modeling one of her outfits for the new school year.

"*Shrunk*," my wife corrected.

"No, *shrank*," I called out, once again proving that I am the most annoyingly correct person in our household—except when my wife is right, which she always is whenever the argument has to do with anything but the English language.

I continued: "You *shrink* your jeans today; you *shrank* them yesterday; and you have *shrunk* them in the past." But nobody was listening anymore. My time to strut upon the stylistic stage had *shrunk* to almost nothing, I realized. So I *shrank* from public view and retired to my home office, there to contemplate how best to explain the proper use of *shrink, shrank,* and *shrunk*.

To begin with, *shrinked* is a Bozo-no-no. (Sorry, Judith, but you'll get over it; you're just a kid.) And *shrunk* is incorrect as the past tense of *shrink*: "Chile's economy shrunk [*shrank*] 4.5 percent in the second quarter" (Reuters). This misuse has undoubtedly been exacerbated by the title of the 1989 Disney movie *Honey, I Shrunk the Kids*, which should have been *Honey, I Shrank the Kids*. But Disney apparently figured proper English would make less money, honey.

In accident-free writing, *shrank* (not *shrunk*) is the past tense of *shrink: My clothes shrank in the dryer. Shrunk* is the past participle, used after *has, had, have,* or some other auxiliary verb: *I was wondering if my husband might have shrunk my clothes, and when I took them out of the dryer I saw to my dismay that they indeed had shrunk. "Honey, you shrank my stuff," I cried in despair, using the correct past tense.*

ACCIDENT 41

Misuse of *shined* for *shone*

The verb to *shine*, meaning "to polish" or "to aim a beam of light," is transitive, which means it has to act on something. That's why you *shine* your *shoes* or *shine* a *flashlight*. But the verb to *shine* meaning "to emit light," "to glisten, be radiant," or "to stand out, excel" is intransitive, which means it performs its action on its own, without an object: the sun *shines*, a diamond necklace *shines*, and a virtuoso musician can *shine* in a performance.

But what do you do when you want to say that something was shining in the past? Do you write *the sun shined* or *the sun shone*? The past tense and past participle of the transitive *shine* is *shined*, so you *shined* your shoes yesterday. But the past tense and past participle of the intransitive *shine* is *shone*, so the sun, that necklace, and that virtuoso musician *shone*.

Writers, and especially sportswriters, frequently have trouble with this elementary distinction, and they misuse the transitive *shined* for the intransitive *shone:* "Despite the loss, Arnaud once again shined [*shone*] for the Cyclones (*Seattle Post-Intelligencer*); "The Florida State women's tennis team shined [*shone*] at the Riviera/ITA All-American Championships" (WCTV-TV, Florida); "For now, Girardi favors Matsui, who shined [*shone*] during a resurgent season" (*Star-Ledger*, New Jersey). Occasionally a writer will confuse *shone* with *shown*, the past participle of *show:* "Then, facing a stiff wind in the second half, the Kent State defense shown [*shone*] brightly, holding the RedHawks to just one shot on goal" (Kent State Athletic Communications).

ACCIDENT 42

Use *incredible* to mean "unbelievable," not "amazing" or "extraordinary"

Is it too much to ask that we strive to rid our writing of the infelicities of informal speech—or, at the very least, the grossest infelicities? *You have an incredible body* and *That was an incredible meal* are pleasant and ingratiating things to say, respectively, to your love interest and your host, but if you sat down to write about that body and that meal, why would you choose to describe them with such a vacuous, hackneyed word?

I'll tell you why: Because it's easier to be lazy and write the way we speak than to struggle for precision. *Incredible* is the lazy writer's way of shirking responsibility and making the reader fill in the details. Consider this sentence written by the syndicated humor columnist Tom Purcell: "Through hard work, he made an *incredible* life for his family, and he unwittingly made an *incredible* life for my grandmother." Were those lives free of hardship, full of adventure, or marked by great achievement? *Incredible* tells us nothing about them except that they were remarkable in some vague way. And after each *incredible* you can almost hear Purcell whispering to the reader, "You know what I mean, so please don't make me go to the trouble of choosing a better word."

As if all this weren't bad enough, whenever writers use *incredible* to mean "amazing" or "extraordinary" there is alway the risk that readers will think they mean "unbelievable," and this misreading can have unintentionally ironic consequences. In a sentence like *Our Jewish community has an incredible history of strength*, the careful reader will discern a disturbing ambiguity: Is the history not to be believed? And in this sentence from an emissive* ostensibly composed by Vice President Joe Biden, the choice of *incredible* makes the poor guy once again vulnerable to ridicule for his diction: "Judge Sotomayor—herself born and raised in a South Bronx housing project—has summed up the American dream in her own incredible story and never once forgotten how the law affects our daily lives." Had someone given that sentence a moment's more thought, we might have had an *uplifting* or *inspiring* story instead of an *incredible* one.

The lesson here is this: Use *incredible* only when you mean "not believable" and you will never have to make excuses or explain yourself.

*My word for a message sent by e-mail, which I coined circa 1999.

USE THE RIGHT WORD, NOT ITS SECOND COUSIN

"The phrase, 'If you do the crime, you do the time' apparently does not apply to judges. That Greer was given no jail time in the first place is incredulous in itself."   —letter to the editor published in *The San Diego Union-Tribune*

When amateur writers compose something for publication in a widely read forum, they are often tempted to toss in a fancy word or two to make themselves look smart. But attempts to impress the reader with elevated diction can backfire badly if writers toss around fancy words they haven't taken the trouble to learn.

In this case the writer has misused the fancy word *incredulous* for the ordinary word *incredible*, perhaps fooled by their similar sound into thinking they must also mean the same thing. But *incredulous* applies only to people—not to facts, events, or circumstances—and means "not inclined to believe, doubting, skeptical": "The brothers looked incredulous, so Campbell showed them the proof" (msnbc.com). *Incredible* means "unbelievable," which was the writer's intended meaning.

ACCIDENT 43
Commas and periods always go *inside* quotation marks
The British put their commas and periods outside their quotation marks, but in American style they belong inside—with no exceptions. Thus: "I'm going to put all my commas inside my quotation marks," the wreckless writer said. "And I'm going to put all my periods there too."

ACCIDENT 44
Misuse of *less* for *fewer*
Though the time-honored distinction between *fewer* and *less* is observed less and less these days by fewer and fewer people, if you want to be a wreckless writer you should strive to get it right. You can start by remembering that the people who have less trouble in life are the ones who make fewer mistakes.

"*Less* means not so *much*" while "*fewer* means not so *many*," says the *Penguin Dictionary of American English Usage and Style*. *Less* modifies mass nouns—quantities, abstractions, things that are considered single or whole: *less* sugar, *less* time, *less* money, *less* freedom. *Fewer* modifies count nouns—things that can be counted, itemized, broken down into individual elements: *fewer* thoughts, *fewer* words, *fewer* writers involved in *fewer* accidents of style. Another way of characterizing the distinction is that *less* goes with a singular noun while *fewer* goes with a plural noun: *drive fewer miles and use less gas; less food feeds fewer people.*

Nevertheless, *less* with a count noun frequently appears in edited writing: "With less [*fewer*] than 3,000 black rhinos left in Africa, geneticists are relying more heavily on DNA markers" (*The San Diego Union-Tribune*); "The city also offered a $10,000 early retirement bonus to veteran city workers . . . which helped to keep layoffs in other city departments to less [*fewer*] than five positions" (*Boston Globe*); "The ocelot in the photograph I'm giving you is one of less [*fewer*] than 100 left in the United States" (fund-raising letter from the Environmental Defense Fund).

Even people you would most expect to know this distinction cold are often clueless: "If you're asking whether I would rather see less [*fewer*] A's, the answer is no" (Joel I. Klein, chancellor of New York City schools, quoted in *The New York Times*).

Less in place of *fewer* is so common nowadays that for many writers *fewer* has come to sound stilted, even if they sense that it's correct. I once edited a business manual that contained this sentence: "As prices increase, producers will offer more products for sale; as prices decrease, producers will offer less (or fewer) products." The writer couldn't decide whether to use *less* or *fewer* and so used both in a desperate attempt to satisfy all parties—those who erroneously offer *less* products, and those who properly offer *fewer* of them.

The American Heritage Guide to Contemporary Usage and Style says that "*less* is often used with count nouns in the expressions *no less than* and *or less*, as in *No less than thirty of his colleagues signed the letter* and *Give your reasons in twenty-five words or less*." These constructions may be common but they are illogical. Because the numbers cited are not quantities considered as a whole but rather a number of items that have been counted in the first example (signatures) and that will be counted in the second (words), *fewer* is the proper choice: *No fewer than thirty of his colleagues signed the letter* and *Give your reasons in twenty-five words or fewer* or *no more than twenty-five words.*

Would the folks at American Heritage also sanction *I have no less than twenty-five reasons* and *Give twenty-five reasons or less?* If so, they would have to bestow their blessing on the wording of the sign above the express lane in almost every grocery store in the land: "Fifteen items or *less.*" But items can be counted, so make that *fewer.*

On the other hand, *less,* not *fewer,* is acceptably and correctly used with amounts of time or money and with specific units of measure or distance because these things are thought of as quantities to be considered as a whole. Thus, we say that someone is *less than thirty years old* and that something takes *less than twenty minutes;* that we have spent *less than $50* or will make *less than $50,000 a year;* that a cup holds *less than eight ounces* and that it took *less than five gallons* to fill the gas tank; that a piece of lumber is *less than six feet long* and that we have driven *less than a hundred miles.*

With fractions, the choice of *less* or *fewer* is best governed by the quantity of the noun. If it's singular, use *less;* if it's plural, use *fewer.* Thus, it's *less* than half the *cake* but *fewer* than half the *pies.* It's *less* than a third of the *class,* but *fewer* than a third of the *students.* This sentence uses *fewer* correctly: "Only half the eighth graders even took algebra and fewer than half of those scored 'proficient' or better" (*Los Angeles Times*). But if the fraction is an amount considered as a whole, *less* is acceptable with a count noun, as in this sentence referring to people who have lost their jobs: "Less than one-third believe they will be employed within four months" (ConsumerAffairs .com).

Less is also the better choice for percentages, which don't refer to a number of things tallied but to an amount taken as a chunk of the whole: *less than 35 percent of voters support the measure; they have sold less than 10 percent of the appliances in stock.* However, if the percentage is a parenthetical part of a construction involving a plural count noun, *fewer* is required: "After three years there were 31 percent *fewer* infections" (NPR's *All Things Considered*).

ACCIDENT 45
Don't write *Thanking you in advance*

This is a stilted cliché that spread from business correspondence to the general population. *We look forward to working with you; it's a pleasure to have you on our team; we appreciate your assistance with this matter*—anything is better than *thanking you in advance*.

ACCIDENT 46
It's *black-eyed*, not *black-eye* or *blackeye*

The Safeway brand sells canned *blackeye peas*—that's exactly how it's printed on the front of the can's label and in the list of ingredients. But the dictionary brand of standard English says they're *black-eyed peas*, with a hyphen in the middle and a *d* at the end. And the flower is a *black-eyed Susan*.

ACCIDENT 47
Write *au jus*, not *with au jus*

Au jus is French for "with the juice," and in English it is best used as an adjective to mean "served with the natural juices or gravy" (*American Heritage Dictionary*) and placed after what it modifies, as in *prime rib au jus*. Our uneasy relationship with French, however, has over the years led many to use *au jus* of the natural juices themselves. This has given rise to such redundant constructions as *au jus sauce* (or *gravy, broth, mix*, etc.) and *with au jus* (literally "with with the juice").

Particularly grating on the ears is the double redundancy *French dip with au jus*. *French dip* is meat inside a roll or bun that you dip in a bowl of broth or gravy. Unless it's served *au jus*, it's just a cold, crummy sandwich. So adding *au jus* to *French dip* restates the obvious, and inserting *with* before *au jus* is the redundant icing on the cake.

Of *French dip with au jus,* a blogger at boingboing.net writes, "EVERY time I see this I cringe. It's the verbal equivalent of being introduced to a society matron and, when she turns to leave, you see she's tucked her dress into her pantyhose. Of course, French isn't the only problem—I once saw a place called the 'Cucina Italiana Kitchen.'"

And I once saw a place called the European Bistro Café—which is about as redundant as you can get, considering that a bistro is a small, European-style café—where, no doubt, they serve *penne pasta* (penne is a type of pasta, as is spaghetti, rigatoni, etc.); *shrimp scampi* (*scampi* are shrimp: it's the plural of the Italian *scampo*); and *soup du jour of the day* (the French *du jour* means "of the day").

For more on redundancy, see "Say It Again, Sam" on page 57.

Misuse of *they'll* for *there will*

In speech, when people condense *there will* into one word it often comes out sounding like *they'll,* the contraction for *they will.* This venial sin, when committed to print, becomes an appalling accident of style. It usually occurs in quoted speech: "Maybe they'll [*there'll* or *there will*] be a simple, innocent explanation" (Mike McCurry, press secretary to former president Bill Clinton, quoted in *The New York Times*). But it also occurs when careless writers mistranscribe what they hear themselves thinking: "But *they'll be* some sparks flying on offense" (NewsOK.com). All I can say to the writer of that sentence is *maybe they'll be and maybe they'll won't.*

It's spelled *arctic,* not *artic*

The mispronunciation AR-tik, which ignores the *c* in the middle of this word, is responsible for the misspelling *artic.* One could make excuses for the mispronunciation, I suppose, but there is no excuse for the misspelling, which is depressingly common on Google News. Here's one example from *The Nation* online: "The Artic ice cap may be about to completely disappear."

Actually, that brief sentence contains three accidents of style for the price of one. The misspelled *Artic* should properly be *arctic* because as an adjective the word is lowercased; it's the noun for the region, *the Arctic*, that is capitalized, as are the names *Arctic Circle* and *Arctic Ocean*. The third misstep is the word *completely*, which is unnecessary because when something disappears it goes away completely.

ACCIDENT 50
Use exclamation points sparingly—or not at all

"The truth was . . . she *wanted* to fall in love with Adam. If only she could! How much tidier life would be!" Those lines are from the novel *I Am Charlotte Simmons* by Tom Wolfe, the bestselling novelist known for his immaculate white suits and his louche love affair with the exclamation point.

Unless you're Tom Wolfe—and, for that matter, even if you *are* Tom Wolfe—don't pepper your prose with exclamation points. It's amateurish. Exclamation points in nonfiction almost always come off as strained and self-conscious, and they make fiction sound juvenile and overwrought. In advertising copy, where they are nauseatingly rampant, they're just a tiresome, heavy-handed way of saying "This is important!" "Pay attention!" "Listen to me!"

Few readers have patience for a writer who is overly fond of the mark of punctuation the British like to call a bang. That's why a soft-spoken chorus of usage experts all advise eschewing the bang. *The New York Times Manual of Style and Usage* sanctions exclamation points only for "shouted or deeply emotional phrases," and in *Woe Is I* Patricia T. O'Conner writes, "The exclamation point is like the horn on your car—use it only when you have to."

ACCIDENT 51
Don't confuse *farther* and *further*

Wreckless writers use *farther* for physical, literal distance: *they drove farther east; he can spit farther; we sat farther away.* They use *further* for nonphysical, figurative distance: *move things further along; make your money go further; nothing could be further from the truth.*

But the words are often used interchangeably, muddying the distinction: "In 1999, ten years after the fall of the Wall, a survey found that East and West Germans were drifting farther and farther [*further and further*] apart" (*The Wall Street Journal*); "Norton says the next rest area was about thirty-five miles further [*farther*] down the road" (WHSV-TV, Virginia).

Further may also mean "more, additional" or "to a greater extent or degree": *further review; further government aid; discussing things further.* Sometimes *farther*'s implication of physical distance and *further*'s implication of a greater extent or degree can seem to coexist, as in this sentence: "Expanding NATO into the Caucasus and *further* along Russia's border reduces rather than increases US security" (*Huffington Post*). In a situation like this, you should base your word choice on whichever implication is more salient. Because the sentence emphasizes geographical over influential expansion, the physical implication is dominant and the writer should have used *farther.*

ACCIDENT 52

Don't use *may* and *might* interchangeably

May and *might* express different degrees of probability. "*Might* is a slightly weaker form of *may*," writes Patricia T. O'Conner in *Woe Is I.* "Something that *might* happen is a longer shot than something that *may* happen. *I may get a raise* is more promising than *I might get a raise.*"

ACCIDENT 53

Overuse of *impact*

If a language genie ever were to appear and offer me one wish, I think I'd ask that we all immediately cease using the word *impact* in place of the nouns *influence* and *effect* and the verb *to affect.*

Stunting the growth of *impact* may not be on your list of priorities for a better world, but I am going a little daft enduring the earsplitting din of this word. Every day, a thousand times a day, something *impacts* something else, and every event has nothing less than a *tremendous impact* on our lives. It's enough to shatter your nerves and rattle your bones. Multiple *impact*s have made our daily discourse

loud and dull, like the sound of ten thousand car horns blowing behind a fender bender on the freeway.

The evil *impactors* have penetrated every corner of society and
are hell-bent on *impacting* our malleable minds. Professors and public officials lecture us about the *social impact*, the long-winded
lawyer pontificates about the *legal impact*, the do-gooder is desperate to have a *positive impact*, the economist drones on about the
fiscal impact—everyone is *impacting* everyone else into a quivering
stupor.

Are we wholly deaf to the subtlety of language? Why do we insist on using a pile driver when a putty knife would do?

Once upon a time we expressed the *effect* or *influence* of something calmly and clearly by saying that it *affected* or *influenced* something else. Now it is hammered into our heads day in and day out
with the word *impact*, which does double duty as noun and verb.
The sad thing is that this powerful word, which traditionally con-
notes considerable force, has lost all its forcefulness through inces-
sant repetition. The only power *impact* has retained is the ability to
cause a headache.

Wherever you turn today you are liable to slam into a sentence
driven to distraction by the overused *impact*. The word is now so
popular that its fans have created a family of spin-offs. To the evil
impactors, that which has an *impact* or *impacts* something else can
now be described as *impactive*, *impactful*, or *impactual*. It can even
have *impactability*. The linguist will praise this prolificacy as a sign
of American ingenuity. The conscientious stylist will condemn it as
the offspring of American mad-scientism, the grotesque result of
unethical experimentation on an innocent word.

Of course, no one can wave a wand and change the course of
language, but a little prudence can go a long way. Using the noun
impact to refer to the striking of one thing against another has always been unimpeachable. Using it as a synonym of the nouns *effect*
and *influence* is now so entrenched that only a few mad-stylists like
me still object to the practice. But using it as a verb—either transitively (*this legislation impacts the elderly*) or intransitively (*decreased
demand will impact on retail sales*)—is another matter. Here is where

the conscientious stylist, wishing to make the vehicle of his prose stand out in the dull, redundant flow of verbal traffic, will prudently draw the line.

I, for one, will continue to boycott this word in all its monstrous forms, using it only for teeth and actual collisions. Though it is perhaps too much to expect you to become an *unimpactful* writer like me, I do hope my mad-stylist's ravings on the effect of *impact* have had a salutary influence on you.

ACCIDENT 54
Prefer *half* to *half of*

Of after *half* is often superfluous and can be deleted: "Only half [*of*] the jobless have health benefits" (ConsumerAffairs.com); "The Charlotte, NC-based bank wants to repay $20 billion, or almost half [*of*] the capital it received from the Troubled Asset Relief Program" (CNNMoney.com).

ACCIDENT 55
Don't use *literally* to mean "figuratively" or as part of hyperbole

If you don't mean "in fact, actually," don't use *literally*. There are a lot of people out there—from English teachers to editors to experts on usage—who will reproach and even ridicule you for it.

In most cases, writers reach for *literally* when they want to punch up an already hyperbolic phrase or create hyperbole out of a hackneyed expression. For instance, they take the hyperbolic *I died laughing* and write *I literally died laughing*, or they take a cliché like *she was bubbling over with gratitude* and turn it into the hyperbolic *she was literally bubbling over with gratitude*. The interpolation of *literally* in these ways can have unintentionally surprising or unfortunate consequences, as when someone gets *literally* blown away or buried alive. So if you're not actually blue in the face, don't say you *literally* are because you don't want to get caught with your pants down—figuratively or literally.

THE ACCIDENTS OF STYLE 49

ACCIDENT 56
Use *shown* as a past participle, not *showed*

The real estate agent showed us the house is good English, but *the real estate agent has showed us the house* is not. When combined with *has, had, have,* or *having,* the preferred form is *shown.*

ACCIDENT 57
It's *verbiage,* not *verbage,* and don't use it to mean "wording" or "language"

The misspelling *verbage* is a result of the common mispronunciation VUR-bij. The word properly has three syllables, VUR-bee-ij, and is spelled with an *i* in the middle: *verbiage.*

Though dictionaries often list *wording* or *diction* as synonyms of *verbiage,* using *verbiage* instead of those words is a preening pomposity. So is using *verbiage* as a synonym of *language,* a sense dictionaries do not record that has become popular among accident-prone writers: "[The] Board of Education will hold a meeting to discuss the official verbiage [*language*] that will appear on the November ballot" (*Waseca County News,* Minnesota); "There was some good verbiage [*language*] about studying hard, staying in school, and being the best you can be" (AssociatedContent.com); "Maybe you sign up for a service and buried in the contract somewhere is verbiage [*language*] saying that you agree to receive robocalls" (ABC News).

In precise usage, *verbiage* is an excess of words, especially an abundance of useless words. So do not write *excess verbiage;* it's redundant.

ACCIDENT 58
Avoid the hackneyed *but hey*

The interjection *but hey* is a trendy and vapid locution much favored by protégés of the What's-Up-Dude School of Insipid Writing. These "casualistas" think that readers want a writer to sound like a regular Joe, so they are enamored of whatever verbal tic makes their writing seem more like speech, especially the most lifeless, laid-back speech. The worst literary sin you can commit, they believe, is to make your writing read like writing—in other words, something you actually thought about and revised before unleashing upon the world.

But hey, maybe I'm going too far with this whole *but hey* thing. I mean, do you have issues with what I'm saying or are you down with it? If you're chill, that's cool, and if you're not . . . well, then be that way. Whatever.

You catch my drift?

But hey is a kind of vacuous shrug that reckless casualistas put in a sentence to signal that an attempt at humor or a smart-alecky remark is on the way: "[The movie] seems to function outside of logic, cohesive plot structure and the laws of gravity, *but hey*—this being the fourth film in the street-racing series, such niceties have long since been tossed out the window" (*Dallas Morning News*); " 'I hate that show,' says Jessie, before departing via Suburban back uptown to her red-velvet-wallpapered home. *But hey*, at least she has parents to go home to" (*The New York Times*). Use the *but* but eschew the *hey*.

AMAZING GAFFE

"Many business [*sic*] are going belly up, even in better times like these"
                                   —headline in *The San Diego Union-Tribune*

Have you noticed lately that many newspapers—along with those "many business"—have been going belly-up? Blunders like this one certainly aren't helping matters.

ACCIDENT 59
Don't use *old* with *cliché, adage, maxim,* or *proverb*–but *old saying* is all right

Clichés, adages, maxims, and proverbs are already old. Repeated use over many years is what made them clichés, adages, maxims, and proverbs. So using the word *old* with any of these words is redundant.

But the word *saying* is neutral and doesn't imply common knowledge or overuse. So it's acceptable to refer to an *old saying.*

ACCIDENT 60
Don't qualify *necessary*
Necessary means "essential, indispensable," and like *essential* and *indispensable* it is an absolute. Something is either necessary or it isn't. There are no degrees of necessariness. So don't follow the reckless writer's example and qualify *necessary;* in other words, don't modify it with an adverb such as *somewhat, particularly, completely, especially,* or *extremely,* and take special care to avoid the ridiculously redundant *absolutely necessary* (for which I got a whopping 950 hits on Google News). If you feel you need more emphasis than *necessary* alone provides, use *essential, indispensable, imperative, inevitable,* or some other stronger word instead.

ACCIDENT 61
It's *handfuls, spoonfuls,* not *handsful, spoonsful*
Because your *hands* can be *full* of something, and because *spoons* can be *full* of something, it's tempting to think that you can have several *handsful* or *spoonsful* of something. But that's not the way we do things in the often illogical, occasionally maddening English language. Words formed from a noun plus the suffix *-ful* always add *s* to form the plural: *handfuls, armfuls, cupfuls, basketfuls, barrelfuls, mouthfuls, forkfuls, platefuls, tablefuls, roomfuls, spoonfuls, teaspoonfuls, tablespoonfuls,* and so on.

ACCIDENT 62
Don't misuse superlative adjectives
Adjectives come in three forms: the positive, as in *big, ugly,* and *stupid;* the comparative, as in *bigger, uglier,* and *stupider;* and the superlative, as in *biggest, ugliest,* and *stupidest.* The positive form of an adjective pertains to one thing (*he's awfully big*); the comparative form compares two things (*Joe's uglier than Jim*); and the superlative form is used when more than two things are compared (*Of all the guys*

I know, Sam is the stupidest). One of the biggest, ugliest, stupidest mistakes that people make is using the superlative when comparing only two things.

In its issue of July 6, 2008, *Parade* magazine published essays by the two U.S. presidential candidates, Barack Obama and John McCain, addressing the question "What is patriotism?" The editors then asked readers to go to the magazine's website and answer this question: "Whose vision of patriotism is closest to your own?" One of two visions will be *closer* to your own. *Closest* requires three or more choices.

We can at least be thankful that the *Parade* editors didn't add the erroneous question "Which candidate is the best?"

ACCIDENT 63
It's *chaise longue*, not *lounge*
Your dictionary won't tell you this, but I will: if you spell it *chaise lounge* and pronounce it *chase lownj*, you will be laughed at by the literati. *Garner's Modern American Usage*, echoing the sentiments of many cultivated writers and speakers, calls the *lounge* spelling and pronunciation "an embarrassing error" and "distinctly low-rent."

Chaise longue, literally "long chair," comes to us directly from French; not surprisingly, because of what it denotes it was corrupted over time into the more English *chaise lounge*, so that now we have two spellings and a variety of pronunciations for this piece of furniture. But in reputable publications and careful speech, the preferred spelling is *chaise longue* and the preferred pronunciation is *shayz long*. The preferred plural is *chaise longues*.

ACCIDENT 64
Don't trip over your *feet* and *foot*
We all know it's one *foot* and two or more *feet*. But is someone five *feet* two inches tall or five *foot* two inches tall? Is a wall twelve *feet* high or twelve *foot* high?

Whenever you're referring to height, length, or distance, use the plural *feet*: *she is five feet two; the wall is twelve feet high; a board that's six feet long; we walked another one hundred feet*. But if the height, length, or distance is part of a phrasal adjective (a hyphenated phrase that modifies a noun), then *foot* is the appropriate word: *a four-foot jump; a twelve-foot-high wall; a six-foot-long board; a one-hundred-foot hose.*

Thus, a basketball player who is six *feet* seven is a six-*foot*-seven player.

ACCIDENT 65
Don't confuse *hanged* and *hung*

A painting or a coat is *hung,* and you can also have a *hung* jury, one unable to reach a verdict. A person being executed is *hanged.* There is one exception to this distinction: if a person is suspended in some way for any reason other than capital punishment, use *hung.*

Since the purpose of hanging is execution, avoid the redundant *hanged to death.*

AMAZING GAFFE

"Some of the most exhilarating cinema to be seen on screen."
—Ann Hornaday, *Baltimore Sun*

As opposed to, say, some of the most exhilarating theater to be seen in a theater, some of most exhilarating TV to be seen on TV, or some of the most exhilarating radio to be heard on the radio? Ms. Hornaday's breathless plaudit is an excellent example of *tautology* (taw-TAH-luh-jee), "needless or useless repetition of the same idea in different words" (*Webster's New International Dictionary,* 2nd ed.).

Also, it should be *on-screen,* with a hyphen, or *onscreen.*

ACCIDENT 66
Avoid *awesome*

The slangy word *awesome* has been so overworked that it has lost all its power to amaze and is now a hallmark of lazy, juvenile writing. It does not belong in serious prose. Serious readers who encounter *awesome* will assume that the writer is underestimating their intelligence, trying too hard to be hip, or twelve years old.

If you mean "inspiring awe," use *awe-inspiring, impressive, imposing, sublime, majestic, formidable, redoubtable.* If you mean "amazing," use *amazing, astounding, astonishing, remarkable, stupendous.*

ACCIDENT 67
The public is an *it*, not a *they*

In standard American English, *public* is a collective noun—like *audience, army, family,* and *jury*—which means that it takes a singular verb (the public *is, votes, wants,* etc.) and should be followed by the singular possessive pronoun *its*, never by the plural possessive pronoun *their: In a democracy, the public decides who its* (not *their*) *leaders will be.*

But *the public* linked with the plural *their* is a common blunder in speech, so it's no surprise that it frequently appears in print: "This . . . will give the public their [*its*] first chance to ask questions of the candidates" (*Spokesman-Review*, Idaho); "The public has their [*its* or *a*] chance to slide into a 1986 beige Jaguar that was once owned by country music legend Conway Twitty" (WSMV-TV, Tennessee).

ACCIDENT 68
You feel *bad*, not *badly*

No one would say *I feel gladly* or *I feel sadly*, so why do so many people say and write *I feel badly*? Perhaps because they do not know that adverbs modify action verbs, but linking verbs connect a subject with an adjective.

Here's how it works. If a verb describes an action, you may use an adverb to describe how the action is performed; e.g., you can *run quickly, eat slowly,* or *sing beautifully.* But linking verbs such as *feel, look, smell, taste, seem,* and *be* do not describe an action; they express a state of being, and they link a subject with an adjective. That's why *you* (subject) *feel* (linking verb) *bad* (adjective), and why *something* (subject) *looks, smells, tastes, seems,* or *is* (linking verbs) *bad* (adjective), not *badly* (adverb).

If you say you feel *badly*, you are describing not your state of being, your mood, which is *bad*, but your manner of feeling, how you are going about the business of feeling. Just as a person who *smells badly* is having trouble smelling and a person who *looks badly* is having trouble seeing, someone who *feels badly* is having trouble feeling—either physically or emotionally. So beware of the safecracker or the actor who admits *feeling badly*. The former can get overemotional about locks while the latter can't get a lock on his emotions.

Sometimes the misuse of *feel badly* for *feel bad* can be unintentionally and deliciously ironic, as when CBS News reported that the attorney for Bernard Madoff said the Wall Street archswindler had "always *felt badly*" for the victims of his billion-dollar Ponzi scheme" (cbsnews.com). The judge was unmoved and did not feel bad at all about giving Mr. Madoff 150 years to ponder his lack of fellow feeling for his victims.

ACCIDENT 69
It's *fall through the cracks*, not *fall between the cracks*

If you think about it, falling *between* the cracks is absurd. You can't fall between two cracks—that's where the board or slat is. You have to fall *through* the cracks. But reckless writers often get it wrong: "State law should be tightened up so future Olmsted-like cases don't fall between [*through*] the cracks of separate state codes" (*Dallas Morning News*); "Welch said many homeless people fall between [*through*] the cracks and don't get some of those simple services" (NanaimoBulletin.com).

ACCIDENT 70
There is no *k* in *renowned* and *renown*

"My band of right-wingers is reknown for its empathy," writes Jim Wooten in *The Atlanta Journal-Constitution*, causing two accidents of style in one fell swerve. *Reknown* is not a legitimate word, and even if it were it would have to be a verb meaning "known again." The word Wooten should have used is the adjective *renowned*, meaning "famous, prominent, well-known" and pronounced ri-NOWND;

the corresponding noun is *renown*, "fame, eminence, distinction," pronounced ri-NOWN.

The same double blunder appears in this photo caption from the *Cleveland Plain Dealer:* "Afternoon sun makes geomatric [*sic*] play on the north and west facades of the Ameritrust Tower, which was designed by the reknown [*renowned*] architect Marcel Breuer." The additional egregious misspelling in that sentence only bolsters the argument that writers, like drivers, ought to be tested for rudimentary competence before being licensed to travel among us.

ACCIDENT 71

It's spelled *consensus*, with an *s* in the middle, not *concensus*

"No consensus is available on how to measure a U.S. high school graduate's readiness for a post-secondary educational career, a report indicated Tuesday," begins an article on the website of United Press International. Now look at the headline for the article: "Report: No concensus on college-ready grad." Apparently, there's either no consensus at UPI on how to spell *consensus*, or the writer of that headline should go back to night school. For the sake of the language, let's hope it's the latter.

ACCIDENT 72

Avoid the phrases *general consensus* and *consensus of opinion*

A *consensus* is a generally held opinion, so *general consensus* and *consensus of opinion* are redundant. Although usage guides and style manuals have long proscribed these prolix phrases, they are regrettably common in edited writing: "And the *general consensus* is if an ABC soap is to go, it should be All My Children" (*Entertainment Weekly*); "After Griffin, there is no *consensus of opinion* of how the draft will unfold" (*Kansas City Star*). In the second example, matters are made worse by following *opinion* with *of* instead of *on* or *about*, which is both repetitive (*of . . . of*) and unidiomatic. Idiom demands that we have an opinion *of* people but an opinion *on* or *about* things.

THE ACCIDENTS OF STYLE

Occasionally, as you cruise the unpatrolled highways of online prose, you may come across an accident of style that is a true scene of horror: *general consensus of opinion*. From this gruesomely redundant pileup it is simply best to avert your gaze.

SAY IT AGAIN, SAM: A RANT ON REDUNDANCY

Redundancy is the unnecessary repetition of an idea, or the use of more words than are necessary to express an idea. It's perhaps the most common error in educated usage; it's also the easiest to correct and avoid, once you train your ear to detect it. In fact, once you start looking for redundancies, you'll find them everywhere—on TV and radio, in your junk mail, in your e-mail, in newspapers, magazines, and books, and yes, even in your own speech and writing.

Every day we are bombarded with redundancies, and many of them have become stock phrases that hack writers reach for without a second thought. For example, how many times a week are you offered a *free gift*? Aren't you glad you don't have to pay for that gift? Have you ever discussed someone's *past history* or your *future plans*? It takes some *preplanning*, better known as *advance planning*, to avoid these common redundancies. Have you ever heard of a *completely unanimous* vote? I'm glad it wasn't partly unanimous. That would mean there wasn't a *general consensus of opinion*, otherwise known as a *consensus*.

Do you have *fellow colleagues* or just plain old *colleagues*? If they're your *fellow colleagues*, when you *interact with each other* do you have *mutual respect for each other* or do you *compete with each other*? Either way, it's a *necessary requirement* that you *confer together*, *cooperate together*, and *collaborate together*. And if you're too many cooks who spoil the broth, you'll *blend* and *combine* your ingredients *together* until you have an *appetite to eat*.

Are you beginning to sense how these ridiculous repetitions, once you're tuned in to them, are so easily *audible to the ear* and *visible to the eye*? That's because they're so *blatantly obvious.*

It's a *real fact,* or perhaps I should say an *actual fact,* that redundancy affects the entire *population of people.* It's not a *passing fad,* or even a permanent fad, and it's not *dwindling down.* It's a *current problem right now* because it can happen *unexpectedly without warning* or *simultaneously at the same time.* It will never recur because it always *recurs again.* For when it comes to redundancy there is no reprieve, just a *temporary reprieve,* and there is no panacea, just a *universal panacea for all ills.*

Redundancy is *large in size.* Examples of it are not *few in number.* It is *radiating out* and *expanding out* every day, and there seems to be no way to *reduce it down* or *cancel it out.* My greatest fear is that it will happen with no *advance warning* and *explode violently* when I am *physically present,* destroying all my *previous preconceptions.* Then I will either have to wear an *artificial prosthesis* or *ascend upward* to heaven.

So here's my *final conclusion:* We must *completely annihilate* redundancy (as opposed to partially annihilating it). I know that's not a *fresh new* idea. It's not even a *new innovation.* But we had better stop *vacillating back and forth* and start doing something about this problem because we are *completely surrounded by it on all sides.* And, *at this particular point in time,* please don't ask me to *repeat that again.*

ACCIDENT 73

Don't confuse *any more* and *anymore*

"Wait a minute—isn't 'Whole Grain White Bread' a contradiction in terms?" asks Michael Pollan in his treatise *In Defense of Food.* "Evidently not any more."

Wait a minute—shouldn't that be *anymore?* Indeed it should.

The two words *any more* apply to quantities (*Are there any more doughnuts?*) or degrees (*She wasn't any more interested in going than he was*). The single word *anymore* refers to time and is used in negative constructions (*She wasn't interested in him anymore*) and in certain questions (*Do you eat doughnuts anymore?*). If the intended meaning is "additional" or "to a greater extent or degree," use the two words *any more: He who does not eat any more doughnuts will not get any more obese.* If the intended meaning is "still" or "any longer," use the one-word *anymore: Are you seeing that guy anymore? No, I'm not seeing him anymore.*

Are you going to have *any more* accidents of style with these words? Evidently not *anymore.*

ACCIDENT 74

Write *a couple of,* not *a couple*

Using *couple* as an adjective followed by a noun—as in *a couple people, a couple dollars, a couple miles*—is excusable in informal speech but unbecoming in careful writing. The circumspect stylist knows that *couple* is properly a noun that requires the preposition *of* to link it to a following noun: *a couple of people, a couple of dollars, a couple of miles.* Without that intervening *of,* the noun *couple* becomes an ungainly adjective modifying the noun that follows, so that phrases like *a couple weeks* and *a couple hundred,* though commonly heard, are, grammatically speaking, as peculiar as *a flock pigeons, a bunch grapes,* and *a number questions.*

The uncoupled *couple,* not surprisingly, often appears in journalism and fiction that affects the cadences of casual speech: "She shows up with *a couple* friends in tow" (*USA Today*); "He plans to close up shop—briefly—for *a couple* weeks in September" (*Seattle Times*); "She touched me for *a couple* hundred to blow town" (Dashiell Hammett, *The Thin Man*). But it sometimes appears in more elevated prose, where the author and copyeditor should have been mindful of this nonstandard colloquialism: "To be safe we need to go back at least *a couple* generations" (Michael Pollan, *In Defense of Food*); "Well, they do give *a couple* examples" (June Casagrande, *Mortal Syntax*).

Like *a handful*—and unlike *a few*—*a couple* must be followed by *of,* with one exception. When the word *more* follows *couple, of* is unidiomatic and unnecessary. This example uses *a couple of* and *a couple more* correctly: "Running back Lorenzo Booker, who dropped *a couple of* passes in Thursday's non-contact practice, dropped *a couple more* in yesterday's first full-gear workout" (*Philadelphia Daily News*).

ACCIDENT 75
Avoid *oftentimes*
Use the shorter and far more common *often* instead.

ACCIDENT 76
It's *converse*, not *conversate*
If you aspire to speak and write standard English, using *conversate* is a surefire way to fail. This recent back-formation from *conversation* will not score you any points with anyone in a position to evaluate how well you are using the language. When people talk to each other, they *converse*.

ACCIDENT 77
Watch out for apostrophe catastrophes
By far the most common accident of style involving apostrophes is the "grocer's apostrophe," so called because it is a frequent fright in supermarket signs: *string bean's; fresh cucumber's; local peach's*. When a writer mistakenly adds *'s* to a common or proper noun to make it plural, a grocer's apostrophe is the result, and this blunder is hardly confined to grocery stores. Here are some hilariously painful examples from the website of the Apostrophe Protection Society, which corroborates each infraction with incriminating snapshots: *cocktail's; toilet's; used car's; taxi's only; tattoo's and body piercing; Four Season's Nudist Resort; Beach Hall Studio's; now open on Sunday's; owner's assume no responsibility for lost, stolen, or damaged articles.* (Why not *article's* for consistency's sake?)

We could just as well call this misuse of the apostrophe to create a plural noun the "restaurant apostrophe," for it appears on countless menus—often miswritten *menu's*—even in chichi establishments. The menu of an Italian restaurant in my neighborhood has some especially outrageous specimens: *pizza's, pasta's, appetizer's, soup & salad's,* and *lunch special's.* You can even order a pizza with sautéed *onion's.* At least this place doesn't have a separate *kid's menu,* which you'll find at scores of family restaurants. Is that a menu for just one kid? Or is it a *kids' menu,* one for all the kids they serve?

The grocer's or restaurant apostrophe also occurs in the curious way some people have of pluralizing their surname. They write *the Simpson's* or sometimes *the Simpsons'* when all they need to do is say *Doh!* and write *the Simpsons.* (Of course, if a plural possessive is involved, a terminal apostrophe is required: *the Simpsons' house.*)

Also, despite what you may see in some newspapers, it's better style not to use an apostrophe to pluralize acronyms, initialisms, decades, and numerals. Just add *s:* PINs; ATMs; CDs; URLs; IRAs; the 1970s and 1980s; temperatures in the 70s and 80s; five AK-47s; two Boeing 727s. But letters in lowercase and abbreviations with internal periods do require an apostrophe to form the plural: *x*'s, *y*'s, and *z*'s; M.D.'s and Ph.D.'s.

The second most common apostrophic accident is the misuse of *it's* for *its* and *its* for *it's,* which I discuss fully in Accident 7. *It's* is a contraction of *it is* or *it has,* while *its* is the possessive form of *it.* But apostrophe catastrophers heedlessly write *its* [it's] *all about passion* and *somewhere a village is missing it's* [its] *idiot.*

Perhaps the third most common apostrophic accident is the missing apostrophe. This occurs when the catastrophers fail to use an apostrophe in a contraction such as *let's* or, more often, fail to use one in a possessive form, so that we see peculiarities like *doctors office* and *farmers market* instead of *doctor's office* and *farmers' market.* "Does your bank pay you back when you use another banks [*bank's*] ATM?" asks an ad for First Republic Bank. And what should we make of the statement *the judges decision is final?* Will that be one judge's decision or several judges' decision?

Finally there is the misplaced apostrophe, which might be called the dartboard apostrophe because it seems to have been tossed at a word in the forlorn hope that it will score a bull's-eye. This catastrophe includes the lone *kid's menu* mentioned above and other random accidents like *lot's of* for *lots of, would'nt* for *wouldn't, gentlemens'* for *gentlemen's, St. Peters'* for *St. Peter's,* and a child's toy called *Touch N' See*—which should be *Touch 'n' See* because the two apostrophes stand in for the missing *a* and *d* in the word *and* (as in *rock 'n' roll*).

If you're unsure about where or where not to place an apostrophe, don't ask someone who knows his *onion's*. Consult a more technical usage guide such as Edward D. Johnson's *Handbook of Good English* or *The Chicago Manual of Style*.

ACCIDENT 78
It's *embarrass*, with two *r*'s, two *s*'s, and an *ass* at the end

The most common misrenderings are *embarass*, with one *r*, and *embarress*. Remember this line and you'll be fine: "Only Barry, who is an ass, misspells *embarrass*."

ACCIDENT 79
Don't use *in my humble opinion*

As far as I know, I've used *in my humble opinion* only once in all my published writing, and I regret it. This phrase—abbreviated to IMHO in that peculiar trimmed-down, puffed-up brand of English known as Blogosphere Blowhardese—is wordy, pretentious, and hackneyed. It draws unnecessary attention to itself, and if the humility it conveys could be converted to a liquid, it might barely fill a bottle cap. Use *I think* or some other more concise and direct phrasing instead.

ACCIDENT 80
It's spelled *remuneration*, not *renumeration*

"Excellent renumeration package with great bonus earnings for right candidate," proclaims the announcement for a position at careersand jobsUK.com. Job applicants, beware: when they call you for an interview, be sure to ask for a *remuneration* package, which will pay you real money, not a *renumeration* package, which, as the old song about Secret Agent Man says, will give you a number and take away your name.

Renumeration (ri-NOO-muh-RAY-shin) is a little-used word meaning "renumbering, recalculation." *Remuneration* (ri-MYOO-nuh-

RAY-shin), from the Latin *rĕmūnĕrāri,* "to reward," is payment for work or service. The trick to both spelling and pronouncing the word correctly is to remember that there is no *renew* in *remuneration.*

USE THE RIGHT WORD, NOT ITS SECOND COUSIN

"I'm having a change of heart about the game [*golf*] I'd always dismissed as a dud.... You, on the other hand, may feel no ambiguity about this game."
—Don Nichols, executive editor of *Southwest Airlines Spirit* magazine

Ambiguity properly refers to language that is vague or capable of being understood in more than one way. You can detect ambiguity (in a word, expression, or passage) but you cannot feel it. It's not a state of mind.

The writer is trying to acknowledge that many of his readers may be golf enthusiasts who never experienced his transformation from a golf-hater into a golf-lover. So he needs a word that denotes conflicting feelings, and that word is *ambivalence,* which sounds much like *ambiguity.* One of my favorite word treasuries, *Webster's New International Dictionary* (2nd ed., 1934), defines *ambivalence* as "simultaneous attraction toward and repulsion from an object, person, or action." When you feel *no* ambivalence, your feelings are clear, one way or the other.

ACCIDENT 81
There is no *pizza* in *pizzeria*

No matter how you slice it, it's spelled *pizzeria,* with an *e* instead of an *a* in the middle, because in Italian the suffix *-eria* denotes a place where something is made or sold: a *panetteria* is a bakery; a *libreria* is a bookstore. If you don't know that Italian tidbit, it can be tempting to put an erroneous *pizza* in *pizzeria.* Even *Pizza Marketing Quarterly,* in a story about an eighty-three-year-old pizza maker named Johnny "Tony" Barrios, identified him as the "owner of Tony's Pizzaria in downtown Ventura."

ACCIDENT 82

Don't use *momentarily* to mean "in a moment" or "soon"

"The plane will land momentarily," says the flight attendant, and the language-savvy passengers aboard wonder if the plane will be on the ground long enough for them to get off. What does *momentarily* mean to you in that sentence?

Momentarily is widely used in American English (though not in British English) to mean "in a moment" or "at any moment": *the doctor will be with you momentarily.* But this sense is at odds with the much older meaning "for a moment or a short while": *the doctor said the shot will hurt momentarily.*

In the present and past tense *momentarily* always means "for a moment": *the pain is momentarily forgotten; she was momentarily distracted.* Only in the future tense do these different meanings compete, and the result can be ambiguous. Does *they will stop momentarily* mean they will stop soon or for a little while?

Discriminating writers and speakers don't just hope that the context will make their meaning clear. They avoid potential ambiguity by reserving *momentarily* for the traditional sense of "for a moment, for a short while," and use *in a moment, at any moment, shortly, presently,* or *soon* when that is what they mean.

ACCIDENT 83

It's an *invitation*, not an *invite*

Though the noun *invite* has been around for more than three hundred years, in all that time it has not been able to work its way up the ladder of linguistic respectability. Today it remains a colloquialism, suitable only for informal communication. In any kind of dignified writing, it is always better to say that you *were invited* or that you *got an invitation.*

ACCIDENT 84

It's *vocal cords*, not *chords*

"The Welsh singer has scratched a number of dates due to strained vocal chords" (*Asheville Citizen-Times*). Was it the singer's music or voice that was strained?

Chord refers to musical harmony, specifically three or more notes sounded together. *Cord* refers to a thick string or thin rope, or anything resembling it, such as a cable or a tendon. In anatomy it's always *cord: vocal cords, umbilical cord, spinal cord.*

ACCIDENT 85

There is no *hair* in *harebrained*

"A wild, rash, heedless, foolish, volatile or giddy person is said to be harebrained because he has or shows no more brains or sense than a hare or rabbit," writes George Stimpson in *A Book About a Thousand Things*. "The word is sometimes incorrectly written *hairbrained*, even by reputable writers, and that spelling, which began to occur before 1600, has misled many into seeking a different origin of the term."

Putting an erroneous *hair* in *harebrained* is such an old mistake because centuries ago *hair* was a variant spelling of *hare*, and *hare* was a variant spelling of *hair*. According to the etymologist Michael Quinion, the variant *hair* for *hare* survived in Scotland until the eighteenth century, giving rise to the false but persistent notion that the word refers to someone with a brain made of hair. You could say, then, that we are historically programmed to tear out our hair over the proper spelling of *harebrained*.

Although *harebrained* writers are rare today on the highways of edited prose, in off-road writing *hairbrained* still runs amok like a March hare. A search on Google Web shows the *hair* misspelling occurring about once in every five times the word is used.

ACCIDENT 86

Don't use *irregardless*

Irregardless came into existence in the early twentieth century, probably as a dialectal blend of *irrespective* and *regardless*. Nobody, but *nobody*, has ever had anything good to say about it. Since the 1920s *irregardless* has been ridiculed for being a ludicrous double negative, like *don't never*, and usage commentators have called it substandard, illiterate, a nonword, a redundancy, and a barbarism that should be shunned or stamped out. Even the notoriously permissive *Merriam-Webster's Collegiate Dictionary* concludes that *irregardless* "is still a long way from general acceptance," a statement that may qualify as one of the greatest understatements of all time.

Yet for all the scorn heaped on this unpopular word—and, yes, it is a word, just not a worthy one—it is alarmingly common in educated speech and it sometimes finds its way past the copyeditors into print: "The roads still need maintenance when vehicles travel on them, *irregardless* of fuel efficiency" (*Arizona Daily Star*); "Multiple chemical sensitivity (MCS) affects men, women, and children *irregardless* of gender, race and economic status" (americanchronicle.com).

As Martha Brockenbrough writes in *Things That Make Us [Sic]*, "*Irregardless* is an irregular word, just as underwear is an irregular hat." So if you don't like displaying your dirty laundry in public, don't never use *irregardless*. (Just kidding, but that's actually not a bad mnemonic device.) It wouldn't hurt to also avoid *irrespective*, which many agree is an unnecessary, pompous synonym of *regardless*—the word that will never get you pulled over by the language police.

One word of caution, though, about *regardless*. It is objectionable in *regardless of the fact that* because the phrase is verbose. Use *though, although,* or *even though* instead: "Since most people aren't familiar with Savagnin, Australian producers are not eager to use it on their labels, regardless of the fact that [*even though*] it's responsible for some of the best wines in the world" (gourmet.com).

ACCIDENT 87

Don't write *in regards to* or *with regards to*

The proper forms are *in regard to* and *with regard to*. Yet the amateurish and awkward *regards* frequently appears in professional writing: "The university's theater department had a culture of permissiveness in *regards to* teacher-student relationships" (*Denver Post*); "With *regards to* healthcare provisions, the chamber is bolstering the use of a healthcare insurance backstop" (*The Wall Street Journal*).

Now for another caveat regarding *in regard to* and *with regard to*. Although they—and even *as regards*—are standard English, why would any self-respecting writer want to use these wordy and stiff constructions? They stick out like a tuxedo at a tailgate party. Your prose will be much smoother and cleaner and free of ostentation if you use *regarding, concerning, about*, or simply begin with your subject—whatever person or thing you want to write about. For example, instead of *In regard to your letter of July 4, wherein you made an offer to buy my widgets at $4 apiece*, write *In your letter of July 4 you offered to pay $4 each for my widgets.*

ACCIDENT 88
Use single quotation marks for quotations within quotations
When you need to quote something within a quotation, use single quotation marks: *Any person with even a vestige of taste has to ask, "What are shows like 'Family Guy' and 'South Park' doing on TV? Don't we know what 'humor' means anymore?"*

ACCIDENT 89
Write *one less*, not *one fewer*
In an editorial in the *Tucson Citizen* lamenting the imminent loss of that afternoon newspaper, Arizona congresswoman Gabrielle Giffords wrote, "Tucson will be very different without the Citizen. Our community will have one fewer voice, one fewer watchdog, one fewer place to go for the news we need to understand our increasingly complex world." That bumper-car sentence commits the same accident of style three times in a row. Instead of *one fewer*, it should have been *one less*.

The congresswoman was clearly aware that *less* applies to mass nouns like *sugar* and *fewer* applies to count nouns like *beets*. So when she put all those singular count nouns in her sentence (*voice, watchdog, place*) she reasoned that *fewer* was the word she should use to modify them. But what she didn't know is there's another, more subtle rule about *fewer* and *less:* we use *fewer* with plural nouns and *less* with singular nouns. Since a singular noun will always follow *one*, you should have *one less* of whatever it is, not *one fewer:* "Angels closer Francisco Rodriguez had one fewer [*one less*] save than San Diego has victories" (*The San Diego Union-Tribune*).

This won't give you *fewer* things to worry about, but it will at least give you *one less* thing.

AMAZING GAFFE

" 'An honorary organization in New York City,' I explained, 'that includes writers, composers, painters, sculptors, and architects. Two hundred and fifty of them, no more and no less. Fewer than one for every million Americans.' " —John Updike, *The New Yorker*

Quandoque bonus dormitat Homerus—literally, "Sometimes even good Homer sleeps," meaning that even good writers are not always at their best. In his last piece for the magazine that had published him since he was a novice writer, the venerable Updike committed back-to-back accidents of style with *less* and *fewer*. He should have written, "Two hundred and fifty of them, no more and no *fewer*. *Less* than one for every million Americans."

See Accidents 44 and 89.

ACCIDENT 90

Don't use *author* as a verb

The verb to *author*, much loved by second-rate journalists, is prententious. You can always use *write*, *compose*, or *create* instead: "Hager has authored [*written*] two books, both of which she promoted on *Today*" (*Seattle Post-Intelligencer*). When referring to legislation or legislators, use *sponsor*: "Bill authored [*sponsored*] by Yee may give cops more money to fight human trafficking" (*San Jose Mercury News*).

ACCIDENT 91

Don't write *first of all, second of all* . . .

Adding *of all* to *first, second, third* in enumerations is wordy. It's excusable in speech—except in formal situations, such as a lecture or presentation—but should be excised from polished prose. Write *first, second, third,* which modern authorities on usage prefer over *firstly, secondly, thirdly.* Whatever you do, don't mix up your adverbial forms and write *first, secondly, thirdly,* or *firstly, second, third,* or some such thing.

One other caveat: *first* is redundant and unnecessary when it's implicit that something is being done for the first time, or when it is paired with a verb (such as *create, invent,* or *discover*) that means doing something for the first time: "When Southwest *first announced* it would fly from Boston to Baltimore for $49 each way, JetBlue added a route there too" (*Boston Globe*); "The model, *first conceived* in 1941, evolved into the touchstone of modern guitars" (*New York Post*). Make that *announced* and *conceived* without *first.*

ACCIDENT 92

Avoid *and/or*

Lawyers, businesspeople, and bureaucrats have a long-standing love affair with *and/or,* but usage experts abhor it. Without listing all the pejorative adjectives they've hurled at *and/or* over the years, let's just say that, contrary to what its users believe, it's not a word-saving shortcut or an economical way of covering all the bases. It's graceless, self-important, and often ambiguous or illogical.

Consider these three examples of the unthinking and unnecessary use of *and/or:* (1) "This loss of perspective sometimes results in unethical and/or ineffective behavior" (*Washington Post*). Sometimes unethical behavior is quite effective, at least until you get caught (just ask Bernie Madoff), so the writer should have used *or* here. (2) "[The doctor] will make a diagnosis [of skin cancer] by visual inspection and/or by taking a skin sample" (Examiner.com). A doctor would never—and can't logically—take a skin sample without a visual inspection, so the diagnosis must be made by visual inspection *and* by taking a skin sample. (3) "[These columnists] reinforce those who believe in their causes and/or intellectually challenge readers who don't agree with them" (*The Herald-Mail*, Maryland). Columnists can't decide to gratify the readers who agree with them *or* exasperate the ones who don't; any opinion piece will of necessity do both, so *and* is the proper word.

Occasionally it's not possible to replace *and/or* with either *and* or *or* and you must reword things. A classic example is *60 days in jail and/or a fine of $25,000*, which can easily be recast into normal prose as *60 days in jail, a fine of $25,000, or both*. Likewise with this sentence from the *New Mexico Independent:* "Use Google Alerts (and/or RSS feeds) to find out when newspapers and other Web sites publish information about you" is better as "Use Google Alerts, RSS feeds, or both to find out when . . ."

ACCIDENT 93
Write *whence*, not *from whence*

Whence means "from where" or "from which," so using *from* with this word is redundant: "Mr. Mendlowitz seemed at ease in his secular life . . . never entertaining the notion of returning from whence [read *whence*] he came" (*Five Towns Jewish Times*). Even when *whence* is used correctly, without *from*, it can make a sentence sound self-consciously literary. Without some legitimate reason to affect an archaic tone (humor perhaps being one), you are probably better off giving *whence* a wide berth.

ACCIDENT 94
Misuse of *tow the line* for *toe the line*

When you *toe the line* you conform strictly; you do your duty or do as you are told. Why is it *toe*, as in your foot, rather than *tow*, "to pull or haul"?

As Robert Hendrickson explains in *The Facts on File Encyclopedia of Word and Phrase Origins*, the expression comes from the "bloody and senseless" prizefights of early nineteenth-century England, before the Marquis of Queensberry rules for boxing were created in 1867. "Fighters firmly placed their toes on a line officials marked in the center of the ring and slugged it out until one man fell, thus ending the round. The fighters then staggered or were dragged back to their corners for 30 seconds and the match continued until one man couldn't come out to toe the line when the bell rang for the next round. . . . That the expression was an early one used in track events, meaning that all contestants must place their forward foot on the starting line . . . also contributed to the popularity of this phrase."

Writing *tow the line* instead of *toe the line* is a fairly common error in edited writing: "Political infighting in Iran heated up yesterday when some of President Mahmoud Ahmadinejad's conservative supporters warned him that he might not get a second term in office if he doesn't start towing [*toeing*] the line" (*Newsweek*); "Souter was one of those old-line Yankee Republicans, a man who had the temerity to exhibit an independent streak and not simply tow [*toe*] the line" (*Dallas Morning News*).

ACCIDENT 95
Write there *are* a handful of things, not there *is*

When the phrase *a handful of* is followed by a plural noun, the verb preceding *handful* should be plural (because it modifies the plural noun, not *handful*): "There is [*are*] a handful of returning starters on that side" (*Tampa Tribune*); "There is [*are*] a handful of titles that are considered the movie masterpieces you must see" (*Time Out New York*). Here's a trick to help you remember this: substitute *a few* for *a handful of*, or simply delete *a handful of*, and the need for a plural verb will instantly become clear.

If a mass noun follows *a handful of*, the verb is properly singular: "There is a handful of malware written for the Mac" (BBC News); "There is a handful of city money as well, but completion is a long way off" (*San Antonio Current*).

ACCIDENT 96
Write *toward*, not *towards*

In American English, the preferred form is *toward*. In British English, it's *towards*. Though American usage manuals, including the style guides of *The New York Times* and The Associated Press, all insist on *toward, towards* often appears in less rigorously edited publications, no doubt because so many Americans pronounce the word with a final *s*. The preferred American pronunciation is *tord*, not *tword* or *too-ward*.

Don't write *more preferable*

Many writers need reminding that *preferable* means "more desirable." So, just as you shouldn't put *more* in front of *better*, you shouldn't put *more* in front of *preferable*: "Many centrist Democrats have long believed that regional co-ops were the ~~more~~ preferable 'other idea'—a stance that has infuriated liberals" (thehill.com). Writers who feel the need for an intensifier make things worse by preceding the offending *more preferable* with *far, much,* or *eminently*. The solution here is to write *much preferable to* (*than* is incorrect): "Those alternatives are far more preferable than [*much preferable to*] risking disrupting or distracting those who are in synagogues to pray for the coming year" (*Jewish Advocate*).

Avoid writing *for free*

I try to avoid writing *for free* because I'd much rather get paid. (Bahdah-bing!)

Although *for free* is now an established idiom in speech and a hackneyed expression in advertising, it has long been criticized by purists as grammatically indefensible. Because *free* is properly an adjective (*free admission*) or an adverb meaning "without charge" (*provided free*), it can't be the object of the preposition *for*. You get something *free*, they say, never *for free*.

At best, *for free* is a casualism that the wreckless writer would be wise to avoid in formal writing. Instead, use *for nothing, without charge, at no cost*—or just *free*: "Subscribers to both the print and online editions would get it ~~for~~ free" (*Baltimore Sun*).

ACCIDENT 99

Don't write *final decision*

The phrase *final decision* is hugely popular (11,645 hits on Google News), but it's a pleonasm: *final* adds nothing to *decision* because decisions are by definition final. (*Decision* comes from the Latin *dēcīdere*, "to cut off, cut down," and so by derivation suggests a cutting off of further deliberation or debate.) Unless the context makes it clear that there have been previous decisions and this is the last of them, delete the word *final* and let *decision* do its work alone: "Canadian Pacific says no ~~final~~ decision has been made to permanently shelve the expansion into the coal-producing region" (*The New York Times*). In that sentence, *yet* could be inserted between *has* and *been*, if desired.

ACCIDENT 100

In order to and *in order for* are wordy

The next time you find yourself writing *in order to* or *in order for*, try deleting *in order*. It won't affect your meaning, and you'll be amazed how much tighter and stronger your sentence will be as a result.

Indeed, you'd be hard put to find a sentence with *in order to* or *in order for* that wouldn't be improved by the removal of *in order*, yet professional writers and editors routinely give these wordy constructions a pass: "Saudi Arabia cut its production last year ~~in order~~ to prop up world oil prices" (*Time*); "But ~~in order~~ for this plan to work, the vaccine would have to arrive earlier than expected" (*U.S. News & World Report*).

ACCIDENT 101

Don't confuse *altogether* and *all together*

Altogether means "completely, entirely, thoroughly, wholly" (*an altogether different situation, altogether wretched weather*), or sometimes "on the whole" (*altogether a success*) or "in all" (*he's written ten books altogether*). *All together* means "all united, all in the same place or at the same time" (*they were all together onstage; we ate all together*).

The misuse of *altogether* for *all together* is rare, but misuse of *all together* for *altogether* is surprisingly common: "I would just as soon avoid him all together [*altogether*]" (Selden Edwards, *The Little Book*);

"Is there someone from this show you love or should we pick a new face all together [*altogether*]?" (AceShowbiz.com); "I have no idea if the world of pro walleye fishing will survive in its current diminished form or disappear all together [*altogether*]" (ESPNOutdoors.com).

101 WORN-OUT WORDS AND HACKNEYED PHRASES THAT WRECKLESS WRITERS SHOULD AVOID LIKE THE PLAGUE

across the board
alive and well (*or* alive and kicking)
as you know
at the end of the day
basically
beat around the bush
bells and whistles
beyond a shadow of a doubt
the big picture
blue in the face
bore(d) to death (*or* to tears)
the bottom line
bring to the table
call a spade a spade
cautiously optimistic
clear as a bell
cold as ice
compare and contrast
conscious effort *or* attempt
cover all the bases
critical

cutthroat competition
cutting edge
dead of night
disappear (*or* vanish) into thin air
each and every
easy as pie (*or* as one, two, three)
enclosed herein
end result
everybody and his brother (*or* mother)
the (simple) fact (*or* truth) of the matter
the fact remains (that)
fame and fortune
final conclusion
final decision
final outcome
final result
firmly establish
first and foremost
for all practical purposes
the foreseeable future

for your information

free gift

full potential

golden opportunity

hard as a rock (*or* as nails)

heart of gold

honest truth

icing on the cake

impact (positive, negative)

in any way, shape, or form

incredible

in harm's way

in my humble opinion

in no time (*or* nothing) flat

in seventh heaven

in terms of

in the first place

in the process of

in the wake of

just what the doctor
   ordered

know for a fact

last but not least

level playing field

a long, hard look

major

make (*or* cut) a long story
   short

meteoric rise

mover and shaker

needless to say

no problem

on the ground floor

on the same page

or what *and* or whatever

(as) per your request

plain as day (*or* as the nose on
   your face)

pretty (as an adverb meaning
   "quite")

pretty (as a) picture

proactive

pure and simple

push the envelope

reality check

really (as an intensifier)

reckless abandon

scare to death

scream bloody murder

sharp as a tack

sick and tired of

the straw that broke the
   camel's back

take a backseat

take the cake

take with a grain of salt

thrilled to death

unique

unless and until

various and sundry

very (*an overused intensifier*)

viable alternative

well and good

you have to understand that

(if *or* do) you know what
   I mean

ACCIDENT 102

There's no need to say *needless to say*

"The phrase *needless to say* is needless nonsense," declares Mark Davidson in *Right, Wrong, and Risky*. "If there's no need to say something, don't say it."

He's right. Enough said.

ACCIDENT 103

Write *why*, not *how come*

Writing that wants to command respect uses *why* to pose a question. Writing that aspires only to imitate the laid-back patterns of speech uses *how come*.

ACCIDENT 104

Don't *commence*—just *begin* or *start*

Sometimes you don't have to speed, cut somebody off, or hit something to have an accident of style. All you have to do is use an annoying word. And *commence* is just such a word. It says to your readers, "I'm too cool to use *begin* or *start*. Henceforth I will *commence*." Find me an instance where *commence* conveys something that *begin* or *start* do not and is demonstrably the better word for the context and I'll send you a hangdog apology and an autographed copy of this book. (Trust me, that will never happen.)

Ostentatious writers can't seem to resist *commence:* "Let the clichés commence" (BBC News); "For now, it will commence on broadcast waves" (*Hartford Courant*); "Court fight could commence this week" (thehill.com); "Greater Manchester has already commenced operations and Lakeside . . . is due to commence this year" (*The Wall Street Journal*). Especially bad, in the eyes of many usage experts, is following *commence* with *to:* "After my morning walk, I make myself comfortable with a cup of coffee and commence to read the syndicated columnists" (*Fayetteville Observer*).

Recently, the craze to ostentatiously commence has extended itself to graduation ceremonies. To *commence* is now sometimes used as a showy substitute for *graduate*—"KVA graduates commence, urged to be happy, not sad" (*Daily Dispatch*, North Carolina)—or to mean "to hold commencement ceremonies": "Drexel's first law grads commence today" (*Philadelphia Daily News*). This is, to put it mildly, inelegant English.

ACCIDENT 105
Don't write *and so on and so forth*
You may use *and so on* to close a thought or a sentence, and if you want to imply impatience or disgust, you may use *ad nauseam*. But *and so on and so forth* is prolix and makes writing sound amateurish.

ACCIDENT 106
It's *cave in to*, not *cave to*
"We can only assume that the administration caved to pressure from coal interests" (*Lexington Herald-Leader*). Much as I'm tempted to mine that sentence for some humor, I will simply point out that whoever wrote it, and whoever failed to copyedit it, can't tell an idiom from a hole in the ground. In standard English we do not *cave to* something, *we cave in to* it. *Cave to* does not belong in serious writing.

A related mistake is writing *cave into* instead of *cave in to*, which improperly gives the idiom the literal suggestion of movement: "City councillors caved into [read *caved in to*] the discriminatory attitudes of homeowners in adopting bylaws that banned more social housing from a central neighbourhood" (*Waterloo Record*, Canada).

ACCIDENT 107
Confusion between *i.e.* and *e.g.*
Many people have trouble with *i.e.* and *e.g.;* the usual mistake is misusing the former for the latter. Both abbreviations stand for Latin phrases: *i.e.* for *id est*, meaning "that is (to say)"; *e.g.* for *exempli gratia*, meaning "for example." We use *i.e.* to reword, clarify, or specify something: "the real estate agent's mantra—i.e., 'location, location, location.'" We use *e.g.* to introduce one or more examples: "I like to read all kinds of fiction, e.g., mysteries, thrillers, and mainstream novels."

Two other points should be noted. First, as you can see from the examples just given, these abbreviations are not italicized; they are also followed by a comma. Second, usage experts generally frown on using them in regular text (as opposed to footnotes, lists, glossaries, etc.) and advise using the more comprehensible *that is* or *namely* for *i.e.* and *for example* or *for instance* for *e.g.* wherever possible.

ACCIDENT 108
Accommodate has two c's and two *m*'s
Accommodate has been called the most misspelled word in the language. I don't doubt it. In the largely unedited writing on Google Web it appears with one *m* (and, far less often, with one *c*) about 10 percent of the time. It may help to remember this: "To avoid an accident of style, put a commode in *accommodate*."

ACCIDENT 109
It's spelled *fluorescent*, not *flourescent*
There is no *flour* in *fluorescent*. The word properly begins with the *fluor-* of *fluoridation* and *fluorocarbon*.

The *floury* misspelling is more common in reputable news outlets than you might think: "The cretin crook's *flour*escent bib meant the game was up before he even had the chance to rob one house" (*Belfast Telegraph*); "Graver is having the jail's old *flour*escent tube lights and fixtures removed" (*Eastern Arizona Courier*).

ACCIDENT 110
It's a *water heater*, not a *hot water heater*
Hot water heater is both redundant—what other kind of water would a water heater make?—and doubly illogical: Why would anyone want a *hot water* heater, one that heats water that is already hot? And if it's a *hot* water heater, wouldn't that be dangerous?

A *hot water heater* is a bit like a *hot cup of coffee*. Is it the cup or the coffee that's hot? Of course it's the coffee, so it should be a *cup of hot coffee*. Yet it's the illogical phrasing *hot cup of coffee* that is more common on Google News and Web.

When people say or write *hot water heater*, they're probably thinking about what the contraption is: a heater that makes hot water. But if you focus on what the thing does (it heats water), you'll always remember it's a *water heater*.

ACCIDENT 111
Write *bored with* or *bored by*, not *bored of*
You can be tired *of* something or sick *of* it, but when something bores you the preferred prepositions are *with* and *by:* "Many kids get bored *with* eating the same thing every day" (*Baltimore Sun*); "They're bored *by* my conversations and I'm bored *by* theirs" (*St. Louis Post-Dispatch*).

ACCIDENT 112
Don't write *all-time record*
It's redundant. A *record* is the best, highest, fastest, most, etc., seen or done in all the time that has elapsed until now. Drop *all-time* and use *record* alone: "Participation in the Supplemental Food Assistance Program . . . reached an all-time record of [*reached a record*] 35 million recipients in June 2008" (Reuters).

ACCIDENT 113
Don't use *most* for *almost* or *nearly*
"Most everyone, at least in the United States, is familiar with the basic facts," writes Dexter Filkins in *The New York Times Book Review*. This use of *most* to mean "almost" or "nearly" has been criticized by numerous authorities on usage, who have called it, *inter alia*, "at best informal," "slovenly," and "a patent illiteracy." The writer who uses *most* for *almost* or *nearly* affects a kind of down-home, mom-and-pop familiarity with the reader, which in any kind of serious nonfiction is inappropriate and should be avoided. The adverb *most* is properly used to mean "to the greatest extent or highest degree" (*this is the most beautiful music*) or "very, quite" (*it was a most unexpected visit*).

NO
SPEED
LIMIT

ACCIDENT 114

Confusion between *wreak* and *reek*

Reek may be a verb meaning "to give off a strong and usually unpleasant odor, smell bad": *He reeked of cigarette smoke.* *Reek* may also
be a noun meaning "a strong smell, unpleasant odor": *the reek of rot-
ting fish on the docks.* The verb to *wreak* means "to cause, bring about,
inflict," and usually appears in the idiom *wreak havoc* (past tense
wreaked havoc).

Because *reek* and *wreak* are homophones (words pronounced
alike), reckless writers often *wreak* [reek] of desperation, *reak* [reek]
of unhappiness, and *reek* or even *reak* [wreak] havoc. Wreckless writers steer clear of writing that *reeks* [stinks] or that *wreaks havoc.*

ACCIDENT 115

It's *wreaked havoc*, not *wrought havoc* or
wrecked havoc

Wreaked is the proper past tense of *wreak*, which means "to cause,
bring about." *Wrought* is an archaic past tense of the verb to *work.*
Havoc is *wreaked*, caused or brought about; iron is *wrought*, manu-
factured in such a way that it can be readily worked.

The misuse of *wrought* for *wreaked* occurs even in the most prestigious publications: "Of course, swine flu has wrought [*wreaked*]
havoc with summer camps in other states, too" (*The New York Times*);
"The region's *peshmerga* militia, jointly controlled by the ruling parties, has largely succeeded in keeping at bay the militants who have
wrought [*wreaked*] havoc elsewhere in Iraq" (*Los Angeles Times*).

The erroneous *wrecked havoc* also appears frequently in edited
writing, perhaps because the notion of wrecking, destroying, is implicit in *wreaked havoc*: "Intermittent rain and swirling winds wrecked
[*wreaked*] havoc at last night's U.S. Open" (*New York Post*); "The bill
was championed by Bronx Sen. Ruben Diaz, who is the Democratic
conference's most outspoken opponent to a bill that would legalize
same-sex marriage—a position that has wrecked [*wreaked*] havoc
on various occasions in the closely-divided chamber" (*New York Daily
News*). (By the way, that hyphen in *closely divided* is a mistake. An
adverb ending in *-ly* combined with a participle should not be hy-

phenated: *Even highly regarded writers sometimes make utterly unthinking errors.* So you just got two accidents of style here for the price of one.)

ACCIDENT 116
Don't surround yourself *completely* or *on all sides*

The verb to *surround* means "to encircle, enclose on all sides." When something is surrounded, it's confined completely; all its sides are covered or closed in. Because the idea of complete coverage is implicit in the meaning of *surround*, all we need to say is that something is surrounded or that it surrounds something else. Yet people feel compelled to dress up the word *surround* and write *completely surrounded* or *surrounded on all sides*. Do they think the word is naked and somehow indecent without this extra verbal clothing?

Poor *surround* may be the most overdressed word in the language. On Google Web, *completely surrounded* appears 936,000 times and *surrounded on all sides* appears 324,000 times. The ridiculously redundant *surrounded all around* appears 2,700 times, and the spectacularly redundant *completely surrounded on all sides* appears 1,470 times. Finally—you're not going to believe this, but it's true—I got 254,400 combined hits for the nonsensical variants *surrounded on three sides*, *surrounded on two sides*, and *surrounded on one side*. It seems we are surrounded by writers who have forgotten the basic meaning of *surround*.

Google News has far fewer hits for these redundancies, thankfully, but *completely surrounded* (65 hits) and *surrounded on all sides* (910 hits) still manage to creep into a number of respectable sources. For example: "The last few hundred members of the Liberation Tigers of Tamil Eelam were completely surrounded by the army early Saturday" (UPI.com).

If you want to pilot your prose smoothly down the page, don't let yourself get *completely surrounded* or *surrounded on all sides*. Keep a safe distance from other words when you use *surround*, and use it only when you mean "to enclose on all sides."

ACCIDENT 117
It's *Welsh rabbit,* not *rarebit*

As Mark Morton explains in *Cupboard Love: A Dictionary of Culinary Curiosities,* "Welsh rabbit contains no rabbit and is not Welsh in origin; instead, it is a dish of melted cheese poured over toast, invented by the British and given its name to mock the Welsh, who were supposedly so gullible that they would accept such a dish as real rabbit." This eighteenth-century culinary jest was forgotten by the nineteenth century, but the dish survived, which left people wondering why they were calling cheese toast *rabbit.* Thus was born the sanitized and euphemized *rarebit,* as in a "rare bit" of food. "This well-intentioned explanation caught on," writes Morton, "promoted, no doubt, by the Welsh themselves and by restaurateurs who feared that a customer might order Welsh rabbit and actually expect to receive a rabbit."

USE THE RIGHT WORD, NOT ITS SECOND COUSIN

"The Dodgers treated yesterday's arrival of [Manny] Ramirez with almost the same folderol that heralded the trade of Wayne Gretzky to the Los Angeles Kings."   —*The San Diego Union-Tribune*

The word *folderol* means "nonsense, foolish talk" or "a useless trifle." Perhaps the writer was thinking of *fanfare.* The words *hoopla* and *ballyhoo* would have worked too.

ACCIDENT 118
Delete *of* after *outside* (with one exception)

The preposition *of* after *outside* is unnecessary: "A baby boy was born in India Thursday with his heart outside of [*outside*] his body" (FOXNews.com); "A man is fighting for his life after being shot Sunday night outside of [*outside*] his home" (KRDO-TV,

Colorado). Remember: You think *outside* the box, not *outside of* the box.

However, when you're referring to the exterior surface of something, *of* is idiomatic. You paint the outside *of* a house and write an address on the outside *of* an envelope.

Outside of is sometimes used to mean "aside from" or "apart from," but it's better style to use one of those phrases instead: "Most men have life insurance outside of [*apart from*] what they get at work" (CNNMoney.com).

ACCIDENT 119
It's *first-come, first-served,* not *first-come, first-serve*
This expression is commonly misunderstood as having *serve* at the end rather than *served*, and the misunderstanding frequently makes its way into edited writing. Here's one example from Reuters: "Space is limited, so attendance will be on a first-come, first-serve [-*served*] basis." But you are not coming first to *serve* first, unless you are playing tennis according to some special rules. You are coming first to be *served* first. It may help to memorize this line: "The first to come will be the first ones *served*."

If you follow this phrase with *basis* or some other noun—that is, if you're using it as a phrasal adjective—be sure to hyphenate the two elements: "Potential winners of the *first-come, first-served* grants are limited to schools transporting students from fourth through 12th grades" (Bizjournals.com). (You may also write *first-come-first-served*, though that is less common.) When a noun does not follow, eliminate the hyphens but keep the comma between the two elements: "That gives them a shot at a better seat, as seats are *first come, first served* on Southwest" (*Arizona Republic*).

ACCIDENT 120
Don't *continue on* or *proceed on,* just *continue* or *proceed*
There is no reason to staple *on* to the verbs *continue* and *proceed* because they both mean "to go on." Yet this redundant practice is common in speech and in all levels of writing: "Despite some dissent

(and a few men who just wanted to escape the ice that threatened constantly) they continued on [*continued* or *went on*] for 600 miles" (*Washington Times*); " 'I'd love to have a debate, just all out, anytime, Oxford-style, if you'd like,' Lahn said to President Obama and then proceeded on [*proceeded* or *went on*] with his question" (ABC News).

ACCIDENT 121
Avoid the redundant *at*

"Where are you at?" asks the guy on a cellphone walking by you, tacking *at* onto the end of his question perhaps because *at* is integral to whatever answer he receives: "I'm *at* the bank, drugstore, supermarket, unisex waxing salon . . ." Ordinary speakers use this superfluous *at* all the time, but careful speakers avoid it for the same reason that good drivers don't honk their horn when the light turns green—it's unnecessary, and it ticks some people off. Wreckless writers avoid it because it's hopelessly poor style and their editors know it.

The redundant *at* is most obvious when it concludes a question, but it can insinuate itself at any point in a sentence: "And that is also the main reason why the stock is where it is *at* now" (Motley Fool: caps.fool.com).

Unless you're using the hackneyed expression *that's where it's at*—and it's hard to think of any reason why you should unless you're quoting the lyrics to the Temptations' "Psychedelic Shack"— just say where it is and leave it at that.

ACCIDENT 122
Misuse of *rob* for *steal*

You *rob* a person or an establishment and you *steal* an object, such as money or property. Thus, you rob a bank or a jewelry store by stealing the bank's money or the store's jewelry. The reporter got it wrong in this sentence: "Lowe is accused of robbing [*stealing*] jewelry with a retail value of about $1 million from the store at 7311 W. Bell Road" (KPHO-TV, Phoenix).

ACCIDENT 123

Can you distinguish *can* and *may*?

Few people can. And that's sad.

In *The ABC of Style* (1964), Rudolf Flesch writes, "Traditional grammar says that *can* should be used only for ability and *may* only for permission, but 20th-century Americans don't care. *Can* for permission is used constantly by everybody."

That may be so but, speaking as a twenty-first-century American, I don't care. *Abusus non tollit usum:* "abuse does not nullify good use." "Everybody does it" is the poorest, lamest excuse for an infraction. It's the last refuge of the speeder, the spitter, the litterer, and the liar. Do you want scoundrels like these to run your language? If they ask, "*Can* I be excused?" will you answer "Yes, you *can*" or "No, you *may* not"?

The saddest thing about the rampant misuse of *can* for *may* is that observing the distinction is no more challenging than stopping when the light turns red and going when it turns green. All you have to keep in mind is that if you're able to do something, you *can* do it, and if you're allowed to do something, you *may* do it. "You can drive your car the wrong way down a one-way street," says *Bryson's Dictionary of Troublesome Words*, "but you may not." You can also drink a quart of booze, but if you do the law says you may not drive (even if you think you can).

In many contexts the notion of being able to do something and the notion of being allowed to do it are closely intertwined, and in those situations it would be unreasonable to object to using *can: In some states you can buy liquor before you're twenty-one; You can deduct those expenses from your income; The sign says we can park here all day.* But when the context is strictly about asking for or granting permission, *may* should be the careful writer's and speaker's choice: *May I offer you some advice? May I have some more key lime pie? Yes, you may, but you may watch TV only after you've cleared the table.*

The most glaring and regrettable misuse of *can* for *may* occurs countless times every day in the simple request "Can I get . . . ?" which, except in the most conscientious writing and speech, has replaced the polite and cultivated "May I (please) have . . . ?"

In negative constructions, *can't* is preferred over the old-fashioned and prissy *mayn't: Mom said we can't go, and I said, "Why can't we?"*

AMAZING GAFFE

"One of Texas' largest universities, UNT offers, many nationally and internationally recognized."   —verbatim from a recruitment letter signed
by the director of admissions at the University of North Texas

There is only one thing you can say about this disaster of an incomplete sentence: *proofread, proofread, proofread.* Don't let anything out the door until you've looked it over thoroughly—especially if it has your name on it. And don't rely just on your spell-checker: I ran mine over that twelve-word mess and it didn't blink. Proofread what you write at least twice, then ask someone else whose skills you trust to read it over. You may be amazed at what another pair of eyes can find that you missed.

ACCIDENT 124
Misuse of *phenomena* for *phenomenon*

If you're talking about one remarkable thing or event, it's a *phenomenon*. If you're talking about more than one, they're *phenomena*. Some writers just can't get their heads around this elementary distinction, so we often see the plural *phenomena* misused for the singular *phenomenon:* "It is difficult and perhaps impossible to explain that phenomena" (*Southwest Virginia Today*); "Buying votes is not a new phenomena in Lebanon" (*Socialist Worker*); "Places like India, China, and Japan will get a great glimpse of this phenomena" (WLTX-TV, Columbia, South Carolina). In all cases, make that *phenomenon*.

Phenomenon is also used informally to mean "a highly successful, talented, or popular person," as in *Michael Jackson was a pop music phenomenon*. In this sense, the plural *phenomenons* is acceptable:

"The Jackson 5 were one of the biggest phenomenons in pop music during the early '70s" (*Florida Times-Union*). But *phenomenons* should never be used for extraordinary things or events.

ACCIDENT 125
Don't write *at this [particular] point in time*

At this point in time is a redundancy that is only made worse by the interpolation of *particular*. This heinous accident of style is especially common among sportswriters, politicians, and police, who use it either to sound important or to pad their prose.

The puffed-up phrase can invariably be reduced to a single word, such as *point, time,* or *now:* "At some point in time [*At some point*], Republicans are going to have to do something other than just vote no"; "There was a point in time [*There was a time*] when we thought we could be artsy photographers"; "At this point in time we expect [*We now expect*] to open approximately 50 stores this year." Sometimes even that solution is unnecessary and the phrase can be deleted: "He feels ~~at this point in time~~ the district should take its time with making a decision"; "Looking back, I'm still amazed at how much talent we had in our small town ~~at that particular point in time.~~"

See "Say It Again, Sam" on page 57.

ACCIDENT 126
It's a *moot point,* not a *mute point*

Hypercorrect speakers—the kind who labor erroneously to say *afternyoon* for *afternoon* and *between you and I* instead of *between you and me*—tend to mispronounce *moot*, which should rhyme with *boot*, as if it were spelled *mute* and rhymed with *cute*. The mispronunciation sometimes spills over into print: "Even if those votes were counted against Fannin though, it would be a mute [*moot*] point" (*Troy Messenger*, Alabama); "At the moment it is a fairly mute [*moot*] point because there are hardly any self-cert products left" (mortgagesolutions-online.com). Pronounce *moot* naturally and you'll avoid this pothole in your prose.

Incidentally, before the adjective *moot* came to mean "hypothetical, academic, of no practical significance," it meant "debatable, open to discussion or debate." In medieval England, a *moot hall* was a building where villagers gathered to discuss the issues of the day, and since the late eighteenth century a *moot court* has been "a mock court for the conduct of hypothetical legal cases, as for students of law" (*Random House Webster's College Dictionary*). The verb *to moot* means "to debate or dispute," and the adjective *mootable*, which dates from 1533, retains the older meaning of *moot*: "open to discussion or debate."

ACCIDENT 127
It's *cut-and-dried*, not *cut-and-dry*

This old phrase, which dates from the early eighteenth century, probably has its origin in the dried herbs that apothecaries sold for medicinal purposes. Although dictionaries list both *dried* and *dry*, the preferred form is *cut-and-dried*, with hyphens. Thus, there are two mistakes in this sentence from *The New York Times*: "I have learned over the years that while my initial reaction is always to question if I or any other doctor missed the diagnosis, the situation is not always so cut and dry [*cut-and-dried*]."

ACCIDENT 128
Avoid the phrase *expensive price*

A price may be high or low, fair or unfair. Only a product can be expensive. Thus, "El Paso had the most expensive price per gallon" (Associated Press) should be either "El Paso had the highest price per gallon" or "El Paso had the most expensive gas."

ACCIDENT 129
Avoid *in the process of*

The phrase *in the process of* is almost always unnecessary; it's just a bit of bloated bureaucratese used to pad a sentence. Yet it manages to appear with knee-jerk regularity, even in the most rigorously edited writing. In the following examples, *in the process of* is superfluous and should have been deleted: "Although the network says it was already ~~in the process of~~ plotting a new direction" (*Los Angeles Times*); "Their home is still ~~in the process of~~ being renovated after Hurricane Katrina" (Associated Press); "MOMA . . . is ~~in the process of~~ retooling the program" (*The Wall Street Journal*).

On those rare occasions when *in the process of* is used to mean "attempting to" or "trying to," it is always better to use one of those phrases instead: "The victim said she was in the process of obtaining [*was trying to get*] a credit report" (*Bowling Green Daily News*).

ACCIDENT 130
Don't use *anniversary* for less than a year

It has become popular in recent years to use the word *anniversary*—which comes from the Latin *annus*, year, and *vertere*, to turn—for dates or occasions that recur in less than a year's time: "With the current rally nearing its six-month anniversary . . . the bears see a day of reckoning soon" (*Los Angeles Times*); "Tuesday marks the five-week anniversary of left-hander John Danks quitting his use of smokeless tobacco" (*Chicago Tribune*).

This is loose usage. An anniversary, like a birthday, comes once a year. Use another word (e.g., *commemoration, celebration, memorial, remembrance*) or revise the sentence: "With the current rally lasting nearly six months . . . the bears see a day of reckoning soon"; "Tuesday marks five weeks since left-hander John Danks quit using smokeless tobacco."

Also, it is better style to use ordinal numbers for anniversaries (*first, second, tenth, twenty-fifth*, etc.) than to write *first-year, second-year*, and so on.

ACCIDENT 131
Don't drop *had* before *better*

"As for men, well, we better get with the program," writes Nick Jimenez, editorial-page editor emeritus of the Corpus Christi *Caller-Times*. If you aspire to be a wreckless writer, you had better get with the program and watch out for accident-prone sentences like that, which omit the requisite *had* before *better*.

"Dropping the *had*," says *Garner's Modern American Usage*, "is acceptable only in informal speech or recorded dialogue." Yet this mistake is all too common in edited prose, probably because of the widespread misconception that writing should imitate speech: "He better not be bluffing" (*Boston Globe*); "I figured I better get his fishing line out there first" (*Des Moines Register*); "They better get used to it" (*Star-Ledger*, New Jersey).

No, we *had* better not get used to it. It's *I had better, you had better, he* or *she had better, we had better,* and *they had better,* not *I better, you better, he* or *she better, we better,* and *they better.* You may also use contractions—*I'd better, you'd better, he'd better, she'd better, we'd better,* and *they'd better*—particularly in less formal writing. However, even in informal writing *it had better* is more appropriate, while *it'd better* is best restricted to transcribed speech.

Headline writers are often guilty of dropping *had*, even when they have space for it. This "is inadvisable," says Garner, which is the Nice Usage Expert Guy's way of saying "inexcusably stupid." There is no excuse for not using *you'd* in this headline: "Have a complaint about your broker? You better have proof" (usatoday.com). And this headline would have been better with a comma before *you'd* or *you had:* "If you work in this Florida city[,] you [*you'd* or *you had*] better wear underwear and deodorant" (*South Florida Sun Sentinel*).

ACCIDENT 132

Write *among, amid,* and *while,* not *amongst, amidst,* and *whilst*

Some British and Canadian writers still cling to *amongst, amidst,* and *whilst,* but in American English these forms are old-fashioned and have been considered overelegant and pretentious since at least the mid-twentieth century. American newspaper stylebooks and usage guides uniformly call for *among, amid,* and *while.* The word *midst* appears only in the set phrases *in the midst of* and *in our midst.*

On a related note, either *unknown* or *unbeknown* is preferable to *unbeknownst,* which strikes an archaic chord in American English.

ACCIDENT 133
It's spelled *memento*, not *momento*
Despite reminders in the stylebooks of The Associated Press and
The New York Times, and despite admonishments in countless usage
guides like this one, many writers have a hard time remembering
that there is no *moment* in *memento*. Those who misspell the word
no doubt also mispronounce it moh-MEN-toh; the proper pronunciation is muh-MEN-toh.

Take a moment to memorize this: "A *memento* is something that
awakens memory." The preferred plural is *mementos* (without any
toes at the end). Also take care not to misspell *memento* in the Latin
expression *memento mori* (a reminder of death, literally "remember
that you must die").

ACCIDENT 134
Don't use *individual* to mean *person*, with one exception
The noun *individual*, writes Rudolf Flesch in *The ABC of Style* (1964),
"is a cumbersome 5-syllable word much overused as a synonym for
person. Usually it can and should be changed to a simpler word like
people, someone, you."

Some examples of the misuse: "Falco introduced several individuals [*people*] who have no health insurance" (*Huffington Post*); "Morris
County Habitat for Humanity is looking for an outstanding individual [*person*]" (*Star-Ledger*, New Jersey); "an individual [*someone,
a source*] with knowledge of the Rockets' decision-making" (*Houston
Chronicle*); "The first step is for the individual [*you, people*] to know
how to make and identify his or her [*your, their*] own sounds"
(tgdaily.com).

This penchant for using the polysyllabic *individual* for *person*,
observes *Garner's Modern American Usage*, can be blamed on "police-
blotter jargon," which so often makes its way into news reports: "At
the Rainbow Lounge, TABC agents placed one individual [*person,
man, woman*] under arrest" (*Dallas Morning News*).

The sole exception to this proscription against *individual* is when
you need to distinguish the person from a group, class, or category:

"Should the individual or society be of primary importance?" (*Jamestown Post Journal*); "It's devoted to . . . securing the rights of the individual against the tyranny of the majority" (*The Nation*).

And here's one more don't, this time regarding the adjective *individual:* Don't pair it with the word *each;* write *each person* or *each thing,* not *each individual person* or *each individual thing.* In the following examples, *individual* is superfluous: "Each individual rider [*each rider*] took only a short break before having to ride again" (*The New York Times*); "In order to check these things properly, you need the results from each individual polling station [*each* or *every polling station*]" (guardian.co.uk.); "While Memphis reports each individual crime [*every crime* or *all crimes*], some cities report only the highest offenses—such as murder" (Scripps Howard News Service).

SHORTER ALTERNATIVES TO LONGER WORDS AND PHRASES

numerous, a lot of, a great number of = many
possess = have
purchase, obtain, procure = buy, get
sufficient = enough
attempt = try
endeavor = try
employ = use
remainder = rest
initial = first
commence = begin
in order to = to
in order for = for
individual (noun) = person, man *or* woman

SHORTER ALTERNATIVES TO LONGER, JARGONY WORDS

facilitate=help, assist; ease, simplify; lead, direct
facility=building (or be specific: hospital, library, school, etc.)
minimize=lessen, decrease, prevent
optimize, maximize=increase, improve, expand
incentivize=motivate, stimulate, move, spur
implement=do, perform, fulfill, carry out
utilize, utilization=use (verb) and use (noun)
eventuate=happen, occur, result
effectuate=effect (verb), accomplish, achieve
differential=difference
methodology=method
technology=device, machine, technique, system

ACCIDENT 135

Don't confuse *comic* and *comical*

The distinction here is between the intentional and the unintentional. If it's supposed to be funny, it's *comic*. If it's funny when it's not supposed to be, it's *comical*. *Comic* acting is funny. *Comical* acting is pathetic.

ACCIDENT 136

Don't confuse *historic* and *historical*

Historic means "making history" or "figuring significantly in history." A historic occasion makes history; a historic building is historically significant. *Historical* means "pertaining to or part of history." Historical evidence relates to history; a historical novel is based on history; a historical event is part of history.

That's a straightforward distinction, yet good writers continually get drunk on the shorter word and drive their sentences into the

Ditch of Bad Diction. Here, for example, is Serge Schmemann, editor of the editorial pages of the *International Herald Tribune*, in *The New York Times Book Review:* "Historians are certainly within their rights in trying to supplement the historic facts with some guesses about the influences of the time and the place. But in 'The Lost Spy,' there are too few historic facts and far too many guesses." Those *historic facts* should be *historical facts* in both cases because facts don't make history; they merely pertain to it.

ACCIDENT 137
A historian or *an* historian? A historical or *an* historical?

If you are unsure whether to use *a* or *an* before certain words beginning with *h*, all you need to remember is this simple rule: If the *h* is sounded, use *a*. If it is silent, use *an*. Thus, use *a* before *humble, hilarious, hysterical, hallucination, hereditary, heroic, huge, homage* (see Accident 291), *history, historic, historical,* and *historian*. Use *an* before *honor, hour, heir,* and *herb*.

Some writers and speakers are tempted to use *an* with *historian* and *historical* because the first syllable is unstressed and the *h* is not distinctly pronounced. But, unless you speak the Cockney dialect, the *h* is far from silent, so *a* should precede *historian* and *historical*.

Nearly all modern authorities on usage and pronunciation favor this "rule of *h*." It's sensible and speech-friendly, it's based on well over a century of good usage, and if you follow it, no one can ever accuse you of affectation.

ACCIDENT 138
Misplacing a question mark with quotation marks

Question marks can go inside or outside quotation marks depending on the form of the question, so you have to be on your guard. If the quotation is itself a question, the question mark goes inside the quotation marks: *"What can I get for you tonight?" the waiter asked.* If the sentence itself is a question, and the quoted matter is merely part of it, the question mark goes outside the quotation marks: *Do you know who said "I came, I saw, I conquered"?*

The accident to watch out for is misplacing the question mark inside the closing quotation marks (or mark) when it is the whole sentence, not just the quoted matter, that is a question. Consider these back-to-back sentences published in *The New York Times:* "Who, reading Maupassant, thinks, 'Oh, there's a Frenchman for you?' Who, reading 'The Death of Vishnu,' thinks: 'I can't relate. I've never slept on a Bombay stairwell?' " Because, in each case, the entire sentence is the question, this is how those sentences should have been punctuated: "Who, reading Maupassant, thinks, 'Oh, there's a Frenchman for you'? Who, reading 'The Death of Vishnu,' thinks, 'I can't relate. I've never slept on a Bombay stairwell'?"

Did you notice that, in addition to moving the question marks outside the closing quotation mark, I changed the colon after the second *thinks* to a comma? I did that so both sentences would be punctuated alike and because it's better to introduce a quotation with a comma unless you have a good reason to draw attention to what follows. (For more on this point see Accident 331.)

ACCIDENT 139

Don't use *unique* to mean "unusual," "special," or "exceptional"

Aren't you sick of the word *unique*? Everywhere you turn you find something that's *very unique, completely unique,* and *the most unique.* Poor *unique* is so overused, and misused, that its uniqueness has worn out. It is perhaps the most banal and feckless word in the language. But hack writers cling to it like a meretricious lover or a life buoy, and soldered to their dull, assembly-line sentences *unique* does only one thing: *bore, bore, bore.*

Unique comes from the Latin *ūnĭcus,* "one, only, sole," from *unus,* "one," and means "unlike anything else, one-of-a-kind." A thing cannot be more or less unique than another thing; it is simply unique— unmatched, unrivaled, incomparable. Yet over the decades all those hack writers, pounding out their advertising and news copy, seized on *unique* as a presumably more stylish substitute for *unusual, special,* and *exceptional.* And when they'd wrung all the unusuality out of this exceptional word, they began to qualify it with modifiers:

somewhat unique, more unique, utterly unique. But while something may be *more unusual* or the *most exceptional*, it cannot be *more* or *most unique.* That is why this sentence, cited in *The American Heritage Dictionary* (2nd college ed.), is so bad it's laughable: "Omaha's most unique restaurant is now even more unique."

After all this abuse, the self-respecting stylist can do little else but boycott this eviscerated word. The next time *unique* is about to spring from your fingers or your lips, take a deep breath and summon something more expressive—perhaps *unrivaled, matchless, peerless, unparalleled, incomparable, singular,* or the delicious *inimitable.* Unlike poor weak *unique,* these are truly stylish words. They will make your sentence sparkle. They will awaken interest in your audience. They will set you apart from the humdrum herd of hack writers.

ACCIDENT 140
Write *precaution,* not *precautionary measure*
Washing your hands frequently is a *precaution* against getting sick, not a *precautionary measure.* Avoid this wordy phrase.

ACCIDENT 141
Don't *overexaggerate*
Something *exaggerated* is already overdone, so adding *over* is redundant.

ACCIDENT 142
You can do without *absolutely*
People have long been fond of using *absolutely* to lend intensity to their speech, but this passion rarely translates into writing, where the word is almost always, as *Garner's Modern American Usage* puts it, "a meaningless intensifier." It may seem more emphatic to say *These charges are absolutely false,* but in writing the adverb is flabby and hollow and the declaration is stronger without it.

"On a night when the Pittsburgh Penguins absolutely had to win, it was the quietly cool Gonchar who delivered" (ESPN.com). Without that *absolutely,* would the Penguins still have had to win that night? "If Pawlenty does sign the election certificate before he absolutely has to" (CBS News). Is there a difference between when Pawlenty has to sign and when he *absolutely* has to?

When quoting speech, *absolutely* must be transcribed: " 'We have to be absolutely uncompromising,' Kuneva said" (Focus News). But in your own writing you must strive to root out all the super-fluities and dullnesses of speech. The unthinking writer who inserts *absolutely* into a sentence adds nothing essential to it and is ten characters closer to a case of carpal tunnel syndrome.

ACCIDENT 143
It's spelled *in memoriam*, not *in memorium*

When you say this Latin phrase, which means "in memory of," it ends with sound of *um*, but when you spell it, be sure it ends with -*am*. Also, the well-worn expression is not *time in memoriam*, as I once heard an interviewer say on NPR's *All Things Considered*. It's *time immemorial*, "beyond the reach of memory or record, ancient."

ACCIDENT 144
It's *delve into*, not *dwell into*

"The aim of the paper," begins an abstract of an academic treatise presented at an international studies conference, "is to dwell into [*delve into*] the relationship between European integration and the evolution of the notion of society." The misuse of *dwell into* for *delve into* is more common than you might think. I once heard it from a learned commentator in a PBS documentary about the Kennedys, and it flourishes like ragweed in blogs and online sources of political and cultural commentary.

When you *dwell on* or *upon* something, you either fasten your attention on it or comment on it at length. You can *dwell on* the past or *dwell on* your favorite subject. When you *delve into* something, you investigate it, dig into it as if with a shovel or spade: "The papers all *delve into* the background of New York's native daughter, Judge Sonia Sotomayor, who has been nominated to the Supreme Court by President Obama" (*The New York Times*).

ACCIDENT 145
There is no *noun* in *pronunciation*

The beastly mispronunciation *pro-noun-ciation* for *pronunciation* has in recent years begun to spread like swine flu from speech into print. For example, here are the first lines of an interview published in the online edition of the *Boston Globe:* "Let's get the pronunciation of your name correct. I've heard it in many ways." As accidents of style go, that deadly opening is like a car driving headlong off a bridge.

People mispronounce and misspell *pronunciation* because of the *noun* in the verb *pronounce*, which leads them by false analogy to change the *nun* in *pronunciation* to *noun*. This error is not yet common in edited prose, but it is pandemic in blogs and other online postings that have not been proofread (701,000 hits on Google Web). Please, please check your pro*nun*ciation of this word to make sure there is a *nun* and not a *noun* in it. And if this word appears in anything you've written, use your otherwise lame spell-checker to make sure your fingers didn't slip and steer your sentence to a watery death.

ACCIDENT 146
Is it *way* or *ways*?

We often hear and read that something has *a (long) ways to go* or is *a (long) ways off*. But this usage is colloquial and inappropriate in serious journalism and other formal writing. The preferred form uses the singular *way: a (long) way to go; a (long) way off*.

ACCIDENT 147
It's spelled *theater* in American English, not *theatre*

The spelling *theatre*, with *-re* instead of *-er*, is British, and any American organization or publication that uses it is guilty of affectation.

American usage experts and newspaper style manuals all prefer *theater*, and American dictionaries all list it first. So why is the British *theatre* so popular in the United States? "Because America's theatrical world was under considerable British influence when the Broadway stage was founded," explains Mark Davidson in *Right,*

Wrong, and Risky, "and American theater owners today seem to think that the British *theatre* adds a touch of class. You may notice the same pretentious spelling at your neighborhood multiplex"—which, I hasten to add, is probably located in a pretentious Shopping Centre.

ACCIDENT 148
It's a *safe-deposit box,* not a *safety-deposit box*
"The note was discovered in a safety deposit box shortly after he [Damon Runyon] died in December 1946," writes Alison Leigh Cowan in *The New York Times,* flouting her own newspaper's style manual, which says it's a "**safe deposit box** (not *safety deposit*)." Other authorities and the dictionaries agree that *safe-deposit* should have a hyphen because it's a phrasal adjective modifying *box.*

Garner's *Modern American Usage* speculates that *safe-deposit box* was corrupted into *safety-deposit box* because when the phrase was spoken the *de-* in *deposit* made it sound like *safety-posit box.* By adding a syllable, this was easily "corrected" to *safety-deposit.*

ACCIDENT 149
It's *home in,* not *hone in*
In *Lapsing Into a Comma,* Bill Walsh makes the point succinctly and well: "You can hone a skill, but you can't hone in on something. The term is *home in.*" If you *home in on* (seek out, focus on) your accidents of style, you will *hone* (sharpen, improve) your writing skills. You can also *hone* this distinction in your mind by thinking of a homing device *homing in* on its target.

ACCIDENT 150
Don't confuse *convince* and *persuade*
"They have to convince at least one of five self-made multimillion-aires—the sharks—to cough up their own cash," writes Gina Salamone in the *New York Daily News,* committing a classic accident of style: using *convince* when the meaning calls for *persuade.*

Simply put, to *convince* is to make someone believe something. To *persuade* is to make someone take action. Properly, the infinitive *to* may follow *persuade* but never *convince*. You do not *convince* people *to* do something; you *persuade* them *to* do it. In the following examples, *convince* is misused for *persuade:* "Meanwhile, the government will try to convince [*persuade*] the holdouts to wait two years" (*The Wall Street Journal*); "He was convinced [*persuaded*] by high-pressure selling to buy several more" (*Philadelphia Daily News*); "Countless millions of dollars have been poured into convincing [*persuading*] youngsters not to smoke" (*Boston Globe*).

Of or *that* may follow *convince:* you *convince* people *of* the truth or *convince* them *that* you're right. But once you've convinced them, you may still have *to persuade* them *to* do what you want. Someone may also be *persuaded to* do something without being *convinced that* it's the right thing to do.

Less often, *persuade* is used where *convince* would be the better word: "I cannot support her [Sotomayor's] nomination because I'm not persuaded [*convinced*] that she has the right judicial philosophy for the Supreme Court" (Senator Chuck Grassley of Iowa). Remember, *convince* is to make someone believe while *persuade* is to make someone act. Had Senator Grassley been *convinced that* Sotomayor had "the right judicial philosophy," he would probably have been *persuaded to* vote in favor of her nomination.

ACCIDENT 151
It's *doctoral*, not *doctorial*, and it's a *doctorate*, not a *doctorate degree*

The *Oxford English Dictionary* shows that the four-syllable *doctorial* had some currency in the eighteenth and nineteenth centuries, but it is now a needless variant ignored by most modern dictionaries, frowned on by usage authorities, and eschewed by careful writers. The proper word in all contexts is *doctoral*, with no *i*, and it is pronounced in three syllables: DAHK-tuh-rul. It's a *doctoral* student, a *doctoral* program, and a *doctoral* dissertation. And if you're a medical doctor, you perform *doctoral* duties and dispense *doctoral* advice.

Also, just as you wouldn't write *Ph.D. degree* or *M.D. degree*, don't write *doctorate degree*. It's redundant. A *doctorate* is the degree of a doctor; you may also call it a *doctoral degree*. Incidentally, a law degree (doctor of law) is a Juris Doctor, abbreviated J.D.—not, as it is often miswritten, a *Juris Doctorate degree*. Note the capital *J* and *D*.

AMAZING GAFFE

"To Mr. Gates, the old-timers are just that: old and fusty guardians of a 'strictly English' English language, the stuff of dead white men and their imperially minded friends, who gaze back with contented nostalgia to a green and pleasant time when everyone knew how to speak well, could tell synecdoche from syntax, would never split an infinitive nor end a sentence with a proposition . . ." —Simon Winchester, *The Wall Street Journal*

No one, to my knowledge, has ever objected to ending a sentence with a *proposition*. Many have long objected to ending a sentence with a *preposition*, but this prohibition is "a cherished superstition," declared H. W. Fowler in 1926, contrary to English idiom and derided by modern authorities on usage. As Theodore M. Bernstein remarked in *The Careful Writer* (1965), anyone who insists that you cannot end a sentence with a preposition "won't have a leg on which to stand."

By the way, a computer spell-checker would never have caught this amusing typographical error. Moral: Relying only on your spell-checker is like putting your car in cruise control and going to sleep. There is no substitute for a keen pair of eyes.

ACCIDENT 152

Misuse of *pour* for *pore*

When you *pour* something, you cause it to flow in a continuous stream: *She poured the sour milk into the sink.* When you *pore over* something (note the obligatory *over*), you read or study it carefully: *Before delivering her speech, she pored over her notes.*

Misuse of the flowing *pour* for the scrutinizing *pore* is a common accident of style, even in reputable media outlets: "As of Sunday evening, homicide detectives were still in the area, interviewing witnesses and pouring [*poring*] over the evidence" (*Toronto Star*); "Inside, Capt. Gene Palka, the American officer in charge, was . . . pouring [*poring*] over a map of the city" (BBC News); "But after pouring [*poring*] over data, it became obvious that breast cancer deaths here are the shocker" (*Staten Island Advance*).

Here's an example of the proper way to *pour over:* "There's also time to watch geese flying south and squirrels collecting acorns and listen to the sounds of water pouring over the water wheel" (*Allentown Morning Call*, Pennsylvania).

ACCIDENT 153
Don't confuse *principle* and *principal*

Principle is a noun that may mean "a basic law, rule, truth, or assumption": *a principle of physics; the principles of a democratic society.* It may also mean "a standard or code of conduct, or ethical conduct itself": *the Golden Rule is our most abiding principle; a woman of principle.* The phrases *basic principle* and *fundamental principle* are common but venial redundancies. The expression *in principle* means "basically, fundamentally."

Principal as a noun means "a head or chief." The *principal* of a school is the head of it, and a *principal* in a play is a leading actor in the play. As an adjective *principal* means "first, foremost, chief": the *principal reason* is the first or foremost reason; the *principal harpist* is the chief harpist.

ACCIDENT 154
Confusion of *ensure, assure,* and *insure*

Ensure means "to make sure, make certain": *Please ensure that this package is delivered on time. Assure* means "to guarantee, promise, put someone's mind at ease": *She assured him she would be there. Insure* means "to protect against loss."

You *insure* a house, a car, or a life by buying an insurance contract. You *assure* people by shoring up their confidence: "Biz Stone, founder of the company, was quick to *assure* users that advertising wasn't imminent" (Geek.com). You *ensure* a thing by making certain that it happens: "Lawmakers need to *ensure* that children will receive either comparable or better benefits" (capitolweekly.net).

Any contractor you hire should be made to repeat this sentence aloud: *I am **insured**, and I **assure** you that I will do everything I can to **ensure** the safety of everyone working on your property.*

Two admonitions: First, restrict *insure* to the insurance business; don't use it interchangeably with *ensure*. Second, remember that *assure* must have a personal object, a person or people to assure. If it's a thing rather than a human being getting assured, it's a safe bet that *ensure* should have been used instead. Here's Iowa governor Chet Culver possibly misquoted in the *Daily Nonpareil*: " 'We must assure [*ensure*] that the film program has the oversight in place to assure [*ensure*] that it operates properly and as intended,' he told reporters in Des Moines."

ACCIDENT 155

Write *these kinds* and *those kinds,* not *these kind* and *those kind*

If you're referring to one kind of thing, keep everything singular: *this kind of thing* or *that kind of thing*. If you're referring to more than one kind or more than one thing, make everything plural: *these kinds of things* or *those kinds of things*. The same goes for when *the* appears in the phrasing: *(that is) the kind of thing I like; (these are) the kinds of things I like.*

The common mistake you should watch out for here is mispairing the plural *these* or *those* with the singular *kind:* "He has overcome these kind [*kinds*] of odds before" (Associated Press); "I'm not going to have these kind [*kinds*] of meetings" (Karl Rove, quoted at FOXNews .com); "So with those kind [*kinds*] of numbers, has Section VI boys soccer caught up with Section V?" (*Buffalo News*); "Those are the kind [*kinds*] of pounds she won't shed with age" (*San Diego Reader*).

Be that kind of writer who doesn't get into these kinds of accidents of style.

ACCIDENT 156
Misuse of *good* for *well*

Athletes are fond of saying that things went *good* or that they played *good*. This accident of style is unpardonable in anything other than direct quotations.

"When it's an activity being described, use *well*, the adverb," writes Patricia T. O'Conner in *Woe Is I*. "When it's a condition or a passive state being described, use *good*, the adjective." In other words, whatever you can do should be done *well*. But if you're talking about how something is, it's *good*. The only time you can *do good* is if you're a humanitarian or philanthropist trying to help people. If you're doing anything else, you do it *well*.

When you dress *well*, you look *good*. When a piano has been tuned *well*, it sounds *good*. When a meal has been cooked *well*, it smells and tastes *good*. And when a parent tells a child to behave *well*, that child had better be *good*.

Have I described this distinction *well*? Does that seem *good* to you?

Sometimes people get confused about using *well* or *good* after the verb to *feel*. Do you feel *good* or feel *well*? they wonder. The answer is that both are correct. *Well* may describe how something is done (*you write well*), but it may also mean "in good health." So you may tell your doctor that you feel *good* or *well*, as you please.

One last piece of advice. In casual speech, *real good* is a pardonable offense, but when you write you should always be *really good*.

ACCIDENT 157
It's *between (for, to) you and me*, not *between (for, to) you and I*

Believe it or not, *between you and I* is not a mistake an ordinary person makes. It takes some education and some presumed refinement to get into this accident of style.

For example, when Massachusetts senator John Kerry was running for president in January 2003, he was quoted as saying, "If I am fortunate enough to share a stage with this president and debate him, one of the first things I'll tell him is there's a defining issue *between he and I.*" The Yale-educated Kerry should have said *between him and me*, but apparently he thought it was infra dig.

Talk to any Joe Blow or Joe Sixpack and I'll bet my last buck he'll say, "Just *between you and me*, pal, there's something screwy going on down at city hall." Or sit down next to him at a bar and he'll say to the bartender, "Hey, howzabout a round *for my friend and me?*" But give him a B.A., a white-collar job, and a house in the suburbs, and by golly the next thing you'll hear pass through his parvenu lips is *Let's keep this between you and I* or *This is a good investment for you and I.*

Just between you and me, why is it that only upwardly mobile types say *just between you and I?* Did their teachers whack them on the wrist for saying *it's me* instead of *it is I?* Did their mothers dock their allowance for telling their friends, "You and me should get together soon?" If you happen to be one of the many who have jettisoned the unpretentious and proper *just between you and me* for the pinkie-in-the-air error *just between you and I*, it's high time you reexamined your grammatical roots.

The problem arises from a misunderstanding of how nominative and objective pronouns function. *I* is always a nominative pronoun and the subject of a sentence: *I am going; I am reading.* The pronoun *me* is objective and must either be the object of a verb (*They can't touch me*) or the object of a preposition: *give it to me; that's for me; this is between him and me.*

If that's so much grammatical jargon to your ear, just remember this rule of thumb: whenever something is *for, to,* or *between* someone else and you, *me* is the correct pronoun—*for her and me; to my friends and me; between you, me, and the lamppost.* You can also eliminate the other person in the clause and consider how it sounds. Your inner grammatical ear should automatically sense that *for I, to I,* and *between I and the lamppost* are hideously unidiomatic.

ACCIDENT 158
Misuse of *myself* for *I* and *me*

Myself has two main uses. It is a reflexive pronoun, meaning that it directs the action of the verb back to the subject: *I hurt myself; I talk to myself; I can't stop myself.* And it is an intensive pronoun, meaning that it emphasizes a preceding noun or pronoun: *I made it myself; I'll do that myself; I myself don't care for it.* Less often, *myself* is used to mean "my sane or normal self," as in *I was beside myself* or *When I get all liquored up, I'm not myself.*

In general usage, that's all *myself* can legally do. But because people are often unsure and self-conscious about how to use the nominative pronoun *I* and the objective pronoun *me,* they extend the grammatical boundaries of *myself* and use it where *I* or *me* properly belongs.

The misuse of *myself* for *I* occurs chiefly in speech and quoted speech: "Steven Spielberg, George Lucas and myself [*I*] are agreed on what the fifth adventure will concern" (actor Harrison Ford, quoted in a syndicated article). But sometimes an erroneous *myself* for *I* sneaks past the editorial security guards and finds its way into print: "My younger sister, kid brother, and myself [*I*] were assigned rooms that were unremarkable" (*Huntsville Item,* Texas).

The misuse of *myself* for *me,* on the other hand, is rampant in both speech and print: "Desmond McCarthy once described to David Cecil and myself [*me*] a typical dinner he had attended" (*The New York Times Book Review*); "What would the difference be, say, between myself [*me*] and a pre-op female-to-male transsexual?" (*The New York Times Magazine*); "I assure you that no one, including Larry Lucchino, Golding and myself [*me*], was anything other than candid and frank" (John Moores, University of California regent and former owner of the San Diego Padres, in a letter to *The San Diego Union-Tribune*); "When I sit at the front porch of our Cape house, in the sunshine and sea-freshened air, I think of them often: my parents and my brothers and sisters, all departed now save for Jean and myself [*me*]" (Senator Edward M. Kennedy, in *True Compass,* his posthumously published memoir).

Two final admonitions: First, never write or say *like myself* or *such as myself.* Make it *like me:* "The company is eliminating the generous annual plans that allowed music fiends such as myself [*like me*] to download 65 songs for about $14 a month" (*Los Angeles Times*). Second, although *myself included* has become a set phrase, it is grammatically eccentric. Careful writers avoid it and use *including me* instead.

ACCIDENT 159

Misuse of *himself* for *him*, *herself* for *her*, and *yourself* for *you*

Pronouns with -*self* are properly used in two ways: reflexively, turning the action back on the subject (*he made himself do it, she excused herself, you told yourself not to*); and intensively, emphasizing a preceding noun or pronoun (*he did it himself, you made that yourself, you yourself are guilty*).

It's a common but nonetheless inexcusable error to use the reflexive/intensive pronouns *himself* and *herself* for the objective pronouns *him* and *her*. Here are two examples of the mistake from Richard Russo's Pulitzer Prize–winning novel *Empire Falls:* "The same girl took up residence in art class with herself [*her*] and the other Boners"; "There were probably leagues set up just for boys like himself [*him*]."

It's also inexcusable to use *yourself* for *you:* "The tour needed a gimmick to entice players like yourself [*you*] and Phil Mickelson to stick around" (miamiherald.com); "As your Vice President, I have had the unique opportunity to travel all across the country and talk to citizens like yourself [*you*]" (Al Gore, in a 1998 fund-raising letter).

Some writers believe that what's wrong with *like yourself* is the word *like* rather than *yourself*, so in a fit of self-consciousness they write *such as yourself* instead. But that's just a hypercorrection for *like you:* "Leaders such as yourself [*like you*] need to be cognizant of how you portray our institutions" (*The Missoulian*, Montana). The same goes for *such as himself* or *such as herself:* "A Carpinteria hot dog seller . . . has won an exemption for peddlers such as himself [*like him*]" (*Los Angeles Times*).

ACCIDENT 160

Misuse of *ourself* for *ourselves* and *theirself* for *themselves*

Ourself is acceptable only if a sentence uses the so-called royal *we*, an old-fashioned (and now stuffy) way of referring to a single person: "*We*, from the mere force of habit, found *ourself* running among the first" (Charles Dickens, *Sketches by Boz*). But when the customary plural *we* is used, referring to more than one person, *ourselves* is required: "Whether we are aware of it or not, we're accountable for everything we do—to ourself [*ourselves*], family and God" (*Mormon Times*).

Theirself, on the other hand, is an illiteracy—the writing equivalent of driving under the influence. Always use *themselves* instead: "Who wouldn't want to put theirself [*themselves*] on the line for him?" (*Montgomery Advertiser*, Alabama).

ACCIDENT 161

It's *supposedly,* not *supposably*

In everyday writing, *supposably* is often erroneously used in place of *supposedly* (formed from *supposed* plus -*ly*): "This social promotion system is supposably [*supposedly*] used to prevent a loss of self-esteem by the student" (school board member's letter to the *Arlington Times*, Washington).

Supposably is a legitimate word, listed in dictionaries, but unless you are a professional philosopher or in some other highly suppositional line of work, it is unlikely that in two lifetimes you would ever have reason to use it in its proper sense of "as may be supposed or imagined."

Take care also to avoid this accident in speech. It's pronounced suh-POH-zid-lee, not suh-POH-zuh-blee.

ACCIDENT 162

It's *could not care less,* not *could care less*

One of the surest ways to show the world that you are a slipshod stylist is to write *I could care less* instead of *I couldn't care less*. If you *could* care less, then you do in fact care, at least a little. If you could *not* care less, then you don't care at all, not one teeny-weeny bit. So *couldn't care less* is the logical phrasing while *could care less* is, quite frankly, ridiculous. Apparently, though, all the slipshod stylists out there plying their trade couldn't care less about this rudimentary point because several searches on Google News revealed that *could care less* is three to four times more common than *couldn't care less* and *could not care less*. That's a lot of carelessness.

Don't be slipshod and say you *could care less*. Be wreckless and say you *couldn't care less*.

ACCIDENT 163

There is no *restaurant* in *restaurateur*

Writers often slip a spurious *n* into the middle of *restaurateur*, so that the word looks like a combination of *restaurant* and the suffix *-eur*, and editors often overlook the mistake. This has happened so often, in fact, that some dictionaries now countenance the misspelling as an acceptable variant. It is not. The word comes directly from the French *restaurateur* and should be so spelled, not tinkered with ignorantly.

Sheer volume of usage does not, by itself, constitute propriety. If that were so, then *I was laying in bed* (Accident 13) and *He should have went* (Accident 23) would be standard. Despite the 421,000 hits that Google Web retrieved for this misspelling, and despite its unfortunate appearance in such respectable sources as *Editor and Publisher* magazine, BBC News, the *Chicago Tribune*, and the website of the Princeton Review, if you wish to be thought of as a careful writer you should heed the advice of *The New Oxford American Dictionary*: "Despite its close relation to *restaurant*, there is no *n* in **restaurateur**, either in its spelling or in its pronunciation."

ACCIDENT 164

Do not *compare and contrast*

The redundant phrase *compare and contrast* was perpetrated and popularized by the educational establishment, of all things, which has misled generations of teachers and their students into thinking that it means "to look for similarities and differences." But *compare* by itself means "to examine for both similarities and differences," while *contrast* means "to examine only for unlikeness or differences."

Sometimes a writer uses *compare and contrast* not as a windy way of saying *compare* but as meaningless filler that can be deleted: "This hastily stitched together educational patchwork makes it difficult to ~~compare and contrast or to~~ draw conclusions about the state of public education in New Orleans and how it is serving its students" (*The Nation*).

Depending on your context, use either *compare* or *contrast*, but never both.

ACCIDENT 165
Use *preventive*, not *preventative*
Though both spellings have been in use since the seventeenth century and dictionaries list both as standard, for the past hundred years or so most authorities have preferred the shorter form, *preventive*. As Mark Davidson points out in *Right, Wrong, and Risky*, it's the *American Journal of Preventive Medicine*, and you would be wise to take your cue from that.

ACCIDENT 166
It's *as best*, not *as best as*
"After explaining to Janet, as best as he could, what they were doing . . . ," writes James Collins in his novel *Beginner's Greek*, then he follows it up on the very next page with "He tried to comfort Charlotte as best he could."

Even with good copyediting, flip-flops like this happen in edited prose. And this flip-flop was perhaps easier to overlook than most because many writers and editors are not aware that the second *as* in *as best as* is superfluous and *as best* is the preferred form. Confusion with the synonymous *as well as* no doubt is largely to blame for the mistake. And that confusion is probably compounded by false analogy with locutions like *as far as*, *as long as*, and *as good as*, which—the alert reader will note—take the positive form of the adjective (*far, long, good*) rather than the superlative (*farthest, longest, best*).

ACCIDENT 167

How to use *between* and *among*

You have probably heard the rule that says you must use *between* for
two things and *among* for three or more. The problem with this rule is
that it's simplistic. It ignores centuries of reputable usage, and it gives
unsuspecting writers and editors a bad excuse to use *among* arbitrarily
where *between* is the proper word. Everyone knows to use *between*
with two—*commuter flights between San Diego and Los Angeles*—and
most people know that you divide something *among* three or more,
but woe unto the reckless rule-follower who flouts idiom and common sense by writing *commuter flights among San Diego, Los Angeles,
San Francisco, and Seattle.*

What the oversimplified rule doesn't tell you is that when you're
dealing with three or more, you may use *between* or *among* depending on how the things you're referring to are related. If their relation
is collective, meaning that you think of them as a group, use *among:*
"Rooftop gardens grow *among* the skyscrapers" (*Christian Science Monitor*); *there is no honor among thieves.* But if the relation is individual
or reciprocal, from each to the others, use *between: NAFTA is a trade
agreement between the United States, Canada, and Mexico. It's hard to
find time to breathe between working, raising the kids, and caring for an
ailing grandparent.*

Here's an example that illustrates the contrast: *After listening to
a debate **between** the six candidates, Amy thought that no one **among**
them stood out as the best choice.* The candidates are debating individually, each against the others, so the debate is *between* them. But
when we consider the candidates as a group from which one must
be chosen, their relation is now collective, so the choice is *among*
them.

Idiom often requires *between* where *among* might seem to be the
proper word. As Bill Walsh observes in *Lapsing Into a Comma*, sand
gets *between* your toes (not *among*), things slip *between* your fingers
(not *among*), and you say *Let's keep this between us* whether there are
two, three, or fifteen people involved. What Walsh refers to as the
"two-at-a-time rule" also calls for *between*, and he gives these examples: *The round-robin tournament featured matches between the top*

four players, and *a disagreement between Bob and Carol and Ted and Alice.*

It's spelled *supersede*, with an *s* in the middle, not *supercede*

Supersede is one of the trickiest words in the language to spell. Even in the most prominent, well-edited publications, it often appears with an erroneous *c* in the middle: "The CEA says it is lobbying state officials in New York to pass legislation that . . . would *supercede* the city ordinance" (*The Wall Street Journal*); "Fear that grand strategies for saving money and improving quality will *supercede* individual circumstances are not new" (*Boston Globe*); "Nicolson's military judgment could be *superceded* by a more senior military commander" (*Foreign Policy*).

If you learn only a few words of Latin, try to make one of them the verb *sedēre,* "to sit, settle," the source of *sedentary, sediment, sedate,* and other English words. It is this *sedēre,* "to sit"—not the verb to *cede,* "to yield"—that sits in the middle of the word *supersede.* Something that *supersedes* by derivation sits, *sedēre,* above, *super-,* and so takes precedence.

Write *until* or *till,* never *'til* or *'till*

You may come across certain soi-disant authorities on usage—the kind whose chief credential is access to dictionaries and style guides they don't read—who will insist that *till* means "to plow the ground," that using it to mean "until" is wrong, and that if you want to abbreviate *until* you should write it with an apostrophe: *'til.* They may even do a search on Google News, as I recently did, to show you that *'til* is more than twice as common as *till*—which of course proves that it's the correct form. After smiling politely and pointing out the word *smug* in the nearest dictionary (preferably the big fat printed one you carry with you at all times), here's what you can tell them.

"*Till* is, like *until,* a bona fide preposition and conjunction," says *Garner's Modern American Usage.* Want some examples from reputable writers? "Fight *till* the last gaspe" (Shakespeare, *Henry VI*, Part One); "Silence, *till* I be silent too" (Alfred, Lord Tennyson, *In Memoriam*). In fact, *till* is at least three centuries older than *until*, and it is not an abbreviation of *until*. The form *'til*, with an apostrophe, "is a variant spelling of *till* used by writers who do not know that *till* is a complete, unabbreviated word in its own right," says *Merriam-Webster's Dictionary of English Usage*. Conclusion: *till* is wholly acceptable, and the variants *'til* and *'till* are substandard.

So remember, it's *shop till you drop, till death do us part*—not, as Kate White, editor in chief of *Cosmopolitan* magazine, mistitled her novel, *'Til Death Do Us Part*—and *it ain't over till it's over*, which this entry is now.

ACCIDENT 170
Write *until,* not *up till* or *up until*

Until means "up to the time of," so it's redundant to write *up until*: "~~Up~~ until now, premium producers like Mercedes-Benz have had an easier time weathering economic storms" (*BusinessWeek*). Because *till* is equivalent to *until*, *up till* is also redundant for *until*: "Many motorists—including those who up till [*until*] now had managed to stretch their dollars by driving fuel-efficient vehicles—will drive less if it costs them more for every mile they drive" (*Bradenton Herald*, Florida).

Up to now is an acceptable alternative to *until now*.

ACCIDENT 171
It's *beyond the pale,* not *beyond the pail*

This accident of style makes me think of the moment in the movie *Annie Hall* when a distraught Woody Allen tries to back a convertible out of a parking space by putting it in drive and stepping on the gas. As the pallid Woody looks to the rear, where he thinks he's headed, the car lurches forward and, in a sense, goes beyond the pale.

The noun *pale* in *beyond the pale* comes to us from the Latin *pālus*, a stake, and denotes a post, fence, or other marker indicating the perimeter of a territory or district, historically one under the protection of some army or government. For example, in the fourteenth century *the Pale* referred to the areas in Ireland colonized by the British, and that which took place outside the Pale was beyond British jurisdiction. At first *beyond the pale* had this literal meaning, then later came to have the figurative meaning "out of bounds, unreasonable, unacceptable."

ACCIDENT 172

Don't interact *with each other* or *with one another,* just interact

Any dictionary will tell you that to *interact* means "to act upon each other." So why do we continually hear and read the redundant phrases *interact with each other* and *interact with one another?*

These are such obvious redundancies that you'd think every copyeditor would be trained from the editorial cradle to pounce on them. Yet they frequently appear in edited prose, and even in some of the most prestigious publications: "She wants to see how the Baker Botts lawyers *interact with each other* and how they manage their time" (*National Law Journal*); "These causes may *interact with one another* and therefore be difficult to isolate" (*The New York Times Magazine*); "Dr. Hansen of the ASPCA advises against applying flea powders and sprays in addition to a spot-on treatment because chemicals in different products could *interact with each other*" (*The Wall Street Journal*).

These redundancies may be perpetuated because people often use *interact* as a snazzier-sounding alternative to *communicate.* But while *communicate* is often and unimpeachably followed by *with each other* or *one another, interact* by itself conveys the idea of reciprocal action or communication (*inter-,* "between, among," plus *act*). If you must use *interact* (and it's not a difficult word to avoid if you try), just remember that people may interact with other people, but they can't interact *with each other.*

See "Say It Again, Sam" on page 57.

ACCIDENT 173

Write (and say) *supremacist*, not *supremist*

Supremacist is formed from *supremacy*, not *supreme*, and is properly pronounced in four syllables: soo-PREM-uh-sist. The misspelling *supremist* is rare in edited prose, but among writers who ignore their spell-checkers and post unfiltered commentary online, it is a frequent blunder—the offspring, no doubt, of the three-syllable mispronunciation soo-PREM-ist.

ACCIDENT 174

It's spelled *ad nauseam*, not *ad nauseum*

"I could go on ad nauseum," writes Lois Kindle in the *Tampa Tribune*—to which I must respond firmly, "Please don't."

The misspelling *nauseum*, with a penultimate *u* instead of an *a*, is regrettably common in articles and blogs on Google News, and on Google Web I was shocked to find that it is nearly as common as the correct spelling. No doubt the pronunciation of *nauseam* (NAW-zee-um) is responsible for the misspelling: we hear a terminal *um* and, influenced by the many classical words ending in -*um* (*minimum, auditorium, equilibrium*, etc.), we spell it -*um*. But the Latin phrases *ad nauseam* and *in memoriam* end with the sound of *um* and are spelled -*am*. Just remember those two phrases or be sure to use your spell-checker (which I was stunned to discover actually catches the misspelling) and you'll be all right.

ACCIDENT 175

It's *for all intents and purposes*, not *for all intensive purposes*

For all intensive purposes is an illogical misrendering of the set phrase *for all intents and purposes*. It occurs more often in speech than in writing, but it occasionally appears in edited prose: "This was, for all intensive purposes, a relationship investment" (*Marin Independent Journal*); "The Bush-era policy . . . remains for all intensive purposes in effect" (*Huffington Post*).

Why does *for all intents and purposes* for some people become *for all intensive purposes*? Because of a glitch in the way our brains work that causes us to hear a different set of words from the ones that were uttered. For example, my daughter Judith recently said, "I want to go to Jack in the Box." My wife and I, who were only half listening, responded in turn with "You want to get a Japanese boss?" and "Who wants dental floss?" When you consider how quickly my daughter's words got garbled in her parents' ears, it's a miracle that *for all intents and purposes* hasn't degenerated into *fallen tents of porpoises*. You could call this phenomenon the Greta Garble Effect, but in fact it already has a name: *mondegreen*.

Mondegreen is itself a mondegreen. It was coined in 1954 by Sylvia Wright, who used it in an article for *Harper's* magazine called "The Death of Lady Mondegreen," in which she recounted how she remembered the lyrics of an old Scottish ballad, "The Bonnie Earl of Morey" (pronounced like *Murray*):

> *Ye Highlands and ye Lowlands,*
> *Oh, where hae ye been?*
> *They hae slain the Earl o' Morey,*
> *And Lady Mondegreen.*

The problem was, as Ms. Wright later discovered to her chagrin, there was never any Lady Mondegreen. The actual words of the last line are *And laid him on the green*.

Recreational linguists and lovers of wordplay have since had a field day identifying scores of amusing mondegreens. Mishearings commonly occur with song lyrics (*the girl with colitis goes by* for *the girl with kaleidoscope eyes*); with Bible verses (*and lead us not into Penn Station* for *and lead us not into temptation*); and of course in everyday speech, where we hear such manglings as *the house is in escarole* (escrow).

Wreckless writers should be on the lookout for the common mondegreens of everyday speech, which can easily creep into print. For example, *take it for granite* for *take it for granted; when all is set and done* for *when all is said and done; nip it in the butt* for *nip it in the bud;* and *for all intensive purposes* for *for all intents and purposes.*

ACCIDENT 176

You don't just *graduate*, you *graduate from*

If you happen to be one of the few Rip van Winkles who are still nursing a mumpsimus* for *She was graduated from* instead of *She graduated from*, it's high time to wake up. The active form has been standard English since the early nineteenth century, and by the mid-twentieth century the passive form was considered old-fashioned. *Graduated from* is "better English" than *was graduated from*, ruled the Evanses in 1957, and preference for the passive, wrote Theodore M. Bernstein in 1965, is "a superstition."

The problem with how people use *graduate* today is that they drop the *from* and say *I graduated college*. This is not good, according to every usage expert I've consulted since the Evanses, who were the first to complain about it. "One may say *he graduated in 1956*," they write. "But if the name of the institution, or some substitute word, is used we must say *from*. *He graduated college* is not standard English."

Subsequent commentators have been far less kind. For example, in *Saying What You Mean* Robert Claiborne calls *He graduated college* "blue-collar," and William Safire, who wrote a weekly column called "On Language" for *The New York Times Magazine* from 1979 until his death in 2009, once imperiously ruled that "to say 'I graduated college' rather than 'I graduated from college' is to be a language slob and a discredit to whatever learning factory mailed you a diploma."

In 1994, *Merriam-Webster's Dictionary of English Usage* observed that *graduate* without *from* "occurs frequently in speech, but its appearance in edited prose is still relatively uncommon." Today it is rampant in speech, blue-collar and white-collar alike, and it has become far more common in edited prose. On Google News I found several hundred citations for *graduate(d) college* and *graduate(d) high school* in newspapers ranging from the *Eagle Valley Daily Enterprise*

---

*The *Century Dictionary* (1914) defines this wonderful word as "an error obstinately clung to; a prejudice," explaining that it is "a term originating in the story of an ignorant priest who in saying his mass had long said *mumpsimus* for *sumpsimus*, and who, when his error was pointed out, replied, 'I am not going to change my old *mumpsimus* for your new *sumpsimus*.'"

to the *New York Daily News*. I found it in a University of Chicago publication, in a U.S. Army press release, and on the websites of scores of TV and radio stations. Those who would interpret this as a sign of growing acceptance do so at their peril. If you wish to be regarded as a careful writer and speaker, take care to say you graduated *from* a high school, college, or university.

ACCIDENT 177

It's *champing at the bit*, not *chomping*

In modern usage, the verb *to chomp* has replaced *to champ* in the general sense of "bite or chew vigorously." But *champ* survives in the centuries-old idiom *to champ at the bit*, which was originally used for a horse that impatiently bites the bit in its mouth and later came to mean "to be restlessly impatient or eager to do something, especially in the face of a constraint or delay" (*Oxford English Dictionary*). The writer with a sensitive ear for language will take care to preserve this venerable idiom.

ACCIDENT 178

It's *(old) stamping grounds*, not *stomping grounds*

Though citations for *stomping* on Google News outnumber those for *stamping* by a crushing 267 to 4, the traditional and etymologically correct form is *stamping*. The expression was used in early nineteenth-century America for a place where horses or other animals were accustomed to gather and, as many animals customarily do, *stamp* the ground. By the 1830s it had come to be used of a place where people customarily gather.

ACCIDENT 179

Write *whether*, not *as to whether*

Whether can usually do its work alone and *as to* should be deleted, especially at the beginning of a sentence: "A̶s̶ t̶o̶ whether it was a mistake to let it fail, Bernanke said, 'We did not have the option; we didn't have the tools'" (npr.org); "The Center for Biological Diversity said that it would poll its members a̶s̶ t̶o̶ [*about* or *on*] whether it should replace Verizon as its cellphone carrier" (*The New York Times*).

ACCIDENT 180
Write *sneaked,* not *snuck*

You could say that *snuck* has *sneaked* up on us. *Snuck* appeared as a variant of *sneaked* in the late nineteenth century, and since then it has become so popular that today you are as likely to read *snuck* as *sneaked*—I got 1,576 hits for *sneaked* and 1,575 for *snuck* on Google News—and *snuck* is probably more common in speech. Does this mean that *snuck* has achieved respectability and deserves to be the preferred form?

The answer is a thundering *no*. An overwhelming number of authorities consider *snuck* nonstandard and a solid 67 percent of the usage panel of *The American Heritage Dictionary* objects to it. Also, if you look closely at those hits on Google News you'll see that *snuck* usually appears in casual writing and quotations of casual speech, while *sneaked* appears in the edited prose of reputable publications.

Conclusion: If you use *snuck* in conversation you're not likely to attract notice, but if you use it in your writing many will consider it an accident of style.

ACCIDENT 181
It's *octopuses,* not *octopi*

Because *octopus* comes from Greek, not Latin, the Latinate plural *octopi*—though it appears in dictionaries—is frowned upon by usage authorities. The preferred plural is the anglicized *octopuses*, formed with -*es* like other regular English plurals. If you want to be true to the Greek you can use the plural *octopodes*, but prepare to be misunderstood and unappreciated by all but a few pedants and marine biologists.

ACCIDENT 182
The problem of *bi-*

We know that someone who is *bilingual* speaks two languages because we know that the prefix *bi-* means "two" or "twice." But if you're being hired for a job and your new boss says you'll get *bimonthly* paychecks, should you infer that you'll be paid twice a month or every two months?

As you can see, the problem with *bi-* is that it's ambiguous. Whereas the prefix *semi-*, meaning "half," is always clear—*semimonthly* is every half month; *semiannual* is every half year—*bi-* can denote either twice or half of what follows. The solution to this ambiguity problem is to use the *semi-* words or a phrase that specifies what you mean. Thus, instead of *biweekly* write either *twice a week* or *every two weeks;* instead of *bimonthly* write either *twice a month* or *every two months;* and instead of *biannual* write *twice a year* or *every two years.*

The word *biennial* is usually not misconstrued and may safely be used to mean "occurring every two years."

ACCIDENT 183
It's *fill the bill*, not *fit the bill*

Those who misconstrue this idiom as *fit the bill*—and that's most of us, judging by the numbers on Google News: 550 hits for *fit* and only 43 for *fill*—no doubt do so for two reasons: because *fit* seems to fit with the way the idiom is used, and because they have no idea what *the bill* is or where this part of the expression comes from. Even Mignon Fogarty, aka Grammar Girl, gets it wrong: "English currently lacks a word that fits the bill" (*Grammar Girl's Quick and Dirty Tips for Better Writing*, p. 61).

"Theatrical companies in the 19th century," explains Robert Hendrickson in *The Facts on File Encyclopedia of Word and Phrase Origins*, "advertised mainly on posters and handbills that were distributed in towns by advance men several weeks before a show came to town. The name of the troupe's star performer was featured on these bills in large letters, to the exclusion of the rest of the company—he or she *filled the bill*, was the show's star." It wasn't long before people began using the expression more broadly to mean "to do all that is desired, expected, or required" or "to be well suited to serve a purpose or fulfill a need."

Don't be a reckless writer and try to wear the shoe that doesn't fit. Wreckless writers remember that *the bill* must be *fulfilled*.

ACCIDENT 184
Don't confuse *imminent* and *eminent*
Imminent means "about to happen": *imminent death*. *Eminent* means "well-known, distinguished, standing out from others in importance": *an eminent scholar*. *Imminent* is sometimes misused for *eminent* in the legal phrase *eminent domain* and in the hackneyed phrase *eminently qualified*. *Eminent* is sometimes misused for *imminent* in the common phrases *imminent threat* and *imminent danger*.

ACCIDENT 185
Write *reminds me of* or *reminds one of*, never just *reminds of*
As Theodore Bernstein reminds us in *The Careful Writer*, "Since *remind* means to recall to one's mind, it must be followed by an object that has a mind." Something cannot *remind of*; it must *remind you of*.

Misuses are regrettably common: "It reminds [*me*] of the Anglo–French attack on Suez in 1956" (*The San Diego Union-Tribune*); "Reminds of [*It reminds me of*] the newswire work I was doing back in the mid-1990s" (TheStreet.com); "Rhett Miller's latest reminds [*one*] of a young Elvis Costello" (*Dallas Morning News*). And here the writer should have used *calls to mind* instead of *reminds*: "Adam reminds of [*calls to mind*] a mixture of Billy Idol, Prince and Freddy Murcury" (website of *Entertainment Weekly*). While we're at it, the spelling *Freddy Murcury* looks fishy too.

ACCIDENT 186
Use *before* instead of *prior to*, *previous to*, and *in advance of*
Usage experts are decidedly down on *prior to*. It is, they say, "an offense against plain English," "a faddish affectation," a "stuffy and pretentious," "terribly overworked" locution. Why use two words where one will do? Why sound like a self-important twit?

Prior to is just a puffed-up way of saying *before*: "Prior to [*before*] today's development, Wall Street analysts had speculated that . . . Coastal did not have its financing package together to buy the casino" (*Philadephia Inquirer*); "Carlyle . . . also led a bid for Silverton prior to [*before*] its failure"* (*The Wall Street Journal*); "Maine yielded just three hits and struck out five prior to [*before*] leaving" (*USA Today*). Improbably, the longer *prior to* appears even in headlines, where space is at a premium: "Williams hunting license stolen prior to N.H. auction" (*Boston Globe*).

If using *prior to* is like running a red light, using *previous to* or *in advance of* is like nailing a pedestrian in the crosswalk. Again, *before* is always better than these deadly phrases, which occur with stultifying frequency in edited writing: "The White House notes that presidents previous to [*before*] Bush . . . were not in the habit of holding White House events for the National Day of Prayer" (*U.S. News & World Report*); "By lining up support in advance of [*before*] a bankruptcy protection filing, GM is likely to find it easier to persuade a judge to apply terms of the sweetened offer to the rest of its unsecured debt" (Associated Press).

ACCIDENT 187

Don't write "According to Webster" or cite *Webster's Dictionary*

This may come as a shock to you, but *Webster's Dictionary* does not exist.

The name *Webster* has long been in the public domain and anyone can use it. Visit any bookstore (while they still exist) and you'll see various dictionaries that incorporate the name—*Webster's New World*, *Random House Webster's*, and *Merriam-Webster's* are the best known. But there is no *Webster's Dictionary*, nor any omniscient language expert named Webster, so don't follow the example of the many shiftless writers out there who try to sound smart by quoting a nonexistent authority.

And just for the record, Noah Webster—whose last name, for better or for worse, is now synonymous with "dictionary"—never wrote a dictionary called *Webster's*. His magnum opus was *An American Dictionary of the English Language*, published in 1828.

---

*Did you notice the ambiguous *its* in this example? It's unclear whether Carlyle or Silverton failed because the pronoun *its* could refer to either one.

ACCIDENT 188
Misuse of *neither*

Neither should always refer to two different people or things. Used by itself in a sentence, *neither* always takes a singular verb: *neither of us is interested.* In the following sentence the writer, distracted by the plural *men*, forgot that *neither* refers to each of the men separately: "Neither of these ~~two~~ men have [has] thought to publicly justify torture" (*Buffalo News*). And because the notion of "two" is implied by *neither*, the word *two* in that sentence is unnecessary.

In a *neither . . . nor* construction the verb should also be singular when the second of the two nouns referred to is singular. These two sentences get it wrong: "Neither Williams nor Earley were [was] prepared to reveal exactly what was said to the lineswoman" (guardian.co.uk); "Neither Pres. Obama nor Kelly Clarkson approve [approves] of Kanye West's grandstanding" (*Hartford Courant* headline). This sentence correctly uses a singular verb: "Neither Joseph Addai nor rookie Donald Brown *is* an elite player" (miamiherald.com).

However, when the second of the two nouns that *neither* refers to is plural, idiom calls for a plural verb. *Bryson's Dictionary of Troublesome Words* gives this example: "Neither the President nor his advisers *were* available for comment."

Finally, don't write *neither (this) . . . or (that).* It should always be *neither (this) . . . nor (that).* In the following sentence, *neither* should be paired with *nor* instead of *or*, and, for proper parallelism, whatever follows *neither* (in this case *the*) should also follow *nor:* "Neither the Bloomfield or [*nor the*] Farmington office has planned vaccination days" (*Daily Times*, New Mexico).

ACCIDENT 189
It's spelled *minuscule*, not *miniscule*

There is no *mini-* in *minuscule*.

The common misspelling *miniscule* is no doubt the result of the popular variant pronunciation MIN-uh-skyool, with the stress on the first syllable, and the false assumption that a word meaning "very small" must begin with the combining form *mini-*, "small." But *minuscule* comes from the Latin *minusculus*, "somewhat smaller," from *minus,* "less." If you pronounce *minuscule* in the traditional and proper manner, with the stress on the second syllable (mi-NUS-kyool), the word is almost impossible to misspell.

ACCIDENT 190
If you use *one* instead of *I* or *you* or *we,* be consistent

These days, except in the most formal of formal prose, it's a bit stuffy and old-fashioned to use *one* instead of *I, you,* or *we.* Yet many academics, doctors, and lawyers, with their penchant for overblown prose, still cling to it: "To understand its genesis, *one* must begin the story further back" (*Harvard Law School News*). Some journalists, perhaps wishing to affect a grander style, are also fond of the regal *one.* But many writers fail to realize that once you commit to using the pronoun *one,* you have to stick with it and be consistent; you can't begin with *one* and then switch indiscriminately to other pronouns, as in these examples: "It is unusual for one's reputation to outlive his [*one's*] work"; "One must convince himself [*oneself*] to join such a program."

Britt Combs of *The McDowell News* scores two out of three in this sentence: "Wherever one goes in America, the people one meets are probably kin, if you look [*one looks*] back far enough." And later in the article, perhaps showing his exhaustion with keeping up the *one* charade, he runs a red light with this sentence: "It's been said that one can pick their friends but not relatives." That should be either *one can pick one's friends* or, much friendlier and more natural, *you can pick your friends.*

ACCIDENT 191

It's *bated breath*, not *baited breath*

This venerable idiom, which dates back at least to Shakespeare's *Merchant of Venice*, is misspelled on Google News a whopping one-third of the time. Why do so many people think it's *baited* instead of *bated*? First, because the words are pronounced the same; second, because *baited* is a common word while *bated* is rare and archaic except in this expression.

Michael Quinion, creator and curator of worldwidewords.org, an excellent resource for language lovers, explains that *bated* "is a contraction of *abated* through loss of the unstressed first vowel (a process called *aphesis*); it means 'reduced, lessened, lowered in force'. So *bated breath* refers to a state in which you almost stop breathing as a result of some strong emotion, such as terror or awe." When you wait for or watch something with *bated breath*, you are almost holding your breath from excitement or anxious expectation.

And if you stop to think about it logically, *baited breath* doesn't make any sense. How can you entice, tease, or torment your own or someone else's breath? I suppose it might be possible to place food in your mouth that would cause your breath to lure an animal or fish, but to do that you'd have to be a predatory creature with an extremely large mouth—a real shark, in other words, as this sentence, read with an ironic eye, perhaps illustrates: "So it is with *baited breath* that value investors await his [Warren Buffett's] annual letter to shareholders" (Motley Fool: caps.fool.com).

ACCIDENT 192

Avoid the word *parameter(s)*

Parameter has a number of specific meanings in mathematics, statistics, and various sciences to which this entry does not apply. If you are a specialist accustomed to using *parameter* in some specialized way, I have no quarrel with you. My complaint here concerns the appropriation of this specialized word by John Q. Public, who thinks it is interchangeable with *feature, element, characteristic, variable,* or *factor,* and Jane Q. Public, who uses it to mean "a limit, boundary" because she thinks it's a fancy alternative to *perimeter.*

Here are some examples of these perversions from John Q. Journalist: "The specifics still may be weeks away, but the *parameters* [read *elements* or *features*] of an independently managed middle school program to raise student achievement are beginning to take shape" (*Richmond Times-Dispatch*). "Barack Obama set forth, in four days, the *parameters* [read *elements* or *characteristics*] of a peace that has never seemed so close and yet so far" (Bernard-Henri Lévy in the *Huffington Post*). "That formula is based on several *parameters* [read *factors* or *variables*], including population, circulation, hours open, and programming" (*Barnstable Patriot*, Massachusetts). "Based on the draft's 7:30 p.m. scheduled start and the time *parameters* [read *limits*] of five minutes per selection" (*Chicago Tribune*). "Within these *parameters* [read *boundaries*] the market demonstrates considerable strength" (artdaily.org).

And then there are the writers who, like Lewis Carroll's Humpty Dumpty, use *parameter* to mean whatever they want it to mean and leave the rest of us scratching our heads. In this sentence from *The Wall Street Journal*, it appears to mean "guidelines" or "justification": "Mr. Yoo is one of those who wrote memos laying out the legal *parameters* for aggressive interrogation of al Qaeda captives." In this sentence from *The Republican* in Massachusetts it appears to mean "details" or "conditions": "The *parameters* are not final, and the company will be allowed to respond and make input to the seven-page list." And in this sentence from the *Washington Independent* it could mean any number of things, from "law" to "authority" to "procedure": "But it's worth recalling that we're in this situation to begin with because the Bush administration, dominated by non-lawyers, had insufficient respect for constitutional *parameters*."

To paraphrase Mark Twain, one could build a very expressive vocabulary simply by leaving the vague and pompous *parameter* out.

ACCIDENT 193
Tiny hamlet is redundant
"I thought of this last week, in a tiny bar in a tiny hamlet in Tuscany," writes Christina Patterson in *The Independent* (UK). That

repetition of *tiny* makes for a nice alliteration with *Tuscany*, but pairing *hamlet* with *tiny* is redundant because hamlets are already as tiny as can be. A *hamlet* is a very small *village*, the word the writer should have used instead. (By the way, this is not an uncommon accident of style. I got more than two hundred hits for *tiny hamlet* on Google News.)

ACCIDENT 194

Personal and *personally* are usually unnecessary

"Have you personally recommended this eye doctor to anyone?" asks a customer-satisfaction survey from Precision Research. How else can you make a recommendation? Certainly not *im*personally.

Personally is almost always a redundant filler word that cries out to be deleted: "*Personally*, I can't believe it's going to be 2010 soon" (post at ESPN.com); "Yuschenko *personally* invites Benedict XVI to visit Ukraine" (interfax-religion.com); "I am *personally* insulted by this intrusion into my campaign and I want it to stop" (candidate quoted in the *Hudson Reporter*); "George parodies politicians who say they are *personally* opposed to abortion but support women's legal right to choose" (*USA Today*). All those sentences would be stronger without the useless adverb *personally*.

The adjective *personal* is also often superfluous. Your *personal secretary* is your secretary, your *personal history* is your history or your story, your *personal style* is your style, your *personal favorite* is your favorite, your *personal opinion* is your opinion, and the cloyingly redundant *close personal friend* is a close friend or a friend.

My *personal* wish is that people would pay *personal* attention to this accident of style, so that we might see fewer sentences like this one from *The Wall Street Journal*: "Mr. Obama's *personal* history still strikes a chord, making him *personally* popular in Egypt and elsewhere in the Muslim world."

ACCIDENT 195

Write *try to*, not *try and*

Try and is a colloquialism that does not belong in serious writing. It also doesn't make much sense, if you think about it. If you *try and do* something, it implies that merely trying will assure accomplishment. When you *try to do* something, it implies making an effort in the hope of accomplishing the deed. If you understand that, then you'll remember what I'm *trying to* tell you.

ACCIDENT 196

Be careful how you use *in the first place*

In the first place, don't use *in the first place* as a sentence opener, as I just did. It's wordy and amateurish. Use *first* or *to begin with* instead, or simply drop the preamble and begin with what you want to say.

The most common accident of style involving *in the first place* is using it when there's no call for it, when it is unnecessary filler, usually tossed in at the end of a sentence: "The president's task is to figure out how to jump-start his agenda and fulfill the promise of change that helped him win the White House *in the first place*" (*U.S. News & World Report*); "It's hard enough to fathom that a man this large and this fast is walking the planet *in the first place*" (*The Wall Street Journal*); "It is very often abuse of human rights that causes humanitarian crises *in the first place*" (United Nations dispatch). Deleting *in the first place* would have made all those sentences stronger.

In this sentence, *in the first place* is unnecessarily used for redundant emphasis: "The agreements were introduced *in the first place* to give the market some stability" (Bloomberg.com). When something is introduced, it is presented for the first time. And in this sentence, *in the first place* is misused to mean "from the beginning": "Redmond cited some numbers, explaining why Fausto Carmona was a tough assignment for him *in the first place*" (*Minneapolis Star Tribune*).

You are on safe ground if you use *in the first place* only to mean "to begin with" or "at all": *That's why we go to the movies in the first place; Microsoft shouldn't have been issued this subsequent patent in the first place.*

ACCIDENT 197

Don't use the phrase *variety of different*

The word *variety* implies difference—"a number of different things thought of together" (*Webster's New World College Dictionary*). Yet even professional writers continually pair *variety* with *different* as if one word couldn't exist without the other: "Banks began offering cards with a *variety of different* interest rates and fees" (*The New York Times*); "Beachwater pollution comes from a *variety of different* sources" (*Huffington Post*); "This team can win in a *variety of different* ways" (*Dallas Morning News*); "And then there's the 'compliance flexibility measures,' which include a *variety of different* credits for other technologies that use CO_2" (*The Atlantic* online).*

And here's one that I was shocked to find in an actual book, with a spine and two covers and, presumably, a history of several sets of critical eyes having pored over its contents: "True, as omnivores—creatures that can eat just about anything nature has to offer and that in fact need to eat *a wide variety of different things* in order to be healthy—the 'What to eat' question is somewhat more complicated for us than it is for, say, cows" (Michael Pollan, *In Defense of Food*). Somebody should have changed that to *a wide variety of things*.

I could cite 875 more instances of this redundancy, and even one from a lexicographer for the *Oxford English Dictionary* who said it on the radio, but I trust you get the point. Don't hitch *variety* to *different* as if the words were a tractor-trailer combination. Use one word or the other depending on which best fits your context.

ACCIDENT 198

There is no *gh* in *straitlaced*, *straitjacket*, *straitened*, and *dire straits*

To *straighten* is to make straight, unbend. But to *straiten*, without the *gh* in the middle, is to make narrow, squeeze, confine tightly. To be *straitlaced* is to be narrow-minded, uptight. To wear a *straitjacket* is to be tightly confined, with your arms squeezed against your sides. And to be in *dire straits* is to be narrowly confined by circumstances that cause great difficulty or distress.

Even professional writers and editors sometimes slip a spurious *gh*

---

*In this last example, note also the misuse of the singular *there's* (there is) with the plural *measures;* it should be *there are*. See Accident 12.

into these words. In the following examples, *straight* should be *strait:* "Martin, the straight-laced, all-American elder statesman" (*The New York Times*); "'Taking Woodstock' is Elliot's coming out, not just as a young gay man in a straightjacket of conformity" (*Seattle Post Globe*); "I don't know much, but I do know the record industry is in dire straights" (syndicated columnist Liz Smith in the *Chicago Tribune*).

Another word, *straitened*, means "to be strapped or squeezed for cash, in financial trouble": "Even in these *straitened* times, gourmands drift into reveries contemplating succulent tidbits" (*Toronto Star*). When you're flush and back on your feet, you're no longer in *dire straits* because you've *straightened* things out.

ACCIDENT 199
Avoid the erroneous *kudo*

Kudos is a singular noun meaning "credit or praise for an achievement; glory; fame" (*Webster's New World College Dictionary*): "Falmouth fireworks earn national *kudos*" (*Cape Cod Times*). The word ought to be reserved for praise given for illustrious, or at least significant, achievement and not used as a pseudoliterary substitute for *congratulations*, as it all too often is: "*Kudos* to Calloway's Nursery, which Garden Center magazine named one of its Innovators of the Year" (*Fort Worth Star Telegram*).

"Sometimes one sees a false singular, *kudo*," wrote Bergen Evans in *Comfortable Words* in 1959. "From this it is simply best to avert the gaze." After more than half a century, this advice is still sound. Despite the notes in certain contemporary dictionaries that artfully apologize for the existence of *kudo*, usage experts have continually dismissed this false singular as a nonword—used, as one guide puts it, "in jest or ignorance"—and good writers have taken care to avoid it.

Today *kudo* tends to appear in the sort of writing that E. B. White, in *The Elements of Style*, calls "breezy." The breezy style, says White, is practiced by "the hordes of uninspired scribblers" who "confuse spontaneity with genius." It "is often the work of an egocentric, the person who imagines that everything that comes to mind is of general interest and that uninhibited prose creates high spirits and carries the day."

Not surprisingly, the breezy *kudo* often appears in writing about the entertainment world, and the breezy writers at *Variety* are especially fond of it; in fact, they seem to be on a singular mission to promote *kudo* as the showbiz alternative to *award*, as these examples illustrate: "John Douglas Thompson won the lead actor *kudo* for his perf in the title role of 'Othello'"; "A dozen play revivals were nommed for a *kudo* from the Drama League"; "Malden was feted with SAG's lifetime achievement *kudo* in 2004."

Perf? Nommed? Feted with a *kudo?* This is the breezy style in action, where, as White explains, writers unnecessarily direct attention to themselves and use nonce words and slang "with neither provocation nor ingenuity." The result is prose that is patronizing or silly.

I would close this entry with that thought, but alas, I have one more accident to report involving the uningenious *kudo.* Those who use it to mean "an honor, compliment, award" have compounded their error by appropriating *kudos* as a false plural meaning "honors, compliments, awards": "In June, Neil Patrick Harris emceed the Tony Awards for CBS, earning good reviews while boosting the audience tuning in to these theater *kudos*" (*Los Angeles Times*). Semiliterate writers have taken this erroneous plural to hideous extremes: "We Newshounds will give *kudoes* to him for being a staunch defender of the rule of law and the US Constitution" (newshounds.us); "You can be the recipient of *kudoes* from your employers" ("Astro-Destiny," a syndicated horoscope column); "*Kudo's* to Benji Cole and Ivedent Lloyd on collecting wins this weekend" (whowon.com). From these dreadful accidents, it is simply best to avert the gaze.

ACCIDENT 200
Prefer *orient* to *orientate*
In British usage *orientate* and the participial adjective *orientated* are common, but authorities on American usage line up solidly in favor of *orient* and *oriented*, which are the older and more concise forms— reason enough to prefer them.

ACCIDENT 201

Misuse of *any time* for *anytime*

When the meaning is "whenever" or "at any time," *anytime* is now preferably one word: Accidents of style can happen *anytime*. You may borrow my car *anytime* you want. *Anytime* you want to visit, let us know.

The two-word *any time* should be preceded by *at*—you may leave *at any time*—except when you are referring to an amount of time: *We don't have any time for that nonsense. Does the doctor have any time to see me today?*

Misuse of *any time* for *anytime* is commonplace: " 'I'm at your disposal any time,' he tells Johnson" (*The New York Times Magazine*); "Just click the 'Edit' links to change your personal information, password, or communication preferences any time you like" (my.t-mobile.com).

A related and surprisingly common error is miswriting *at anytime* for *at any time:* "In addition, you can speak with a licensed agent at anytime" (Reuters); "He was told the disk could go out at anytime" (Associated Press).

ACCIDENT 202

Write *the same* or *exactly the same*, not *the exact same*

The exact same may be a venial sin in informal conversation, but in any kind of writing more dignified than a text message it's a sinful accident of style.

In print, *the exact same* is a clumsy way of adding unneeded emphasis to the word *same*. Sentences are always stronger when *exact* is deleted and the stress falls on *same:* "Then I flipped to MSNBC, and lo! . . . they had the ~~exact~~ same two clips" (*The Atlantic*); "Seventy-one percent said that they would choose a private insurer when given the choice to purchase the ~~exact~~ same health insurance policy at the ~~exact~~ same price from either a private insurer or the federal government" (press release at market watch.com).

Sometimes this unnecessarily emphatic *exact* can be ambiguous or sound foolish: "I am *the exact same* age as Michael Jackson" (comment at the *Washington Post* website). It's doubtful the writer meant she was born at the same time on the same day as Michael Jackson, only that she and the pop star were the same age: fifty.

On the rare occasions when special emphasis is called for, the proper phrase is *exactly the same:* "When we come to vote on the Lisbon Treaty in October, we will be voting on *exactly the same* treaty, with *exactly the same* consequences" (*Irish Times*). In that sentence, the writer chose to use *exactly the same* instead of the more docile *same*—and to repeat it in the next phrase—to add rhetorical punch to his argument for voting against the treaty. *Exactly the same* is also permissible when calling attention to a precise correspondence, especially a surprising one: *the twins were exactly the same weight; they spoke in exactly the same way.*

You should also be on the lookout for another accident involving both the incorrect *exact same* and the correct *exactly the same*— qualifying them with *almost:* "She showed clips that proved that he has been saying the same thing since the Monday after the elections, using *almost the exact same* words" (comment posted at msnbc .com). "It is abundantly clear to me that you and I see the world fundamentally in *almost exactly the same* way" (comment posted at *The American Conservative* website). Those two examples should make it abundantly clear that something can be *almost the same* or *exactly the same* as something else, but it cannot be *almost exactly the same.* Don't try to be in two places at once or you'll be *almost completely* wrong. If you mean a close but not exact similarity, eschew *exactly* and write *almost the same.*

ACCIDENT 203
It's *daylight-saving time*, not *daylight-savings time*

In reputable media outlets the plural *savings* appears in this phrase considerably more often than the singular *saving*—I got 128 hits for *savings* and only 47 for *saving* on Google News. But *abusus non tollit usum:* "abuse does not nullify good use." The mistake is so common probably because of false analogy with *savings account.*

The Associated Press Stylebook and *Garner's Modern American Usage* prescribe a hyphen: *daylight-saving time. The New York Times*

Manual of Style and Usage and Mark Davidson's *Right, Wrong, and Risky* leave it open: *daylight saving time.* The hyphen makes more sense to me because it shows that *daylight-saving* is a phrasal adjective modifying *time,* thus reinforcing the proper spelling without the final *s.*

By the way, has it ever occurred to you that the expression *daylight-saving time,* taken literally, is absurd? Not one second of daylight is actually saved.

ACCIDENT 204
With *the number* and *a number,* watch the number of your verb

This distinction is easy to get wrong, but it's also easy to remember how to get it right. The phrase *the number*—with the definite article *the*—always takes a *singular* verb: "*The number* of women arrested for driving drunk *is* on the rise" (*The New York Times*). The phrase *a number*—with the indefinite article *a*—always takes a *plural* verb: "*A number* of schools in the area *are* renovating or building with eco-friendly methods" (*St. Louis Post-Dispatch*).

Here's an example of a missed connection between *the number* and the ensuing verb: "As far back as 1992, Bruce McEwen and colleagues at Rockefeller University found that *the number* of synapses, or nerve connections, in rats' brains *rise and fall* with their estrous cycle" (*Yale Alumni Magazine*). It's not the brains that rise and fall here; it's the number of synapses. So the verbs in the sentence should be singular: *The number of synapses in rats' brains rises and falls* . . .

ACCIDENT 205
Don't use *rarely ever,* but *rarely if ever* is okay

Rarely means "seldom," and tacking on *ever* after it is pleonastic—in other words, unnecessary. But perhaps because of the hackneyed phrase *never ever,* writers are often tempted to use *rarely ever,* not realizing that when you *rarely ever* see something that *rarely ever* changes you *rarely* see it because it *rarely* changes. If you must use *ever,* use the phrase *hardly ever* instead. The phrase *rarely if ever* (or *rarely, if ever*), meaning "seldom, if at all," is also acceptable: "Rarely, if ever, do sports reporters give us this information" (*Cleveland Leader*).

ACCIDENT 206
Misuse of *allegedly*
Writers must use the word *allegedly* when there has been a charge of wrongdoing, the truth of which is still unknown. But overcautiousness, perhaps because of the fear of legal consequences, sometimes leads writers to use *allegedly* of something known (rather than merely asserted) to be true, as in this snippet from a TV newscast: *where the girl was allegedly killed*. That the girl was killed is not in question; it's her murderer's identity authorities are still unsure of. Take care to use *allegedly* only of that which has not been verified or proved.

ACCIDENT 207
Comma catastrophes
In reckless writing, the most common abuse of the comma is the comma splice, which occurs when complete sentences (independent clauses) are linked by a comma: "That's never happened before, most kids are frightened of the homeless"; "Roberts is in there doing the job, he's got some specific ideas"; "Students exhaust themselves during exam week, many of them stay up for days." In those examples, a period should have been used instead of a comma. But when the ideas expressed by back-to-back sentences are closely related, a semicolon is the right choice: "Keeping the faith is one thing, [;] paying for a ticket is something else entirely." A comma would be acceptable in that sentence only if the writer had used *but* after it to link the two independent clauses. Finally, here's a sentence where either a semicolon or a period would have worked, but not a comma: "Improved libraries are not a luxury, they are essential to our future."

Another frequent misuse of the comma is placing it between the subject and the verb, creating a bump in the flow of the sentence: "A lead story in the *Wall Street Journal* yesterday, had the words *vision* and *dream* about ten times" (Noam Chomsky, *Imperial Ambitions*). Didn't that comma before *had* make you hit the brakes when there was no reason to slow down?

In these sentences the comma also intrudes between subject and verb, creating a speed bump that should be deleted: "The sun shining through the unshuttered window[,] woke her early"; "The cavalry, artillery, and light infantry[,] were drawn up in order"; "The only thing more luxurious than the ostrich look[,] is the way these mats feel under your feet." And in this sentence the comma separates the verb from its complement and should be deleted: "But the biggest compliment is[,] not tooting your own horn." The lesson here is don't place a comma where there is no plainly audible pause. (Notice how I didn't put a comma after *the lesson here is?*)

Only a clodpate would write *you silly, goose* and separate the adjective from the noun it modifies. But decent writers are often tempted to do just that when two or more adjectives modify a noun. Take care not to put a comma between the final adjective and the noun it modifies: *a strong, unwavering, committment to reform* should not have a comma before the noun *commitment,* and *a vast, warehouse-size, computer called Unicomp* should not have a comma before the noun *computer.*

Writers are often unsure whether, and how, to use commas to set off a phrase from the rest of the sentence. *My brother, you will be pleased to hear is in perfect health* needs a comma after *hear* to set off the parenthetical *you will be pleased to hear* from the sentence *My brother is in perfect health.* And *He said that,"regardless of cost" he would pay* needs a comma after *cost* to set off the parenthetical *regardless of cost* from *He said that he would pay.* But the wording is even smoother with *regardless of cost* at the end and no commas at all: *He said that he would pay "regardless of cost."*

A classic mistake is using commas to set off a phrase that shouldn't be set off. This can alter the intended meaning of the sentence: "Among the Reagan supporters, who read the *Times* account, the consensus was that the newspaper should not have given the story front-page coverage." As written, the sentence suggests that all the Reagan supporters read the *Times* account. But the writer surely meant that the consensus was among only those supporters who read the account, so the first of the two commas should have been deleted: "Among the Reagan supporters who read the *Times* account, the consensus was . . ."

When an opening phrase is connected to the main part of the sentence by *that*, writers sometimes mistakenly think it's necessary to place a separating comma before *that*: "The senator argued during the committee hearings[,] that the tax cut would not have the desired effect on the economy"; "But it turned out[,] that planes leaving Lindbergh Field set off the ear-piercing bark every few minutes." This comma interrupts the proper flow of the sentence and is always wrong.

Also don't put a comma before a quotation that is run in to the sentence when there is no obvious pause in the flow of words. For example, the commas in *He called him, "the best teammate I've ever had"* and *My father always said that, "the worst thing you can do is lie"* are serious accidents of style.

If you cannot logically put *and* between two or more adjectives that modify a noun, don't put a comma between the adjectives. The comma in the headline "Lunt has little, old ladies running laps" implies that Lunt has both little ladies and old ladies running laps when what is meant is that the ladies are all little and old. Remember, there's a big difference between *a dirty, old man* and *a dirty old man*.

Now for a quick lesson on nonrestrictive and restrictive elements. Nonrestrictive elements are supplementary and omittable; restrictive elements are essential and not omittable. In the sentence *My first husband, Clifford, loved to pick his nose* the name *Clifford* is supplementary information; the sentence can get along just as well without it. And in *Clifford, my first husband, loved to pick his nose* the phrase *my first husband* is also supplementary, a clarification that could be omitted. But in the sentence *My friend John is a software engineer* the name *John* is essential because it specifies which of my many friends we're talking about, so it should not be set off by commas. And in the sentence *John Steinbeck's novel* The Grapes of Wrath *is one of my favorites* the title of the novel should not be set off by commas because Steinbeck wrote many novels and we need to know which one we're referring to.

The point of this minilesson is to say that you should not set off restrictive elements—the essential ones, which can't be omitted—with commas. The opening of this blunderful sentence in the *Washington Post* incorrectly sets off two restrictive elements with commas: "The British essayist and self-confessed workaholic[,] G. K. Chesterton[,] suggested in his 1928 essay[,] 'On Leisure[,]' that . . ." No commas are needed here at all because the names of the author and the essay are restrictive elements; they are essential, not supplementary, information.

Thus, moreover, and *for example* at the beginning of a sentence need a comma afterward, but have you ever heard the precept that introductory phrases of three or more words should have a comma? That is only an invitation to overpunctuate. *Throughout this book I have tried to help you avoid accidents of style* does not need a comma after *book*. When the pause after the introductory phrase is brief or imperceptible, don't use a comma: "In the late 1700s the norms of comma placement" (Barbara Wallraff, *Word Court*); "In these examples you would probably omit the comma" (Claire Kehrwald Cook, *Line by Line*).

"The tendency these days," writes Theodore M. Bernstein in *The Careful Writer*, "is to use a minimum of commas." Unfortunately, comma-laden sentences are not hard to find, and they are usually the by-product of overly fussy editing. Here's an example from an article by Alan M. Dershowitz in *The New York Times Book Review*: "To raise the stakes even further, Junger tells us, in his mother's words, about the day, before the Goldberg murder, when DeSalvo was alone with his mother in the Junger home." That poor wheezer is the literary equivalent of an asthma attack. The sentence would breathe much easier if three of the five commas were deleted: "To raise the stakes even further, Junger tells us in his mother's words about the day before the Goldberg murder, when DeSalvo was alone with his mother in the Junger home."

As Claire Kehrwald Cook writes in *Line by Line,* "Commas call attention to words. They make readers pause and take notice. Unless you want that effect, don't use commas that the sentence structure doesn't require."

ACCIDENT 208
Don't confuse the verbs *serve* and *service*
"Serve people. Service things."

So says Mark Davidson in *Right, Wrong, and Risky,* and I can't possibly improve on the sensible succinctness of that advice. A mechanic *services* your car and a repair technician *services* your appliances. But businesspeople *serve* their customers, even if they're in customer *service.* The only established exception to this distinction that I know of is prostitutes *servicing* their clients.

ACCIDENT 209
Recur and *reoccur* are not synonyms
In *The Careful Writer,* Theodore M. Bernstein explains the difference between the words *recur* and *reoccur.* Both mean to happen again, he says, but *reoccur* "suggests a one-time repetition," whereas *recur* "suggests repetition more than once." Thus you would say *the revolt is not likely to reoccur,* but *as long as these skirmishes recur, the revolt will continue.* A onetime repetition is a *reoccurrence,* while periodic or frequent repetition is *recurrence.*

Writers often misuse *reoccur* for things that happen more than once: "It will reoccur [*recur*] every two years, with the next one scheduled in 2011" (*Dayton Daily News*); "The condition can reoccur [*recur*] in times of excess heat or humidity" (*Mid-South Horse Review*); "Of particular concern to the study authors is how frequently these combinations of external stressors might reoccur [*recur*]" (University of British Columbia science website).

If economists predict that a recession will *reoccur* in fifty years, that means they're predicting it will happen again in fifty years. If economists predict that recessions will *recur* for fifty years, they're predicting it will happen several times in that period.

"It is the ability to feel a fine distinction such as this," writes Bernstein, "and to choose the word that precisely expresses the thought that marks the writer of competence and taste."

ACCIDENT 210
Alumni is plural, not singular

Using *alumni* as a singular noun—for one person—is semiliterate. Yet members of the media often make this embarrassing mistake: "She is an alumni of Notre Dame" (*U.S. News & World Report*).

To avoid this classical accident of style, you must learn to distinguish four Latin words: *alumnus, alumna, alumnae,* and *alumni. Alumnus* refers to a male graduate or former student; *alumni* is the plural. *Alumna* refers to a female graduate or former student; *alumnae* (pronounced uh-LUM-nee) is the plural. Traditionally, *alumni* refers to men or, more often today, to a group composed of both sexes; this use is still widespread and respectable, and I recommend it.

Sometimes, to avoid any suggestion of sexism, both plurals are used for mixed groups—the *alumni* and *alumnae* of Indiana University—but some commentators (count me among them) consider this wordy or redundant. If you object to using *alumni* for both men and women, the noun *graduate* and the plural *graduates*, though not quite equivalent in meaning to their Latin counterparts, offer a convenient, gender-neutral alternative.

Headline writers are in love with the chummy, unisex abbreviation *alum:* "Prison Break Alum Bares (Almost) All for New Fox Drama" (*Seattle Post-Intelligencer*). In writing that aspires to any sort of dignity, you would be wise to avoid it. If you must use an abbreviation, try *grad* instead.

ACCIDENT 211
Don't hyphenate words beginning with *non-* (with 1.5 exceptions)

Sticking unnecessary hyphens in words beginning with the prefix *non-* is one of the most common accidents of style. It is rampant in all forms of writing and at all levels of expertise, and—pay close attention now—it is nonstandard, which is the nonjudgmental way of saying wrong, wrong, wrong.

Consult any contemporary dictionary and you will find scores of words, from *nonabrasive* to *nonzero,* in which the prefix *non-* appears without a hyphen. Yet a vast number of people (including the addlepates who program your spell-checker and even some copyeditors) are in thrall to the delusion that most words beginning with *non-* should be hyphenated.

On Google News I found considerably more hits—sometimes more than twice as many—for the nonstandard hyphenated versions of *nonstandard, nonstop, nonskid, nonresident, noncommittal, nonbeliever, nonmember, nonverbal, nondenominational, nonessential, nonentity, nonunion, nonsexist, nonprofessional, nonpayment, noncompliance, noncombatant,* and *nonaligned,* while *nonprofit, nonfiction, nonviolent, nonconformist,* and *nonstick* were hyphenated almost as often as not. Of the thirty-odd common words I searched, only *nonfat, nonpartisan,* and *nonsectarian* seemed relatively safe from the hordes of harebrained hyphenistas.

A word beginning with *non-* requires a hyphen only when what follows is a proper noun, meaning a noun beginning with a capital letter: *non-Marxist, non-Christian, non-Danish.* You may also get away with inserting a hyphen to avoid creating a weird-looking, unpronounceable word (e.g., *non-nerd* instead of *nonnerd*) or a confusing phrasal adjective (e.g., *non-life-threatening situation* rather than *nonlife-threatening situation*). But the wreckless writer, wishing to steer clear of the ditch of dull diction, will instead rephrase any such ponderous construction so it is *not nerdy* and *not a life-threatening situation.*

ACCIDENT 212
Don't write *separate out*

Out after *separate* is always superfluous—or, as *Garner's Modern American Usage* puts it, "baggage that doesn't add to meaning." The wreckless writer or editor should hasten to delete it: "Thrift has always been a morally charged category, used to define a vision of the good life and to separate ~~out~~ the upright and righteous from the prodigal and wayward" (Lauren Weber, *In Cheap We Trust*); "The challenge . . . is to always try to separate out the raw data from the assumptions that guide interpretation of the data" (evolutionnews.org).

If the intended meaning is *remove, eliminate,* or *delete,* use one of those words instead: "Separate out [*remove*] anything that is not a seed—which can include leaves, stems, chaff and other plant debris" (*San Francisco Chronicle*); "A group of these Democrats have said they'd prefer to separate out [*delete*] climate change language from the legislation" (politico.com).

Finally, don't be lazy and sloppy and use *separate out* to mean "consider as separate or different": "It is a curious cultural trait that Americans tend to separate out [*consider, single out*] artists as something different and perhaps less legitimate than other professionals" (WDBO Radio, Florida); "The increases are relatively small, but you can't separate out [*single out, isolate, point to*] one or two expenses and ask if they're reasonable" (*Las Vegas Review-Journal*).

ACCIDENT 213
Avoid using *home* for *house*

A *house* is a physical structure, a building or dwelling: *the house at the end of the street; a summerhouse at the lake; an apartment house.* A *home* is a place where you live. It can be any sort of place (a mansion, condo, houseboat, tent), and it can also be a location (*California is my home; going home to New York City*). But a *home* must have something a *house* does not: "connotations of domestic comfort and family ties" (*Random House Webster's College Dictionary*). You buy a *house* and make it your *home,* hence the hackneyed saying *It takes a lot of living to make a house a home.*

Developers and real estate agents long ago realized that it made more sense, from a marketing standpoint, to build and sell places to live that you are emotionally connected to rather than impersonal buildings of so many square feet. That's why we see ads for *homes* for sale rather than *houses* for sale, and when we buy a *house* we become a *homeowner.* We also tell people they have a lovely *home* when we mean they have a nice *house,* and we read about fires, hurricanes, and tornadoes destroying *homes* rather than *houses.* But these uses, where the reference is clearly to a physical structure, are loose usage. *"Home* where *house* will do is imprecise," writes Barbara Wallraff in *Word Court*. "And it's a genteelism—like calling an office a *business establishment* or a man, apropos of nothing in particular, a *gentleman.*"

ACCIDENT 214
Don't use *anxious* to mean *eager*
One day at the end of a long, hot, lazy summer, my twelve-year-old daughter, Judith, grew pensive and said, "Y'know, Dad, I think I'm eager to go back to school."

"That's great," I replied perfunctorily, while the voice in my head was exulting. "Thank goodness you're not *anxious* about going back to school," I thought, "and thank goodness you know the distinction between *eager* and *anxious.*"

If I were a dictionary editor assigned to write a usage note on *anxious* and *eager*, the finished product would probably read something like this:

> Since the early 17th century, ANXIOUS has been used to mean "worried, uneasy, troubled, full of anxiety": *an anxious look; anxious for their safety.* Since the mid-18th century ANXIOUS has also been used as a synonym of EAGER: *anxious to see the new movie; anxious to meet you.* This usage is common today, especially in speech, but modern authorities are sharply divided over its acceptability. Some commentators consider it fully established while others consider it slipshod. Those who take pains to distinguish these words use EAGER to suggest keen interest or impatient desire (*eager to learn, eager for a raise*) and reserve ANXIOUS for situations that involve anxiety or apprehension (*anxious about losing my job, anxious about the test*).

All that is true, of course (because I wrote it). But since I'm not a dictionary editor and merely one of the commentators that these notes so often treat superciliously, I'm free to offer you more candid advice. Observing the distinction between *anxious* and *eager* qualifies you as a conscientious user of the language, a person who makes decisions about usage based not on how words are habitually used but on how they are intelligently used.

Wreckless writers always bear in mind that an *eager* person is expectant and desirous while an *anxious* person is worried, nervous, or fearful: *He was eager to get there on time but anxious about getting a speeding ticket.* And they know that when *to* follows *anxious* (rather than *about* or *over*), it's a warning sign of probable misuse: "Since signing up with the Celebrity Boxing Federation last month King has been anxious [*eager*] to step into the ring to face some challengers" (Reuters); "Chris says that he is anxious [*eager*] to get his acting career going again" (babychums.com).

ACCIDENT 215

Don't confuse *emulate* and *imitate*

The following sentence, from a story about an Ernest Hemingway look-alike contest that aired on WLS-TV, Chicago, improperly uses *emulate* as an ostentatious substitute for *imitate*: "David Douglass wore the sweater to help him emulate Hemingway's look in a *Life* magazine cover from 1957."

To *imitate* is to copy, resemble, or mimic. A contestant in a Hemingway look-alike contest wants to *imitate* Hemingway. To *emulate* is to try to do as well as or better than, to rival or compete with. Aspiring novelists often try to *emulate* Hemingway.

ACCIDENT 216

Don't write *and etc.*

Etc.—properly pronounced in four syllables (et-SET-uh-ruh), not three (et-SET-ruh)—is the English abbreviation of the Latin *et cetera*, which means "and other things." Unaware that *et* means "and," the unschooled writer sometimes veers down the road of redundancy and sticks the word *and* before *etc.*, creating a stuttering phrase that means "and and other things": "But there is still the usual mountain of work to do at home—homework, laundry, dinner, dishes *and etc.*" (*Austin American-Statesman*). Some incautious writers compound this error by failing to put a period after the abbreviation: "After checking us out, driver

licenses *and etc,* the polite officers apologized for the inconvenience
and went on their way" (*American Thinker*).

Etc. refers to things; *et al.* (from the Latin *et alii*, "and others")
refers to people. Both abbreviations should be followed by a period and printed in roman type (except when referred to as words,
as they are here). A comma should not follow *etc.* or *et al.* when they
precede a verb. These sentences are punctuated correctly: "You
said that police, firefighters, etc. were not laid off" (*Charleston
Gazette*); "Nancy Pelosi et al. are trying to push through a vote on
so-called healthcare reform before the August recess" (*American
Spectator*).

One other caveat. Many usage guides recommend avoiding *etc.*,
arguing that it is a crutch for writers who are too lazy to finish a
thought themselves. It is never a good style choice to make the
reader fill in the missing pieces; it is also abrupt and clunky to end a
sentence with *etc.* rather than a phrase such as *and others* or *and so
on*. Reserve *etc.* for those rare situations when you need to spare yourself the trouble, and your reader the tedium, of slogging through a
protracted list of similar things.

THE LONG AND SHORT OF IT

Like the compulsive eater who keeps taking another and yet another
bite, we are addicted to using too many words to say what we mean.
Perhaps we think it makes us sound more serious or seem more intelligent, but alas, it only makes us appear more self-important and less
articulate. To help you cut the unwholesome fat from your writing and
speech, here is a hit list of some of the verbose phrases we love to
regurgitate, with concise alternatives.

prior to *or* previous to=before
in advance of=before

subsequent to=after, following

with the (possible) exception of=except (for)

on a daily basis *or* on a regular basis=daily, regularly

on the basis of=based on

to be indicative of=to indicate, show, predict

in regard to, in regards to (*nonstandard*), with regards to (*nonstandard*),
    as regards=regarding, concerning, about

in order to=to

each and every=each, every, everyone, *or* us all

for the purpose of=for, to

to be in possession of=to have, own

a significant part *or* (pro)portion=many, most, much, a lot, a great deal

in the event that=if

in (*or* with) reference to, in (*or* with) respect to=about, concerning,
    regarding

to take into consideration=consider

to be of the opinion that=to think, believe, feel

until such time as=until

as a result of=because

in the immediate future, for the foreseeable future=now, for now,
    at the moment, for the time being

in the neighborhood of=around, about, approximately

for the (simple) reason that=for, because, considering

of great importance=important

after the conclusion of=after

by means of=by

come in contact with=meet, see

I would appreciate it if=please

inasmuch as=since

insofar as=because, since, as

for the amount of=for

in accordance with=by

in connection with=with

during the time that=while, when

it is interesting to note that=delete phrase, begin with the word after *that*

in spite of the fact that, despite the fact that, regardless of the fact
  that = though, although
due to the fact that, owing to the fact that, because of the fact that, in
  light of the fact that, in view of the fact that, by virtue of the fact
  that = since, because

ACCIDENT 217

Don't *congregate together* or *congregate in groups*

The word *congregate* means "to gather or come together in a crowd,
assemble in large numbers," so pairing *together* or *group* with *congregate* is redundant: "When children get sick with the flu they tend to
spread it quickly because they congregate *together*" (WALA-TV,
Alabama); "Students should stay home and not congregate *in large
groups* for 7–10 days, according to the health department" (San Diego
Unified School District website).

ACCIDENT 218

It's between this *and* that, not between this *to* that

Don't write that something is *between . . . to*: "Adults, on average,
lose *between* one *to* two hours of sleep each school day as they adjust
to the back-to-school routine" (Cox Newspapers). In this construction *between* should always be paired with *and*, so make that *between one and two hours*. You may also write *from one to two hours*.

ACCIDENT 219

Avoid *fun* as an adjective

The headline in *Newsday* reads, "Workaholic Boomer is having a fun
time," and my immediate question is why. Why would a headline
writer use *fun* as an adjective modifying *time* when you get a shorter,
snappier headline if you use *fun* in the traditional way, as a noun?
There's just no denying that "Workaholic Boomer is having *a fun
time*" is a deadbeat, slacker headline compared with "Workaholic
Boomer is having *fun*."

So why do so many people, particularly younger adults and children, use *fun* as an adjective? Why does the wordy *a fun time was had by all* seem to be gaining on the simpler *everyone had fun*? And why the heck did Mignon Fogarty let her publisher put the sentence "Find your grammar groove with *fun* advice from online sensation Grammar Girl" on the back of her book *Grammar Girl's Quick and Dirty Tips for Better Writing*?

Here's how *Garner's Modern American Usage* sees it: "Because *fun* is always a mass noun, it never appears with an article. So although we may say *This is a pleasure* or *a joy*, we cannot say *a fun*. Instead we say *This is fun*—and this predicate noun looks as if it might be a predicate adjective." From there it's a short step from *this trip is fun* to *this is a fun trip*, and many have made the excursion.

But wreckless writers who don't want to be pulled over by the language police should avoid tagging along for the ride. The adjectival *fun* is still a risky usage; most authorities are wary of it, and some are downright hostile. *This is so fun* and *we had a fun vacation* may be gaining some acceptance in educated speech, but they are guaranteed to elicit a frown from your English teacher or your editor. And don't even think about using the comparative *funner* and superlative *funnest* in your writing (unless you're quoting casual speech). They're verboten.

ACCIDENT 220
Don't confuse *clamor* with *clamber*

"Driven from their towns by machete-wielding mobs of Christians," reads a photo caption in *The New York Times Magazine*, "panicked Muslims clamor up the gangplank to a ferry, lugging whatever possessions they can manage." The writer of that caption confused two similar-sounding words: *clamor* (KLAM-ur) and *clamber* (KLAM-bur), with a *b* in the middle.

To *clamor*, from the Latin *clāmāre*, "to cry out," means "to shout, create an uproar": "Hundreds *clamor* for state fair jobs" (WRTV, Indiana). To *clamber*, from a Middle English word related to *climb*, means "to climb with difficulty, using the hands and feet": "At Jumping Kids . . . children no longer *clamber*, climb and bounce over inflatable toys" (*Houma Courier*, Louisiana).

ACCIDENT 221
Don't *shuttle back and forth*

To *shuttle* means "to move or travel back and forth repeatedly." Just as you would not write *commute back and forth* because *commute* means "to travel regularly between two locations," it is redundant to write *shuttle back and forth*. You should *shuttle between* two places, not *shuttle back and forth between* them. If you want to use *back and forth*, drop *shuttle* and use a different verb, such as *go*, *move*, or *travel*: "Bus commuters who *shuttle back and forth between* [read *shuttle between* or *travel back and forth between*] south Mumbai and the western suburbs daily" (*Economic Times*).

ACCIDENT 222
Watch out for danglers

You've probably heard of the infamous "dangling participle," and if you're not sure exactly what it is, this entry should help you sort things out.

A participle is a form of a verb. There are present participles, which end in *-ing* (*coming*, *making*), and past participles, which usually end in *-ed* (*opened*, *picked*) but with irregular verbs take other forms, as in *broken*, *brought*, *done*, and *swum*. A participle is said to dangle when it is not logically connected to the noun it modifies, which is usually the subject of the sentence.

If that sounds a bit technical, a few examples should make things clear. Here are some choice ones from Edith H. Fine and Judith P. Josephson's *More Nitty-Gritty Grammar*, along with the authors' comments (the underlined portion of each sentence is the dangler, which improperly modifies the boldfaced noun): "Blessed with superior stamina, Marie's **sneakers** pounded the pavement. (Sneakers in training?)"; "Wearing a black negligee, **he** noticed her. (Ooo-la-lah!)"; "Nestled between Providence and Fall River, **Ned** saw the fishing boats. (Hope the water was warm!)." Of course, it's Marie who is blessed with superior stamina; it's she rather than he who is wearing the black negligee; and it's the boats that are nestled, not Ned.

Here's another egregious dangler: *Walking down the street, the hat flew off his head.* That's some hat if it can fly off someone's head while walking down the street. This problem is easily solved by putting the person doing the walking closer to the participle: "While he was walking down the street, the hat flew off his head."

Lest you think the dangling participle is but a factitious construct of an evil English teacher's mind, consider this example from the world of professional writing: "Without condoning all of his conduct, some of [his] promises have surely been misremembered or misconstrued" (*The San Diego Union-Tribune*). Promises can't condone anything; only people can. It's the writer who is not condoning this person's conduct, so the sentence should have been written with the writer in it, like this: "I'm not condoning all of his conduct, but some of [his] promises have surely been misremembered or misconstrued." Perhaps the writer was spooked about using the first-person *I*—a common and irrational phobia affecting many journalists.

Here's another dangler from a publisher's press release for the novel *The Twelve* by William Gladstone: "Not speaking until age six, his world is filled with numbers and colors." A world that cannot speak for six years? Revision makes the person, not his world, the logical subject of the sentence: "Not speaking until age six, he lives in a world filled with numbers and colors."

Bear in mind that an opening phrase doesn't have to have a participle to be a dangler. Any introductory element that connects illogically to the subject of the sentence can dangle: "Perhaps the world's most famous mime, Marceau's performance is expected to be a total sellout" (*The San Diego Union-Tribune*). Marceau is the world-famous mime, not his performance. Revision: "Marceau is perhaps the world's most famous mime, and his performance is expected to be a sellout." (*Total sellout* is tautological.)

By the way, reckless writers are not the only ones who commit this accident of style. They're just the ones who get caught for doing it. In an early draft of this book's entry on *fewer* and *less*, your intrepid usage guide composed this faulty sentence: "When referring to fractions, the choice of *less* or *fewer* is best governed by the quantity of the noun." How can a choice refer to fractions? When I had finished polishing the entry, that sentence read, "With fractions, the choice of *less* or *fewer* is best governed by the quantity of the noun."

ACCIDENT 223

It's *full complement*, not *full compliment*

To *compliment*, with an *i* in the middle, means "to praise, say something nice about." To *complement*, with an *e* in the middle, means "to make complete, make whole," and the expression *full complement* means "the entire amount or number, complete array." Writers often mistake what is praiseworthy for what is complete: "Mixing his full compliment [*full complement*] of pitches, Hudson hit 90-plus miles per hour with his fastball and successfully worked the corners with his cutter and slider" (*Atlanta Journal-Constitution*).

ACCIDENT 224

Don't write *unless and until* (or *until and unless*)

Lawyers are notorious for overwriting, perhaps because they were taught that it's better to say everything twice rather than leave something out. *Unless and until* is a bit of lawyer jargon that has made its way from the verbose and recondite language of contracts and legislation into mainstream prose: "Trenton should not return the keys to the city to local officials *unless and until* they are able to take responsibility for adopting such a plan" (*Philadelphia Inquirer*). The phrase is tautological: it repeats the same idea in different words. Use *unless* or use *until* as it suits you, but not both.

ACCIDENT 225

Close proximity is redundant

"Some locutions, such as *close proximity*, have become so well established that criticizing them may seem petty," says the fourth edition of *The American Heritage Dictionary* in a usage note about redundancy. One man's petty is another man's poison.

Proximity means "closeness, nearness"; therefore *close proximity* means "close closeness" or "near nearness." It is "inescapably tautological," says *Bryson's Dictionary of Troublesome Words,* echoing scores of authorities on usage who have for years decried this redundancy. The second college edition of *The American Heritage Dictionary,* published just fifteen years before the fourth edition, agrees: "Strictly speaking, the expression *close proximity* says nothing that is not said by *proximity* itself." Apparently, one dictionary editor's pet phrase is another dictionary editor's redundancy. But now I'm being petty and straying from the point: the careful writer gets *close* or *in proximity,* but never *in close proximity.*

Usually *close proximity* is a long-winded way of saying *close* or *near:* "Style guides should be kept in close proximity to [*near* or *close to*] your writing station" (thesunlitdesk.com); "There should be more to a cabin than simply an inexpensive motel room built in close proximity to [*near*] lots of trees" (*The New York Times*). But sometimes it's a fancy-pants way of saying *close together:* "He said that with five grade crossings in close proximity, train engineers tend to blare their horns almost without stop" (*Boston Globe*).

ACCIDENT 226
It's the *Democratic Party,* not the *Democrat Party*

During the 2008 presidential campaign, a full-page ad for Kraft salad dressing appearing in *Bon Appétit* pictured two opposing salads—"the Republican salad," with the vegetables on the right side of a plate, and "the Democrat salad," with the vegetables on the left side of the plate. An inventive ad, you might conclude, except for one thing: it should have been a *Democratic* salad.

The New York Times Manual of Style and Usage says, "Do not use *Democrat* as a modifier (*the Democrat Party*); that construction is used by opponents to disparage the party." Whether disparagement was Kraft's intent in the ad is a matter of debate; what is certain is that Kraft's copywriters, in trying to start a food fight, caused a full-page accident of style. The word *democrat,* whether capitalized or lowercased, is a noun, never an adjective, so—in nonpartisan prose, at least—it should never modify another noun. The adjective is *democratic* and the name of the party is the *Democratic Party.*

A related accident that has been cropping up more and more is using the adjective *democratic* as a noun to mean "a member of the Democratic Party." I've been coming across this mistake all over the place, from reputable newspapers to louche locations online: "*Democratics* Choose November Slate" (*Hartford Courant*); "The Alabama *Democratics* on the Elections" (*The New York Times*); "Countering the Republicans, Pelosi convenes *Democratics* to talk faith" (*The San Diego Union-Tribune*); "Who are the *Democratics* running for president in 2008?" (WikiAnswers.com).

There is no such thing as a *Democratic.* Members of the *Democratic Party* are *Democrats.*

ACCIDENT 227
Avoid the Latin *per* with English words, except in certain stock phrases

Here are two good rules of thumb for the aspiring stylist: (1) When a non-English word or phrase has no special purpose or effect, avoid it. (2) When an English word or phrase works just as well or better than a non-English one, use English.

There is no reason to use the Latin *per* with English words like *day, share,* or *square foot;* use the ordinary English *a.* There is no reason to use *per annum* or *per year* when you have the English *a year, each year,* and *annually* at hand. And there is never any reason whatsoever to write *per your request* (*instructions,* etc.), or worse, the redundant *as per your request;* this is an example of the lowest form of inflated business jargon. *Per* means "according to," and you should use that English phrase or *as you requested* (*instructed,* etc.) instead. *Per* may also mean "for each," so don't write *per each,* which is redundant: "A sitting parent, for example, might earn one point per each [*for each*] child" (Associated Press).

Per is established and acceptable in the stock phrases *miles per hour, miles per gallon,* and *per person,* and in the fully assimilated Latin phrases *per diem, per capita,* and *per se.*

ACCIDENT 228
Don't write *self-confessed*
"As a self-confessed multitasking addict, I've incurred the wrath
of enough irritated friends and ruined many a romantic evening to
know," writes Jenna Wortham in *The New York Times*. Sorry, but
make that a *confessed* multitasking addict; adding *self-* to *confessed* is
redundant. As Theodore M. Bernstein points out in *Dos, Don'ts, and
Maybes of English Usage*, "Only the person who is confessing can
confess, so why the *self-*?"

This accident is regrettably common in reputable publications:
"While he is still the country's most popular politician, Berlusconi
has lost support since a self-confessed [*confessed*] prostitute said she
spent the night with him in Rome" (*Business Day*); "His inside account threatens to be as damaging to Mr Gotti as the 1992 testimony of the self-confessed [*confessed*] hitman Salvatore 'Sammy the
Bull' Gravano was to his late father, John Gotti Sr, who died in jail"
(timesonline.co.uk).

ACCIDENT 229
Specie* is not the singular of *species
The word *species* is both singular and plural. You may write *This
species is endangered* or *These species are endangered*. There is no singular *specie* meaning "one species," but accident-prone writers often
believe there is: "The magnolia tree is the designated specie [*species*]
planted along Halstead Street" (*Pasadena Star-News*). The unusual
noun *specie* means "money in coins, usually of gold or silver," and is
unrelated to *species*.

ACCIDENT 230
**When you mean "agree," it's *jibe with*–not *jive*
or *gibe with***
If you play or dance to swing music, you *jive: They were jiving to the
beat*. If you tease or kid someone, you also *jive: Don't jive with me*.
If you mock, taunt, jeer, or utter reproachful words, you *gibe*, as in
Shakespeare's line "You . . . with taunts did *gibe* my missive out of
audience." If you agree with someone or something, you *jibe*: "But

what to do when your vision doesn't *jibe* with that of your customers?" (*Indianapolis Star*).

Jive and *gibe* are frequently misused in edited prose for *jibe*, "to agree." Some examples: "The team also removed a few elements that didn't jive [*jibe*] with this year's theme" (*San Jose Mercury News*); "In Smoltz's mind, the bottom line—six runs in 5⅔ innings—did not jive [*jibe*] with his self-evaluation" (*Boston Globe*); "Margaret Lutostanski, who lives in Community Board 10, says that doesn't gibe [*jibe*] with her experience" (*New York Daily News*); "People tend to believe rumors that gibe [*jibe*] with their preconceptions" (*Publishers Weekly*).

Syndicated columnist James J. Kilpatrick had some fun with this accident of style in a piece about commonly confused words: "Following the presidential campaign of 2000, according to *U.S. News*, Republicans began drafting a health-care bill 'to *jive* with Bush's wishes.' Come now! Republicans never jive. They rarely even swing. The writer wanted 'jibe,' to agree."

ACCIDENT 231
There is no *tendon* in *tendinitis*
Although tendinitis afflicts tendons, it is properly spelled with an *i* in the middle, not an *o*. The misspelling *tendonitis* frequently occurs in edited writing; about 14 percent of the citations for this word on Google News get it wrong. Here's one from Reuters: "The abdominal injury came after Nadal had been forced to miss his Wimbledon title defense because of tendonitis [*tendinitis*] in both of his knees." (Also, that *of* after *both* is unnecessary.)

ACCIDENT 232
Each and *every* take singular verbs, and *each and every* is redundant
Would you write *each of you is* or *each of you are*? How about *every one of you is* or *every one of you are*? If you answered *is* to both questions, your usage is impeccable. In these constructions, *each* and *every* are singular and must take a singular verb.

If you think of *each* as meaning "each one" and *every* as meaning "every single" you'll always get it right. Phil Stacey, an entertainment blogger for the *Los Angeles Times*, failed to use that mnemonic device and got snookered by the pronoun *them* into using a plural instead of a singular verb: "But it seems that each of them are [*is*] being a bit weighed down by the criticism the judges have given them over the course of the competition."

Now, what about the common expression *each and every*? It is, says *Bryson's Dictionary of Troublesome Words*, "at best a trite way of providing emphasis, at worst redundant, and generally both." Bryson echoes many other usage experts who have denounced the phrase as a cliché and a pomposity. Compounding that problem is the tendency among those who use *each and every* to pair it with a plural verb when, like *each* or *every* alone, it should have a singular verb: "'Each and every one of you are [*is*] my heroes [*hero*],' said Thomas, who served as a commander at Abu Ghraib from April 2004 until February 2005" (SunHerald.com); "Each and every one of them are [*is*] proud to be part of ensuring the Youth Ranch will continue to help the children of Florida" (ChipleyBugle.com). In these examples, *All of you are* and *All of them are*, or *You are all* and *All of you are*, would have been better and more concise.

ACCIDENT 233
It's *without further ado*, not *adieu*

Ado is busy or troublesome activity, fuss, commotion, as in *much ado about nothing*. *Adieu* is a frenchified way of saying good-bye. *Ado* is pronounced uh-DOO, and *adieu* is pronounced uh-DYOO (the preferred pronunciation) or uh-DOO.

If you pronounce *ado* and *adieu* alike as uh-DOO, take care not to make the mistake of writing *further adieu*. If you pronounce *adieu* as uh-DYOO, take care not to make the mistake of saying *further* uh-DYOO.

ACCIDENT 234
Misuse of *continuous* for *continual*

Just as using your turn signals and allowing people to merge ahead of you are signs of a considerate driver, the ability to distinguish *continual* and *continuous* precisely is a sign of a careful user of the language.

Continual means "happening again and again at short intervals": *continual* reminders, *continual* attempts, *continual* laughter, the *continual* ringing of the telephone. *Continuous* means "uninterrupted or unbroken": *continuous* noise, *continuous* rain, a *continuous* effort, the *continuous* rotation of the earth.

The misuse of *continual* for *continuous* is common. In a review of Pat Conroy's novel *South of Broad*, a writer for the *Milwaukee Journal Sentinel* committed this accident of style twice in the same paragraph: "In a bid to infuse the story with continual [*continuous*] drama, Conroy aggregates tragedies to an implausible degree"; "Examples include Leo's continual [*continuous*] battle to retain his sanity in the years after his brother's suicide."

Here is a sentence (borrowed from Rudolf Flesch's *The ABC of Style*) in which the writer uses both *continual* and *continuous* correctly: "The connection he *continually* draws between Shakespeare's written lines and the social and political mutations of the era is the essential value of his lively, *continuously* fascinating book."

ACCIDENT 235
Do periods go inside or outside parentheses?
When the words in parentheses are part of a larger sentence, even if they constitute a sentence themselves, the period goes outside the closing parenthesis: *You can't go home again (that's what Thomas Wolfe wrote).* When a word, a phrase, or a full sentence is enclosed in parentheses and is not part of a larger sentence, the period goes inside the closing parenthesis: *(Right.) (You bet.) (I'm not kidding.)*

ACCIDENT 236
You have *problems*, not *issues*
One of the great virtues of a prose stylist—by which I mean a writer who is not only a fine craftsman but whose way of putting words together shows dignity, grace, and respect for the reader's intelligence—is a steadfast resolve to steer clear of any word or phrase embraced

by uninspired scribblers and the indiscriminate herd. The best stylists strive not to sound like everyone else, so they cast a cold eye on whatever happens to be in vogue.

The vogue word at issue here is *issue*, which in its plural form *issues* has become the kinder, gentler way to say *problems* or *concerns*. This trendy euphemism, which may have come from the jargon of psychology or from the lingo of politics, avoids the perceived stigma and sting of *problems* and allows us to allude to difficulties without admitting that they exist.

And therein lies the rub. Why do we shrink from saying what we mean? Why are we so reluctant to be specific? With so many good words out there, why do we reach for this mealymouthed, weasel word *issues*? Perhaps it's just easier to follow the herd and not think too hard about what we mean to say.

But if you are an aspiring or practicing stylist who doesn't want to invite problems, you would be wise to avoid "having issues." Remember that *issues* are things to be discussed or debated, while *problems* are things to be addressed and resolved. Your city council can debate the *issue* of dilapidated sewer lines, then vote on whether to spend money to fix the *problem*.

The next time you feel you're having issues with something, challenge yourself to find a more expressive, specific word—*problems, difficulties, troubles, impediments, conflicts, disagreements, disputes, controversy, concerns, worries, misgivings*, and *qualms* are among the many possibilities.

ACCIDENT 237
Don't use *due to the fact that* or *owing to the fact that*
These wordy phrases can invariably be replaced with *because:* "Due to the fact that [*because*] sexual organisms exchange and mix their genetic material when they breed, their traits can be more easily manipulated artificially" (Reuters); "Neither video is particularly convincing as a piece of documentary evidence, owing to the fact that [*because*] you can't really tell who's standing where when they throw the ball" (*Washington Post* blog).

ACCIDENT 238
Misuse of *nauseous* for *nauseated*

Many writers use the word *nauseous* to mean "sick to one's stomach, feeling nausea": "Worse, he woke that morning almost *nauseous* with the understanding that the night before he'd actually eaten a snail" (Richard Russo, *Empire Falls*). This usage is so common today that it can no longer be called an outright error. But it is still a general misunderstanding—a "peccadillo," as *Garner's Modern American Usage* puts it—disapproved of by most modern authorities. Writers who aspire to be wreckless should consider whether it's in their best interest to heed those authorities or to attach themselves to the bumper of the car in front of them and follow the speeding herd down the highway.

The traditional meaning of *nauseous* is "causing nausea, sickening," as *a nauseous odor* or *nauseous language*. The traditional word meaning "sick to one's stomach" is *nauseated*. That which is *nauseous*, sickening, makes one *nauseated*; it may also be described as *nauseating*, sickening. In *Right, Wrong, and Risky*, Mark Davidson advises us to "say that a nausea-*causing* person is *nauseating* and that a nausea-*suffering* person is *nauseated*." And in *Woe Is I*, Patricia T. O'Conner offers this smoke-free mnemonic sentence: "I'm *nauseated* by that *nauseous* cigar."

ACCIDENT 239
Don't *focus in on*

When you focus, you concentrate your attention *on* something. The word *in* is unnecessary after *focus:* "Both author and illustrator focus in on [*focus on*] the boy as he wonders aloud what life will be like for him when he's grown" (*The New York Times*).

If you mean "to bring into close-up, as with a photographic lens," use *zoom in on* instead: "Before eyes can focus in on [*focus on* or *zoom in on*] any one area of her living room, they process and absorb the entire space in all of its flea-marketlike appearance" (*Baltimore Sun*). That sentence would also have been improved by tightening *all of its* to *all its*.

ACCIDENT 240

Misuse of *volume* for *number*

The word *number* denotes things that can be itemized or counted: *a number of people, a great number of books.* The word *volume* denotes a mass or quantity, something considered as a whole: *sales volume, the volume of mail, trading volume on the stock market.* A higher *number* of sales will increase the sales *volume;* an increase in the *number* of letters sent will affect the *volume* of mail; and the *number* of shares traded on a given day will determine the trading *volume.*

Writers sometimes misuse *volume* for *number:* "State law requires identification of the driver before a ticket is issued, meaning cities can't rely on a high volume of tickets to pay for the program" (*The San Diego Union-Tribune*). Tickets are individual items that can be counted, so it should have been *a high number of tickets.*

ACCIDENT 241

Don't use *comprise* to mean "make up"

"If words were automobiles," writes Mark Davidson in *Right, Wrong, and Risky,* "a special license would be required for the use of the much-abused verb *comprise.* That license would be granted only after the applicant memorized the following instructions: The whole *comprises*—consists of—all its parts. The United States *comprises* fifty states."

Many other usage guides are sticklers on this point, cautioning that it is an unpardonable accident of style to use *comprise* to mean "to make up, constitute, compose." Yet all manner of writers, from the rank amateur to the seasoned professional, continually abuse *comprise* in this way: "At some large airports, regional jets comprise [*make up*] more than 50 percent of the total number of flights" (*The New York Times*); "Liberals comprise [*constitute*] about 21 percent of the population" (*San Francisco Examiner*).

Even worse in the eyes of many authorities is using the passive construction *comprised of* to mean *composed of.* Yet this transgression is legion in edited prose: "Many influential gay rights groups fear a fight in federal court will ultimately end up before a U.S. Supreme Court comprised of [*composed of*] a socially conservative majority that could deal the same-sex marriage campaign a significant setback with an adverse ruling" (Associated Press); "After taking two days of testimony on diet and killer diseases, the committee's staff—comprised [*composed*] not of scientists or doctors but of lawyers and (ahem) journalists" (Michael Pollan, *In Defense of Food*).

What has caused this widespread abuse of *comprise*? Perhaps a predilection for what H. W. Fowler, in *Modern English Usage* (1926), called "elegant variation," which tempts the unsuspecting writer to substitute a fancier, similar-sounding word for a more ordinary word. "It is the second-rate writers, those intent rather on expressing themselves prettily than on conveying their meaning clearly . . . that are chiefly open to the allurements of elegant variation," wrote Fowler. "There are few literary faults so widely prevalent." The abusers of *comprise* may have convinced themselves that *comprise* simply sounded better than *compose*, which was reason enough to use it instead.

In the hands of a conscientious writer, *comprise* means "to include, contain, consist of," as in this sentence: "The unified Jerusalem authority would *comprise* representatives from the boroughs, the Israeli and Palestinian governments, and all major religious authorities in the old city" (Azeem Ibrahim, CBSNews.com).

ACCIDENT 242
Don't confuse *childish* and *childlike*

These words are not interchangeable. The wreckless writer is careful to distinguish between *childish*, which means "immature, silly, foolish," and *childlike*, which means simply "like a child, characteristic of a child." *Childlike* suggests the favorable qualities of childhood, such as innocence, playfulness, and trust, whereas *childish* suggests the negative qualities, such as silliness, selfishness, and stubbornness.

Reckless writers often misuse the pejorative *childish* for the positive or neutral *childlike*: " 'Paper Heart' sets the dials on the way-back machine even further, giving us adult characters so childish [*childlike*] you want to give them milk and cookies" (*Star-Ledger*, New Jersey); "There's nothing wrong in childish [*childlike*] things appealing to grown-ups, if they remind them of their childhood or are beautifully done" (*Daily Mail*, UK); "This story is only heart-breaking if you still retain any sentimental sense of democracy and an admittedly childish [*childlike*] yearning for good government" (TheBostonChannel.com).

Israel Gutierrez of the *Miami Herald* gets it right in this sentence: "It's the only way LeBron James can come out of this hidden-video fiasco without looking like the most *childish*, egomaniacal, embarrassingly self-absorbed superstar athlete ever."

ACCIDENT   243
Confusion between *flaunt* and *flout*
To *flaunt* is to show off, display ostentatiously or boastfully. You can *flaunt* your wealth or good fortune, your brand-new $60,000 sports car, or your hot bod in a bikini: "Cindy Crawford is happy to *flaunt* her body in skimpy swimwear, even though she knows her lumpy thighs will be criticised" (stuff.co.nz). To *flout* is to show contempt for, disregard disdainfully, smugly ignore. You can *flout* the law, a convention, a claim, or the rules: "To repeal the tax now would require legislators to *flout* the will of the people" (*Arkansas Times*).

Writers frequently use *flaunt*, "show off," when they mean *flout*, "show contempt for": "Traffic officers will go after drivers who flaunt [*flout*] the state's hands-free cell phone law" (*Santa Cruz Sentinel*). Misuse of *flout* for *flaunt* is uncommon but does occur: "Some moms have even organized public 'nurse-ins' to flout [*flaunt*] their right to feed their babies" (*Utne Reader* online).

Reckless writers will continue to *flout* traditional usage and muddy the meanings of these two words. Wreckless writers, without *flaunting* their superiority, will strive to preserve the distinction.

ACCIDENT   244
It's spelled *sacrilegious*, not *sacreligious*
When I checked Google News, this word was misspelled only 4 out of 143 times. But on Google Web it was misspelled more than

THE ACCIDENTS OF STYLE

59,000 times. Moral: If no one is copyediting what you write, at least use your spell-checker (*and* a dictionary, to make sure your spell-checker gets it right).

You will never have to atone for this orthographic error if you remember that *sacrilegious* is formed from the word *sacrilege*. There is no *religious* in *sacrilegious*.

ACCIDENT 245
Don't write *included with it*

The phrase is pleonastic—it uses more words than are necessary to express an idea. Usually *included* alone can do the job and *with it* should be deleted: "A keyless chuck is included ~~with it~~" (*Pittsburgh Post-Gazette*); "A nighttime snack almost always included ~~with it~~ milk or a soft drink" (*The San Diego Union-Tribune*); "Many try to argue that not all the fixes are for Mac OS X, but rather for other software that might be included ~~with it~~" (*PC World*).

Sometimes eliminating the pleonasm is not so straightforward and requires revision. Take this sentence, for example: "The Web browser *included with it* is rather fast and provides support for Adobe Flash videos" (Softpedia.com). Just deleting *with it* could create a miscue for the reader, and using *included* as an adjective— "The *included* Web browser is rather fast"—sounds awkward, so changing the wording is the best solution: "The *accompanying* Web browser is rather fast" or "The Web browser *that comes with it* is rather fast."

ACCIDENT 246
Not everything is *major*

Have you noticed how everything these days is *major*? Everywhere you turn a writer or a broadcaster is trotting out this little word for something big.

For example, every day at work you face a *major* challenge or a *major* test. You make your *major* concern your *major* priority; you take on *major* problems and take a *major* step. Your company undergoes a *major* expansion, necessitating *major* budget cuts, a *major* reorganization, a *major* overhaul, and *major* layoffs. So you lose your job, which of course is a *major* disappointment. Then you fall into a *major* depression and get into a *major* car accident in which you suffer *major* injuries.

Do you think it might be time to put the brakes on this *major* accident of style before we experience a *major* blowout?

Sometimes writers get so accustomed to using a certain adjective with certain nouns that they forget there are other adjectives out there waiting to step in and freshen things up. Using *major* whenever you're talking *big* is a recipe for stale writing. Try to give the overworked *major* a rest and rejuvenate your prose with words like *formidable, daunting, redoubtable* (challenge); *arduous, exacting* (test); *chief, foremost, paramount* (concern, priority); *important, significant, meaningful* (step); *sizable, broad* (expansion); *extensive, considerable, substantial* (budget cuts); *sweeping, far-reaching, wholesale* (reorganization, overhaul, layoffs); *serious, severe, grave* (depression, car accident, injuries); *outrageous, intolerable, gross, grievous, egregious* (accident of style).

There are a few contexts in which *major* is customary and acceptable; for instance, a company can have a *major stake* in another company, an airline can be a *major carrier*, and you can have *major medical* insurance. Apart from established uses, however, give *major* a break and choose a more pointed or evocative adjective.

ACCIDENT 247
Don't confuse *enervate* and *energize*

The unwary writer, noticing that *enervate* looks and sounds so much like *energize*, may be tempted to substitute the former word for the latter in an effort to seem more literary and refined. But the words are antonyms: *energize* means "to stimulate, fill with energy, invigorate," while *enervate* means "to weaken, drain of energy, debilitate."

Even the people you'd most expect to know this distinction often get it wrong. My longtime colleague in language punditry, Richard Lederer, once delivered the keynote address at a conference of Illinois English teachers, after which one of the group's officers thanked him for his "enervating performance."

Here's an example of the correct use of *energize* and *enervate* in back-to-back sentences: "Obama wants to avoid *energizing* conservatives. He'd prefer to *enervate* them" (*The Atlantic* online).

Don't confuse *sometime* and *some time*

Sometime denotes an indefinite moment in time: "It remains to be seen whether, *sometime* later this year, a compromise can be crafted" (*The New York Times*). *Some time* denotes an amount or interval of time: "Once I've had *some time* being a mom, I'll figure out how to go back to work" (*The New York Times*). You can take *some time* off work to devote *some time* to your family, but chances are you'll have to go back to work *sometime*.

Misuses of *some time* (an amount of time) for *sometime* (at an unknown time) are common. Here are two examples from the *Boston Globe*: "The H1N1 shot will be given some time [*sometime*] in November during school"; "Some time [*sometime*] this month, a truck will pull up to a loading dock at Brigham and Women's Hospital in Boston and deliver human lung tissue samples."

If you can put *quite* before it or *to* after it, *some time* is probably what you want: "They've been sticking by that line for *quite some time*" (Council on Foreign Relations); "These tools take *some time to* customize to suit your purposes" (*The Wall Street Journal*). Otherwise, use *sometime*.

Misuse of *crisises* as the plural of *crisis*

"What were the crisises in 1846?" asks WikiAnswers.com, proving that the questions posed there can be as suspect as the answers posted. For all I know there may have been several *crises* in 1846, but I can assure you there were no *crisises*.

Just as the plural of *thesis* is *theses* and the plural of *neurosis* is *neuroses*, the proper plural of *crisis* is *crises*, pronounced in two syllables: KRY-seez. The change from *-is* in the singular to *-es* in the plural for these words comes to us from Greek. The anglicized plural *crisises*—perhaps modeled after *processes*, the plural of *process*, which comes through Old French from Latin—is erroneous.

.As *crisises* has become a more common accident in educated speech, its appearance in edited writing has increased: "He has also been at the helm through a number of high-profile crisises" (*San Francisco Examiner*); "McCain says he can best handle crisises" (FOX News.com); "No shortage of crisises have besieged the Friars' Welsh" (*Providence Journal*). Remembering that *crisis* and its proper plural, *crises*, have two syllables, not three, will help you avoid this accident in your speech and writing.

On another note, it is redundant to write *crisis situation*, just as it is redundant to write *emergency situation*. A *crisis* is a critical situation and an *emergency* is an urgent situation. Drop *situation* and use *crisis* or *emergency* alone.

ACCIDENT 250

Misuse of *illicit* for *elicit*

Illicit is an adjective meaning "illegal," as in *illicit activity, illicit drugs*. *Elicit* is a verb meaning "to draw or bring out, coax," as *to elicit interest*. Reckless writers sometimes ill-advisedly make the adjective do the work of the verb: "I was hoping simple intellectual engagement might illicit [*elicit*] responses" (*Orange County Register*); "First, Rosie cracked jokes about 'The View,' illiciting [*eliciting*] roars of laughter from the audience" (FOXNews.com).

ACCIDENT 251

Misuse of *verbal* for *oral*

People often use phrases like *a verbal agreement, a verbal commitment*, and *a verbal understanding*. Have you ever stopped to ask yourself exactly what they mean? It's often assumed that anything verbal is conducted through conversation, that it is spoken but not written down—and therein lies the problem.

The word *oral* means "spoken, not written," and the precise meaning of *verbal* is "pertaining to or expressed in words, whether spoken or written." So those agreements, commitments, and understandings are *oral*, not *verbal*. *Oral* communication is speech, conversation. *Verbal* ability is one's skill with words, and the *verbal* section of the SAT, the college entrance examination, tests a high school student's knowledge of written language.

Verbal, "pertaining to or expressed in words," is continually misused to mean *oral,* "spoken," and the result is rampant ambiguity and confusion: "He has verbal offers from Oklahoma, Michigan, Virginia Tech" (ESPN.com). The writer assumes you'll infer that the offers are not yet in writing, but the choice of *verbal* implies that they could be. "Ensure all promises made *verbally* are included, in writing, in the contract" (*The San Diego Union-Tribune*). The writer wants to say that we should put all spoken promises in writing, but to convey that meaning precisely the sentence should read like this: "Ensure all promises made *orally* are included in the contract."

Sometimes the misuse of *verbal* can be unintentionally amusing: "Even babies can recognize a dog's verbal and physical cues" (Examiner.com). Who's more remarkable for their ability with words—the dogs or the babies?

Verbal and *oral* are now so inextricably confounded that the tautological phrase *verbal and written* has become entrenched: "The position requires . . . strong *verbal and written* communication skills" (RenewableEnergyWorld.com); "If staffers don't abide by the training schedule, they risk *verbal and written* warnings and, ultimately, dismissal" (*Chicago Tribune*). Even putative authorities will mislead you about these words. In my version of Microsoft Word, the thesaurus offers these synonyms for *verbal: spoken, oral, vocal,* and *unwritten.*

This may seem like a morass, but don't despair. Avoiding this accident of style is easier than you may think. Just remember that *oral* refers to spoken words, *written* refers to written words, and *verbal* refers to anything expressed in words, whether spoken or written: "We deal here with both written and oral presentation" (Antonin Scalia and Bryan A. Garner, *Making Your Case*); "Their disputes are at least verbal. Far more dangerous threats come from . . . insurgent gunmen and bombers" (*The New York Times*).

ACCIDENT 252

Prefer *use* to *utilize*

The verb *to utilize* is unobjectionable if the intended meaning is "to put to good use, make practical or profitable use of." Thus, if a country *uses* its natural resources it may do so either conscientiously or wastefully, but if it *utilizes* its natural resources it does so beneficially. When you *use* your vocabulary you put it into service for the purpose of speaking or writing; but when you *utilize* your vocabulary you muster all your verbal tools and turn them to profitable account.

Most of the time, however, *utilize* is used not in this precise way but as a pretentious substitute for *use*, as in *She utilized a spoon to eat the soup*. Here are some real-life examples from edited writing: "Stone . . . will direct again, utilizing [*using*] a storyline based on contemporary economic events" (*The San Diego Union-Tribune*); "Rangers to utilize [*use*] Pudge as DH" (MLB.com); "Do you utilize [*use*] Clayton's libraries?" (*Atlanta Journal-Constitution*); "I've asked him to utilize [*use*] spell-checking and re-read his e-mails" (*The Wall Street Journal*); "The Intermedia Arts Program focuses on conceptual, critical, and aesthetic explorations in artistic production, utilizing [*using*] a variety of current technological means" (Mills College course catalog).

Use can stand in for *utilize*, but *utilize* should not stand in for *use*. If you are unsure whether you are using *utilize* properly, it is better to avoid the appearance of evil. You will never go wrong with *use*.

ACCIDENT 253

Don't use *again* after words beginning with *re-* that mean "to do something again"

We hear the question *Could you repeat that again?* so often that it seems innocuous and idiomatic. But its phrasing disguises a redundancy that careful users of the language take pains to eradicate from their speech and prose.

Perhaps the most common meaning of the prefix *re-* is "again," as in *rewrite*, "to write again," and *remake*, "to make again." Because the idea of doing something again is implicit in these words beginning with *re-*, there is no need to follow with *again*. *Repeat* means "to say again," so to *repeat again* is redundant.

There are scores of words beginning with *re-* that should not be paired with *again*. Here is a short list of some of the most commonly abused specimens: *repeat, rewrite, remake, recur, remarry, reiterate, reinvent, reuse, reapply, relive, replay, reemerge, reformulate, reinfect, rerecord, reprogram, resell, retell,* and *resubmit.*

Of course, if you prefer to use *again*, just drop *re-* when you can and write *make again, use again, marry again, play again, tell again,* and *submit again.*

See "Say It Again, Sam" on page 57.

ACCIDENT 254
Misuse of plural *criteria* for singular *criterion*

Criteria is a plural noun. *Criterion* is a singular noun. "Remember: one criterion, two criteria," says *Bryson's Dictionary of Troublesome Words.*

That simple lesson is lost on many writers, who misuse *criteria* as if it were singular, pairing it with a singular verb: "Neither criteria is [*criterion is*] mentioned in Durbin's letter" (*Chicago Sun-Times*); "The main criteria was [*criterion was*] the music had to be original" (*Colorado Springs Independent*).

The oxymoronic phrase *sole criteria* is also a popular solecism among the ditzerati: "But it was not the sole criteria [*criterion*] on which the group based its endorsement decisions" (*New York Daily News*); "Corrections officials agreed to stop using race as the sole criteria [*criterion*] for assigning bunks in the reception centers" (*Los Angeles Times*).

One more piece of advice. Avoid the variant plural *criterions*, a feeble attempt at anglicization that is thankfully moribund (only nine hits on Google News), and the ghastly variant plural *criterias*, which is illiterate.

ACCIDENT 255
Confusion between *rack* and *wrack*

These words should be easy for you to distinguish because the preferred form is *rack* in all but one uncommon sense. The noun *wrack* means "ruin, destruction." It's "an archaic variant of *wreck*," says

Bryson's Dictionary of Troublesome Words, that nowadays appears legitimately only in the expression *wrack and ruin*.

In all other familiar contexts, the proper spelling is *rack*. The frame you place something on to stretch it is a *rack*. When you strain or stretch something, such as your brain, you *rack* it. And when something rattles your nerves, it's *nerve-racking* (as if your nerves had been placed on a rack and stretched). Dictionaries list *nerve-wracking* as a variant spelling, but don't be bamboozled by that; dictionaries recognize anything that occurs frequently, even if it is considered a mistake. Modern authorities on usage, including the style manuals of *The New York Times* and The Associated Press, are staunchly in favor of *nerve-racking* and opposed to *nerve-wracking*.

ACCIDENT 256
Drive carefully with *both*

There are several things you should do and should not do with *both*.

First, don't use *both* when the idea of *both* is implied by the context: "The two are ~~both~~ recently divorced" (*Buffalo News*); "Throwing them ~~both~~ together in a series is what we think makes 'Fringe' special" (*Los Angeles Times*).

Don't use *both* when you mean "each." The result can be ambiguous, as in this example from Mark Davidson's *Right, Wrong, and Risky*: "Both suits cost $300." Do the suits cost $300 together or, more likely, does each one cost that much? *Bryson's Dictionary of Troublesome Words* gives this example of a ludicrous *both*: "a supermarket on both sides of the street." Of course you can't have one supermarket on both sides of the street, so it should be *a supermarket on each side* or *supermarkets on both sides*.

You must use *both of* before a pronoun (*both of them, both of you, both of us*), but it's better style to drop *of* whenever it is nonessential: *they liked both ~~of~~ your ideas; I love both ~~of~~ my daughters; she has appointments on both ~~of~~ those days*. Also, *both of the* can often be beneficially reduced to *both*: "Both ~~of the~~ protesters were later released" (Associated Press); "No matter, say both ~~of the~~ dads" (*Worcester Telegram*).

In *The Careful Writer*, Theodore M. Bernstein cautions us not to use *both* with *as well as* because "the *as well* part of the phrase *as well*

THE ACCIDENTS OF STYLE

as means virtually the same thing as *both*." So a construction like *the drug wars both in Mexico as well as in Colombia* should be changed to *the drug wars both in Mexico and in Colombia*.

Finally, when you follow *both* with *and* in a construction that means "this as well as that," you must make sure that whatever follows *both* and *and* is grammatically parallel. In the following sentence, note how the elements after *both* and *and* have the same structure: "Germany's ready public acceptance of homosexuality is the product of recent sea changes both *in the character of society* and *in the letter of national law*" (*Foreign Policy*). If the writer of that sentence had decided to place *both* after *in*, to keep the structure parallel it would have to read *in both the character of society and the letter of national law*, with *the* instead of *in the* introducing each element.

The parallellism is askew in *He is known both for his pragmatic style and his political value*. For proper balance, the sentence needs another *for* before the second *his*, or else *both* should be placed between *for* and *his*. These sentences are also out of whack: "Adam Duritz, the Counting Crows frontman famous for both his dreadlocks and [*his*] dating record, is back in the spotlight" (*People* magazine); "Vargas came out in the first, scoring good combinations to both the body and [*the*] head of the hard charging Nelson" (Boxing Scene.com). (Incidentally, *hard-charging* should be hyphenated because it's a phrasal adjective modifying the proper noun *Nelson*.)

ACCIDENT 257

Confusion of *prone* with *supine*

As I noted in the introduction, *prone* means "lying facedown, on one's belly" while *supine* means "lying on one's back, faceup."

Writers who are lying down on the job frequently flip-flop these words and misuse *prone* for *supine:* "Then she tells parents to lie prone [*supine*] and place their babies on top of them, face-to-face" (*South Florida Sun Sentinel*). That sounds like a painful position for baby and mother alike. "Many women will . . . scurry frantically round the house while he lies prone [*supine*] in front of the telly" (*Daily Mail*, UK). You can't watch much telly when you're flat on your face, so that bloke either had too much to drink or he's dead.

Misuse of *supine* is rare, but occasionally a writer will apply it in a peculiar way, in this case anthropomorphically: "Shown are a tree uprooted and lying supine" (*Chesterton Tribune*, Indiana). A tree lying on its back? Take care to use *supine* and *prone* only of a creature that is capable of lying on its back (*supine*) or on its belly (*prone*).

ACCIDENT 258
It's spelled *millennium*, not *millenium*

Remember: double *l*, double *n*. *Millennium* comes from the Latin *millĕ*, a thousand, and *annus*, a year. For some reason this word continually confounds professional writers and copyeditors; out of 10,774 hits for it on Google News a whopping 1,680 were misspelled with one *n*.

AMAZING GAFFE

Misspelled words in journalism and institutional prose are usually the result of hasty writing and poor proofreading. Occasionally they're the result of insufficient education. But would you believe that they can also be a consequence of a college education?

"Melon Media, an e-mail marketing company based in Australia, sells a Web-based application called Spellr.us that checks spelling on Web sites," reports the October–November 2009 issue of the newsletter *Copyediting*. "The company released a survey on July 7, 2009, asserting that an average of 14.2 percent of the pages on the Web sites of the world's top 20 universities contain at least one spelling error....

"According to Spellr.us, the top five misspelled words were *accommodation, university, harassment,* and *research*. The word *university* was misspelled by 13 of the universities surveyed. McGill University, ranked number 20, had the fewest errors, with 34; Duke University, ranked number 13, had the most, with 300."

ACCIDENT 259
As far as needs a verb

If you use *as far as* to mean "as for, regarding," be sure to follow it
with a verb: "As far as the first teams *are concerned*" (*Baltimore Sun*);
"As far as memorable plays in modern UConn football history *go*"
(*Hartford Courant*).

Omitting the verb after *as far as* is a common accident of style:
"As far as the claim for Leonard's front door [*is concerned*], Guglielmi said the estimate for repairs was high enough that the claim
will have to go through the Board of Estimates" (*Baltimore Sun*);
"As far as his mini-boycott of the media [*goes*], it's not about us and
it didn't really affect the coverage of the event" (*New York Daily
News*).

But even if you use *as far as* correctly, it's better style to use *as
for* or *regarding*. And it's even better style to skip all these prelimi-
naries and begin your sentence at the beginning: "Guglielmi said
the estimate for repairing Leonard's front door . . ."; "His mini-
boycott of the media is not about us . . ."

ACCIDENT 260
Use *presently* to mean "soon," not "currently" or "now"

Presently is often used interchangeably with *currently* or as a pompous substitute for *now:* "Presently [*Currently*], if you're rich or smart
enough to work for a company that provides health coverage, then
you're safe" (*Chicago Daily Herald*); "He believed that he could
achieve more than he was presently [*now*] achieving" (*The Times*,
Johannesburg, South Africa). This is inferior and ambiguous usage.
The New York Times Manual of Style and Usage and many other authorities recommend restricting *presently* to the meaning "soon"—
as in *She will arrive presently*—and using *currently, at present, at the
moment*, or *now* when you mean "now."

Another stylistic blunder involving *presently* is using it unnecessarily or redundantly. *Presently* is superfluous in the following examples: "The UK ~~presently~~ has more primary care physicians per capita
than the US" (*North County Times*, San Diego); "All were reading, going through donated clothing, playing on the one computer ~~presently~~

there" (*News-Leader*, Springfield, Missouri); "Lynchburg is ~~presently~~ facing a $500,000 free-speech complaint from a city detective" (*Lynchburg News & Advance*, Virginia).

ACCIDENT 261
Don't use *reticent* to mean "reluctant"

A common vice of many writers, even some of the best, is the temptation to replace an ordinary word with a fancier one that sounds somewhat like it and seems to convey the same meaning in a snazzier way. This temptation is what causes people to write *reticent* when they mean *reluctant*.

"His campaign is cheapening his greatest strength—and making a mockery of his already dubious claim that he's reticent to talk about his P.O.W. experience," writes Maureen Dowd in *The New York Times*. Like so many other writers today, Ms. Dowd seems to believe that *reticent* and *reluctant* are interchangeable, and that, given a choice between them, any sentence will be improved by using the more impressive, literary word. But a sentence is improved only by using the proper word.

Regrettably, writers have confused *reticent* with *reluctant* so often in recent years that dictionaries now record this poor usage. But the words are not synonyms. *Reluctant* means "unwilling, hesitant, disinclined." *Reticent*, from a Latin verb meaning to be silent, means "reluctant to speak"; a person who is reticent doesn't want to talk.

This excerpt from an article in the *MetroWest Daily News* (Massachusetts) shows how *reticent* ought to be used: "Police say that could alienate an already reticent immigrant community. 'We want them to report crimes,' said Police Chief Steven Carl. 'We want them to call us when they're victims. We don't want them to be afraid of us.'"

If you find yourself tempted to use the phrase *reticent to* (do something), stop, take a deep breath, and write *reluctant* instead. This simple act of reluctance will spare you a solecism and help preserve the precise meaning of a useful word.

ACCIDENT 262

Don't confuse *immigrate* and *emigrate*

Immigrate and *emigrate* both mean to leave a country and settle in another, but they differ in their emphasis and direction. The *im-* in *immigrate* means "into," and the word means literally "to go into a new country, migrate in." The initial *e* in *emigrate* is short for *ex-*, which means "out"; to *emigrate* means "to leave or go out of one's country, migrate out."

Immigrate is followed by the preposition *to*. You *immigrate to* a country, go into it to resettle. *Emigrate* is followed by the preposition *from*. You *emigrate from* a country, go out of it, leave it to settle in another. When you emigrate from your native country, you immigrate to another. An *emigrant* is a person who emigrates from his native country to another country; he immigrates to the country in which he will resettle. When the emigrant settles in a new country, he becomes an immigrant to it.

ACCIDENT 263

It's *heartrending*, not *-wrenching* or *-rendering*

National Public Radio tells "the tragic, *heart-wrenching* tale of Jaycee Lee Dugard." CBS News online reports on "Farrah's *heartwrenching* battle with cancer." *BusinessWeek* asks, "What is the least *heartwrenching* way . . . to handle layoffs?" And *Booklist* says Robert Hicks's novel *A Separate Country* is "as beautifully written and *heart-wrenching* as its predecessor."

Apparently, *heartwrenching* is the new *irregardless*—the nonstandard word that everyone loves to use. *Heartwrenching* has become popular so fast that dictionaries do not recognize it, unlike *irregardless*, which occupies an unhallowed place in their pages. But dictionary recognition can't be far off if Google News is any measure, for this illegitimate marriage of *heart* and *wrenching* is now about eight times more common in edited writing than the traditional *heartrending*. Even President Barack Obama, in his May 2009 commencement speech at Notre Dame, showed the world that, on certain issues, he would rather *wrench* than *rend:* "Maybe we won't agree on abortion, but we can still agree that this is a *heart-wrenching* decision for any woman to make."

It used to be that reckless writers were all aflutter about *rendering* hearts instead of *rending* them. They would miswrite *heart-rendering* instead of *heartrending*, as if the heart were a big piece of fat being melted in a cast-iron pan rather than a repository of tender emotion that can be easily torn or broken. But this error, which for years usage mavens had a hearty laugh or a heart attack over, has mysteriously abated (only twenty-eight hits on Google News), and by a twist of fate we now have in its place the contorted *heartwrenching*.

My wild surmise is that *heartwrenching* came into being through a confused coupling of *gut-wrenching*, for which the *Oxford English Dictionary*'s earliest citation is 1972, and *heartrending*, which we've been using for more than three hundred years. It makes perfect sense that we *wrench* our guts (twist them violently so as to cause distress or nausea) and *rend* our hearts (tear them apart because of anguish or grief). But if our hearts can now be *wrenched*, how long will it be before we start *rending* our guts? Frankly, it all sounds like the kind of linguistic mayhem that only a lexicographer with a chain saw could instigate.

Careful writers who, like me, are heartsick and heartbroken over this thoughtless, clumsy displacement of *-rending* by *-wrenching* will tastefully refrain from throwing a wrench in the works and hew to the traditional *heartrending*.

ACCIDENT 264

Proper use of *demise*

The noun *demise*, because it comes to us from law, is a formal, euphemistic, and sometimes pretentious word for death: "Windows Mobile's demise greatly exaggerated, iSuppli says" (*ComputerWorld*). Thoughtful writers should always ask themselves whether *death* or some other word—*decline, failure, collapse, closure, bankruptcy, dismissal, extinction, elimination, disappearance, dissolution, discontinuation*, etc.—is the more precise and sensible choice.

ACCIDENT 265

Don't dangle *having said that*, or don't use it at all

Contemporary writers love to use the phrase *having said that* perhaps because, as a wise old literary woman once told me when I was young and full of spark but had yet to publish a word, "Writers don't like writing. They like having written."

Having said that is usually used to signal a transition from one statement to another that qualifies or contradicts it. The phrase is wildly popular these days among writers who strive to be fashionable by sporting the latest verbal finery and consigning to charity the old and threadbare words in their closets. In the case of *having said that*, the cast-off goods include *however, nonetheless, on the other hand, in spite of that*, and the splendidly concise *still, but*, and *yet*. Any of these can effect a transition more handily than the trendy *having said that*, but if you want to be a fashionable writer it's always out with the old and in with the new.

Having said that, I will now show you the proper way to use *having said that*. And I just did. Did you notice? The subject of the sentence following *having said that* was a person ("I"), and that person—which can be anyone—ties the modifier to the sentence by supplying a speaker who has just *said* whatever came before. *Having said that* is acceptable when a speaker ties it to the main clause: *Having said that, he stressed that he has no doubts the plan will work.* But without a personal subject to anchor *having said that* to the sentence, the phrase becomes a dangling modifier, grammatically incorrect and rhetorically useless: "Having said that, there will be a natural decline in new-vehicle sales for the rest of the year" (*Time*); "Having said that, a fair amount of the growth we've experienced in the last two or three quarters is really the reflection of technology and development" (StreetInsider.com). Sometimes this dangling modifier can produce a ludicrous effect: "Having said that, our cameras will continue to roll at the jury house" (*Entertainment Weekly*). So the cameras can speak? Now that's entertainment.

To sum up, *having said that* is a vogue phrase that says little more than that the writer who uses it is fond of vogue phrases. It is best avoided, but if you must use it make sure that you or some other speaker is the subject of the main clause.

ACCIDENT 266
Don't confuse *economic* and *economical*

"The alarm clock is set to give us precisely enough time to rise, shower, get ready for work and grab some breakfast before hitting the road," writes Jim Bradford in the *Kansas City Star.* "We're very economic with our time."

Change that *economic* to *economical.* When you mean "thrifty, frugal," or "inexpensive, money-saving," the word you want is *economical.* For every other sense pertaining to the economy or to economics, use *economic: economic growth, economic crisis, economic forecast.*

ACCIDENT 267
It's *to the manner born,* not *to the manor born*

You are *to the manner born* because you are accustomed to behaving in a certain *manner,* as if you were born to act that way. The expression has nothing to do with being born into privilege, with a silver spoon in your mouth, a misconception that has tempted many to write *to the manor born.* The source is Shakespeare's *Hamlet:* "Though I am a native here / And to the manner born."

ACCIDENT 268
Don't write *Is it just me, or . . .*

Whenever I see a sentence beginning with *Is it just me, or . . .* I stop reading immediately. This rhetorical device, which the "opinionati"* have fetishized, is a red flag signaling that whatever follows—even if you agree with it—will be arrogance sugarcoated with humility. When someone begins a sentence with *Is it just me, or . . .* you can be certain that a smug attempt to patronize, manipulate, or intimidate you is in progress.

Opinionati: my nonce word for people who believe they have a moral obligation to express their opinion on matters of the day in some public, and usually obnoxious, manner.

THE ACCIDENTS OF STYLE

"Is it just me, or does calling someone you just met 'my friend' sound a bit condescending?" writes the conservative commentator Bill O'Reilly in a syndicated column. Had he begun the sentence with *does* or *doesn't*, we would be free to answer the question for ourselves and then digest his analysis. But by beginning his query with *Is it just me* he sets you up to look like an idiot for not agreeing with him.

If you're unwilling to "place yourself in the background," as *The Elements of Style* famously advises, at least avoid alienating your readers with the disingenuous *Is it just me, or . . .*

ACCIDENT 269

It's *suffice it to say*, not *suffice to say*

There are two ways you can properly say it with *suffice*—the usual way, *suffice it to say*, or the unusual way, *it suffices to say*. Despite the frequency of *suffice to say*, this abbreviated form without *it* is non-standard: "Suffice [*it*] to say, it was not exactly ladylike" (guardian .co.uk); "Suffice [*it*] to say, the Red Sox and Wagner will be feeling their way through this together" (*Boston Globe*).

ACCIDENT 270

Don't write *ATM machine*, *PIN number*, or *HIV virus*

Before I tell you why you should never write those phrases, let me explain the difference between an acronym and an initialism. Both are abbreviations of a phrase formed from the initial letter of each word in the phrase. The difference is that you can pronounce an acronym as a word, while an initialism is pronounced as a series of letters. So *PIN* is an acronym, but *ATM* and *HIV* are initialisms. *MEGO* ("my eyes glaze over") is an acronym, but *LOL* ("laugh out loud") is an initialism. The world of medicine teems with both kinds of abbreviations: for example, *SIDS* ("sudden infant death syndrome") and *SARS* ("severe acute respiratory syndrome") are ac-ronyms; *ER* ("emergency room") and *ICU* ("intensive care unit") are initialisms.

Now here's why you should never write—or say, for that matter—*machine* after *ATM*, *number* after *PIN*, or *virus* after *HIV*: adding those words is redundant. The *M* in *ATM* stands for *machine* ("automated teller *machine*"), the *N* in *PIN* stands for *number* ("personal identification *number*"), and the *V* in *HIV* stands for *virus* ("human immunodeficiency *virus*"), so these accompanying words are repetitive. *ATM, PIN,* and *HIV* should always stand alone: *Can you believe that idiot thought he could get HIV from punching in his PIN at an ATM?*

Don't use *transpire* to mean "happen"–in fact, don't use the word at all

The traditional and precise meaning of *transpire* is "to leak out, become known, come to light, pass from secrecy into common knowledge." Thus: "When the facts about the Watergate scandal *transpired*, it became clear that President Nixon had been lying to the American people"; "Then it *transpired* that they were not married; they were merely living together" (James J. Kilpatrick). But for more than two centuries *transpire* has also been used as a pompous alternative to *happen, occur, go on,* and *take place,* as in "Watching the play, he wondered what would *transpire* next" or "They told us what had *transpired* while we were gone."

To the people who edit your dictionaries, that long history makes this use of *transpire* acceptable. But there is usage, and then there is conscientious usage. To the seasoned writers and editors who compose style guides to help you write with greater clarity and grace, using *transpire* to mean "happen" marks you as a member of the scribbling army of second-rate writers who compensate for their lack of skill by resorting to turgidity and affectation. These writers, who consider themselves *individuals* rather than *people,* loftily *commence* when others *begin, endeavor* when others *try, purchase* when others *buy, indicate* when others *show, utilize* when others *use, facilitate* when others *help,* and finally *meet their demise* rather than *die.*

But I digress. Back to *transpire:* "To use *transpire* as a substitute for *happen* is to engage in blowfish prose, by which an ordinary word is puffed up to a more pretentious word," writes James J. Kilpatrick in *The Writer's Art. Transpire* "is how a stuffed shirt says *happen* or *occur* or *take place*," writes Patricia T. O'Conner in *Woe Is I*. Mark Davidson, in *Right, Wrong, and Risky*, calls *transpire* "a snooty substitute for the perfectly good word *happen*," and *Garner's Modern American Usage* says it is "a mere pomposity displacing an everyday word." I could go on, but I think I've made it clear that no usage expert with a reputation to lose is sweet on this inflated use of *transpire*.

What should a writer do, then, with this troubled word? You can use it in its traditional sense of "leak out, come to light, become known," but there is always the risk that most of your readers will misunderstand you. If that's a risk you're unwilling to take, don't use the word at all. "The risk-free way to deal with the verb *transpire*," advises Mark Davidson, "is to avoid it."

ACCIDENT 272
Misuse of *borne* for *born*

Born refers to birth, whether actual or figurative: *born on the fourth of July; born to be free; a born-again Christian; "a terrible beauty is born"* (W. B. Yeats). *Borne* may refer to giving birth or producing (*she has borne many children, the tree has borne fruit*); to something carried by something else (*mosquito-borne diseases*); or to something burdensome that must be tolerated or endured: *How much of the cost will be borne by employees?*

Because these two words are both past participles of the verb to *bear*, and because they both have something to do with birth or birthing, writers sometimes get confused and misuse *borne*, the word for birthing or enduring, for *born*, the word for birth: "Allred filed a lawsuit Monday demanding a guardian be assigned to steward the money generated by the octuplet infants borne [*born*] to Octomom Nadya Suleman" (*San Jose Mercury News*); "Thought is borne [*born*] of quiet, of internal talk" (Robert Hartwell Fiske, *Silence, Language, and Society*).

In *The Appropriate Word*, J. N. Hook offers these helpful examples of the proper use of *born* and *borne*: "Melba was *born* in Missouri. Her mother had *borne* two other children; one of them, a boy, was *born* deaf and crippled. Melba's mother has *borne* that burden with patience."

ACCIDENT 273

Don't call a *lectern* a *podium*

If you look up *podium* in any current dictionary you are bound to find contradictory definitions, one saying it's a raised platform for a speaker or conductor and another saying it's a stand for a speaker's notes, a *lectern*. The American Heritage Dictionary even goes to the trouble of putting a photo in the margin of a woman in academic garb standing at a lectern, under which is printed the word *podium*. Curiously, neither *The American Heritage Book of English Usage* (1995) nor *The American Heritage Guide to Contemporary Usage and Style* (2005) has anything to say about *lectern* or *podium*. Apparently the editors at *American Heritage* have concluded that the promiscuous use of one word for the other is not any cause for concern.

I disagree, as do nearly all other modern authorities on usage. "A lectern is the stand on which a speaker places his or her notes," says *Bryson's Dictionary of Troublesome Words*. "A podium is the raised platform on which the speaker and lectern stand." The style manuals of The Associated Press and *The New York Times* support that time-honored distinction and insist, as the latter puts it, that "a speaker stands *on* a podium and *at* or *behind* a lectern." Though using *podium* for *lectern* "has become commonplace," concludes *Garner's Modern American Usage*, "careful writers should avoid it."

Maureen Dowd of *The New York Times* got it right when she wrote, "You knew he [Obama] would never inspire alarm as W. did, that if Condi walked too far away or his notes blew off the lectern, he'd be utterly lost." President Barack Obama got it wrong when in his eulogy for Senator Edward M. Kennedy he said, "We can still hear his voice bellowing through the Senate chamber, face reddened, fist pounding the podium." As the *Harper Dictionary of Contemporary Usage* observes, the only speaker likely to grasp or pound a podium "would be one who had fallen flat on his face."

The conscientious writer instinctively understands that words are both more stable and more supple when useful distinctions are maintained. And the distinction between *podium* and *lectern*, as Roy H. Copperud affirms in *American Usage and Style: The Consensus*, "should be maintained."

USE THE RIGHT WORD, NOT ITS SECOND COUSIN

"The notion of decamping to Paris to 'find yourself' without having the vaguest idea of what that self might be can sound quaintly old-fashioned."
—Kenneth Turan, *Los Angeles Times*

The first thing you must do if you want to be a wreckless writer is know the precise meanings of the words you use. Since *quaint* has long meant not simply "odd" or "unusual" but "charmingly odd, especially in an old-fashioned way" (*American Heritage Dictionary*, 4th ed.), it is infelicitous and pleonastic to use the phrase *quaintly old-fashioned* when *quaint* alone would convey the intended meaning.

ACCIDENT 274

Don't use *fortuitous* as an elegant variation of *fortunate*

Writers routinely use *fortuitous* when they mean *fortunate* because they imagine that the two words must be interchangeable because they're similar in sound, and they think that by replacing an ordinary word with a fancier one they'll appear more intelligent. But this arbitrary and thoughtless substitution does not enhance anyone's prose; it only has a deleterious effect on the language.

Fortuitous means "happening by chance, accidental, unexpected." Though we usually use *fortuitous* to refer to what are sometimes called "happy accidents," and though we rarely use it to refer to a chance event of an unfortunate nature (you wouldn't say *a fortuitous earthquake*), in precise usage *fortuitous* is not interchangeable with *fortunate* or *lucky*. For example, it's not unreasonable to infer from the phrase *a fortuitous meeting* that the meeting was fortunate or lucky. But consider how the meaning of *fortuitous* becomes clear when it's part of this sentence: "A fortuitous meeting with Mr. Percival Sneed was the cause of his death." There's no way you can use *fortunate* or *lucky* in that sentence, unless you are trying to be droll.

ACCIDENT 275

Don't confuse *admission* and *admittance*

Admittance refers strictly to physical entry, *admission* to acceptance into a group or institution or to a fee paid to enter. If the intended meaning is that no one may come in, the sign should read "No admittance." If the intended meaning is that no money will be charged for entrance, the sign should read "No admission" or "Free admission."

Use *admission* for any figurative entry, such as membership: *his admission to college; her admission to the bar; the country's admission to the European Union.* It is a common error to use *admittance* in this figurative sense: "His admittance [*admission*] to CU, however, was delayed" (*Rocky Mountain Independent*). Use *admittance* only for physical entry that does not involve membership or special standing. Thus: *Admittance to the pool requires admission to the club.*

An *admission* may also be something admitted, something acknowledged or conceded as true. *Admittance* is sometimes improperly used in this sense: "It's a simple admittance [*admission*] that I will no longer worry about keeping up with changing regulations" (*Seattle Post-Intelligencer* reader blogs).

ACCIDENT 276

It's *hark back,* not *hearken back* or *harken back*

When you *hark back*, you refer to or recall an earlier topic, time, or circumstance: "Italy . . . wore new light blue retro jerseys and brown shorts that *hark back* to the Azzurri's first two World Cup titles in 1934 and 1938" (*Chicago Tribune*). The archaic word *hearken* (variant spelling *harken*) means "to listen, give one's attention to": "Whenever it is whistled to, it stops to hearken," wrote Oliver Goldsmith in 1774.

Perhaps because *hark* by itself is an old-fashioned synonym of *hearken* ("Hark, the herald angels sing!"), people became confused and began writing *hearken back* and *harken back* instead of *hark back.* These unidiomatic forms have infiltrated educated speech (for example, I have heard NPR political reporter Scott Horsley say *hearken back*) and they are increasingly seen in print: "The Birds proudly harken [*hark*] back to the glory days of riff-heavy rock" (*Hartford Courant*); "Still others hearken [*hark*] back to MTV's *The Real World*" (npr.org).

If you wish to avoid this subtle but serious accident of style, you will *hearken* to my advice and hew to the idiomatic and preferred *hark back*.

ACCIDENT 277
Don't use *peruse* to mean "to skim, browse"

Traditionally and by derivation, *peruse* means "to read carefully, examine closely, study" (from the verb to *use* + *per-*, "thoroughly"). Although there is historical precedent for using *peruse* as a synonym for *read*, many modern authorities consider this pompous, and I agree. If you wouldn't say it's *algid* when you mean it's cold, and you wouldn't say you're *discalced* when you mean you're barefoot, then don't say you've *perused* an article or book unless you have read or studied it carefully.

In recent years writers have also begun using *peruse* to mean "to skim, browse, dip into or glance through"—the opposite of the word's traditional meaning: "Buying at the rate of 50 books a week has clearly made it impossible for him to read most of his purchases, though he strives at least to peruse [*skim*] each one" (*San Diego Reader*).

As you can imagine, this contrary usage has only bred confusion. Some examples: "In the thriller, the president of the USA gets to *peruse* the mysterious volume" (*USA Today*). Does the president read, study, or skim the mysterious volume? There's no way to tell what the writer intends *peruse* to mean. And in this sentence *peruse* is also ambiguous and tacked on merely for show: "This is a very slick diving magazine that . . . is well worth your while to read and *peruse*" (scuba-doc.com).

As if that weren't distressing enough, *peruse* is now used not only of cursory reading but of any sort of browsing or superficial inspection: "Folks out shopping for a vehicle can also peruse [*browse*] displays of firearms as well" (*St. Louis Post-Dispatch*); "Whether you're in the mood to chow down or just want to peruse [*look around*] the shops" (WTVY-TV, Alabama). This slovenly corruption of the word's meaning has become so prevalent that if you right-click on *browse* in Microsoft Word, the thesaurus gives *surf* and *peruse* as synonyms.

So what is a devotee of precise usage to do? Use *read, browse,* and *skim* when that is what you mean, and reserve *peruse* for contexts where you mean "to read carefully, study or examine closely," as in this sentence: "Teachers and content specialists spent four years discussing what they wanted from the math program, *perusing* textbooks and materials . . . and finally picking a favorite" (*Grand Junction Daily Sentinel*, Colorado).

ACCIDENT 278
Write *one of the few*, not *one of the only*

The popular expression *one of the only* is "strange and illogical," say Richard Lederer and Richard Dowis in *Sleeping Dogs Don't Lay*, because "there is no meaning of *only* that fits in *one of the only*."

The adjective *only* means "without others of its kind or class; being the single one": *She was the only woman there and the only person I could talk to.* When writers use *one of the only* they are literally saying *one of just one.* But it's clear that they mean *one of the few* because the phrase is always followed by a plural noun: "It doesn't help that one of the only [*one of the few*] ways to fund parking lots is through parking fees and tickets" (*Los Angeles Times*); "Luckily, next door they have one of the only [*one of the few*] foods that actually grow on one" (Minnesota Public Radio); "The President has been one of the only [*one of the few*] honest brokers in this entire process" (msnbc.com).

The wording *one of only a few* is acceptable when special emphasis of *fewness* is desired: "The school was *one of only a few* high schools in the city that African-Americans were allowed to attend during the era of segregation" (*Baltimore Sun*).

ACCIDENT 279

Use a plural verb after the construction *one of the* [plural noun] *who* or *that*

In an op-ed piece published in *The San Diego Union-Tribune*, Randy Ward, superintendent of schools for San Diego County, summed up his case for the importance of public education by writing, "Public education is one of the things that matters most." Besides being platitudinous, does anything about that sentence seem amiss to you?

If you guessed that *matters* should have been *matter* because a plural verb has to agree with the plural noun *things*, pat yourself on the back. You're well on your way to becoming a wreckless writer because you've learned to spot one of the most frequent accidents of style that occur (not *occurs*) on the highway of words.

No one would write *These are the things that matters most*. But as soon as the words *one of* get mixed up in a sentence, many people wrongly persuade themselves that *one* now governs the verb so the verb must be singular. The grammatical truth is that when *one of* is followed by a plural noun and *who* or *that*, the verb that follows must agree in number with the plural noun: *This is one of those <u>blunders</u> that <u>are</u> [not *is*] easy to make.*

You can see the logic of this immediately if you invert any sentence where *one of* is followed by a plural noun: "Of the *things* that *matter* most, public education is one"; "Of the *blunders* that *are* easy to make, this is one"; "Of the *accidents* of style that *occur* on the highway of words, this is one of the most frequent."

Another way of thinking about the problem is that in this type of sentence you're talking about many things, not one thing. It's not the *one* blunder that *is* easy to make; it's one of the *many* that *are* easy to make.

Authorities on usage have tried to inculcate this basic rule of the road for generations, yet writers of all levels of ability continue to misread the signs. To put that another way, this is one of the grammatical errors that trip [not *trips*] up even professional writers, as evidenced by these faulty sentences: "John Moores is one of those owners, though, who makes [*make*] it difficult to view baseball in a vacuum" (*The San Diego Union-Tribune*); "This is one of those rare works that does [*do*] equal justice to the standards of the academy and to an intelligent reader's desire to be both edified and entertainingly engaged" (*Los Angeles Times*); "Photography . . . is one of those courses that sounds [*sound*] great and then turns [*turn*] out to be an absolute bitch" (K. Crafts and B. Hauther, *Surviving the Undergraduate Jungle*).

Let's get some cash for those clunkers by closing with a touching example of correct usage: "Lovers kiss in the Saxon Gardens of Warsaw, one of the many areas of the city that conjure its glorious past" (photo caption in *The New York Times*).

ACCIDENT 280
Don't write (or say) *If I would have . . . I would have*

Whenever you start a sentence with an *if* clause expressing the earlier of two past actions, you must use the past perfect tense—the one with *had* before the verb. In other words, write *If I had . . . I would* (or *could*) *have*. Many writers and speakers, perhaps unaware that they are trying to describe one past action taking place before another, are lured by false parallelism into the grammatically incorrect *If I would have . . . I would have*. Thus, instead of *If he would have thought of it, he would have told you* it should be *If he had thought of it, he would* (or *could*) *have told you*.

This accident of style is a recurring flat tire in media outlets, usually in quotations (especially from athletes) but sometimes in edited prose: "If she ~~would have~~ [*had*] deep-fried them, we could have sold them at the fair" (*Austin Daily Herald*); "I know if we ~~would have~~ [*had*] been at Acadia on Sunday, there would have been a lot of arguing over how close to get" (*Allentown Morning Call*, Pennsylvania); "If they ~~would have had~~ [*had had*] solid play out of their quarterback, this would have been a winnable game" (*Emporia Gazette*, Kansas).

Wreckless writers should also be on the lookout for sentences that invert this sequence of tenses, proceeding not from what *had* happened to what *would have* happened but from what *would have* happened or been done *if* something *had* or *hadn't* happened or been done: "Justice says she thinks things *would have* been different if she ~~would have had~~ [*had had*] a helmet" (KWQC-TV, Iowa); "He ~~would have been asking~~ [*would have asked*] for police protection after the game if he ~~would have~~ [*had*] caused an injury" (ESPN.com blog).

Finally—and if you've followed things so far, this should be easy—when you express a wish, always use *had* and not *would have*. Don't say *I wish they <u>would have</u> left earlier.* Say *I wish they <u>had</u> left earlier.*

Don't write *what it is, is*

"What it is, is meat pounded thin, coated in egg and bread crumbs and sautéed in butter—yum," writes Heidi Knapp Rinella in the *Las Vegas Business Press*.

Excuse me, but *yuck*. There is no excuse—ever—to allow *what it is, is* (with or without a comma) to disgrace your prose. This "ungainly construction," as *Garner's Modern American Usage* puts it mildly, is a verbal tic that has become a virus. It has migrated from speech into print at an alarmingly rapid rate, apparently because so many writers today suffer from the delusion that it's acceptable, even preferable, to write as you speak. (Someday, I continue to hope, the numskulls who have been disseminating that half-witted bit of literary advice will be justly punished by being forced to transcribe the incoherent inanities of daytime television talk shows while being tickled senseless with a feather pen.)

Speech is to writing as dough is to bread. To become bread, your dough must rise, be kneaded, and then baked. To become digestible writing, your speech must be elevated, then shaped, then subjected to hot scrutiny. Without this laborious transformation, your writing will be as raw and unpalatable as unbaked dough.

Once you learn to recognize a bad speech habit in your writing, it's not that hard to get rid of it. *What it is* is a noun clause that needs a verb to follow it—as you can see from how I had to word that. But the noun clause itself is pleonastic and your sentence is best begun straightforwardly. In other words, you can easily fix the *what it is, is* problem by replacing that phrase with *it is* or *it's*. Thus, "What it is, is payback time" (*Chicago Tribune*) becomes "It's payback time," and "What it is is a goofy exercise in showboat tourism" (*The New York Times*) becomes "It's a goofy exercise in showboat tourism."

Most of the time *what it is, is* is just a writer's clumsy way of stumbling into a sentence without first thinking about where it's going. But for some writers this viral pleonasm has become a kind of rhetorical device that they reach for to presumably add punch to a sentence that closes an elaborated thought: "*Being Human* . . . is not the silly sitcom its premise—a vampire, a werewolf and a ghost rooming together—suggests. Neither is it a Gothic slice-and-dice of politics and culture like HBO's *True Blood*. What it *is* is darkly funny, deeply affecting and utterly cockeyed" (Glenn Garvin in the *Miami Herald*). The idea here was to rhetorically contrast what something is not with what it is, but it's clear from the writer's use of italics in "What it *is* is" that even he suspects the wording falls flat. He would have been better off concluding with *Instead, it is darkly funny, deeply affecting and utterly cockeyed.*

Here's another example of this rhetorical *What it is is:* " 'Homecoming' is coldly efficient for what it is. But what it is is trash" (Stephen Holden in *The New York Times*). What the writer takes for emphatic diction is merely repetitive and verbose. Remember: the fewer the words, the greater the emphasis. If you cut the stuttering *what it is . . . what it is is,* you get half the words and twice the punch: " 'Homecoming' is coldly efficient. But it's trash."

The *what it is, is* construction is still clumsy and pleonastic even when the writer tries to disguise it by inserting some filler between the noun clause and the verb: "What '*til* is, unarguably, is a variant spelling of *till* used by writers who do not know that *till* is a complete, unabbreviated word in its own right" (*Merriam-Webster's Dictionary of English Usage*). Why would the editors of that usage guide phrase it that way when they could have written " '*Til,* unarguably, is a variant spelling of *till*" or "Unarguably, '*til* is a variant spelling of *till*"? And if they had to begin the sentence with *what,* they could have written "What we do know is that '*til* is a variant spelling of *till.* . . ."

Here's another example in the past tense: "What he was, in fact, was a first-rate personality" (*The New York Times Book Review*). Make that "In fact, he was a first-rate personality" or, if you want *in fact* to create a pause in the middle, "He was, in fact, a first-rate personality."

The lesson here, perhaps, is this: "*What* at the beginning of a sentence," says *Bryson's Dictionary of Troublesome Words*, "often indicates a statement that could do with another look."

ACCIDENT 282

Penultimate does not mean "ultimate" or "final"

Some writers think that *penultimate* is a more emphatic way of saying "ultimate" or "perfect": "The passive voice is the penultimate weapon of denial" (*Irish Times*). Other writers think the word means "last" or "final": "So here's hoping she makes the producers Draw Four as she lays down her penultimate card and punches the air defiantly" (*BlackBook Magazine*). Both these uses are wrong.

The correct meaning of *penultimate* is "next to last, being the last but one in a series." The penultimate round of a tennis tournament is the semifinal round, the one before the final round. And J. K. Rowling's *Harry Potter and the Half-Blood Prince* is the penultimate novel, the next to last one, in her wildly popular series.

ACCIDENT 283

Don't use *anticipate* to mean *expect*

Writers with a proclivity for using long words for no good reason have appropriated *anticipate* as a magniloquent substitute for *expect:* "Fewer consumers anticipate [*expect*] prices will rise"; "Drivers should anticipate [*expect*] area roadwork"; "We anticipate [*expect*] committee action on health reform in the coming weeks." This loose and pompous usage has become so prevalent in all forms of writing that it's hard to find someone who can tell you why these two words are not interchangeable. But open any reputable manual of style published since Fowler's *Modern English Usage* (1926) and you'll see this misuse decried and the distinction explained.

For example, here's what *The Associated Press Stylebook*, often called "the journalist's bible," has to say about it: *"Anticipate* means to expect and prepare for something; *expect* does not include the notion of preparation: *They expect a record crowd. They have anticipated it by adding more seats to the auditorium."*

Although the style manual of *The New York Times* says that *anticipate* "means foresee and prepare, not merely expect," it's not hard to find this directive flouted by writers for that newspaper: "While the announcement had been anticipated [*expected*] for weeks, the official word nonetheless put the administration's imprimatur on a corps of big banks considered healthy enough to extricate themselves from Washington's grip." But *Times* writers also get it right, using *anticipate* properly to mean "foresee and prepare for": "Others try to *anticipate* his moves but are often left performing jumping jacks in vain, staggering off balance or twisting into a human pretzel."

A related misuse of *anticipate* is using it to mean "to expect or look forward to eagerly": "Dan Brown's much-anticipated 'The Lost Symbol' is a hair-raising, fun ride"* (*New York Daily News*). The announcement of a politician's candidacy, the opening of a Broadway play, or the publication of a new novel by almost anyone but Dan Brown should be *eagerly* or *long-awaited*, not *highly* or *much-anticipated*.

ACCIDENT 284
Use *plethora* to mean "too much" or "too many," not simply "a lot"

Plethora comes from an ancient Greek word meaning "fullness," and its original English meaning is "an excess of blood in the body." Today *plethora* properly means "an excess, overabundance, superfluity," as *a report with a plethora of dull statistics.* In loose usage, however, *plethora* is often just a fancy word for *abundance, a lot,* or *many.*

This misuse is especially popular with headline writers: "Fall brings a *plethora* of new clubs to Dallas area"; "There is [*are*] a *plethora*

*For a discussion of this adjectival use of *fun,* see Accident 219.

of things to do in Edson"; "Sennheiser announces a *plethora* of new headphones." Surely whoever composed those headlines didn't mean to say that there were *too many* new clubs in Dallas and an *excess* of things to do in Edson, or that Sennheiser was manufacturing an *overabundance* of headphones. But that's what *plethora* means in precise usage—*too much* or *too many*.

Yet a plethora (not just a lot but an excessive number) of citations for *plethora* meaning "a lot, many" can be found with just a few clicks on Google News. What are we to make of the unintentional irony implicit in a school that offers a *plethora* of classes, a company that offers a *plethora* of benefits, and a football team that sends a *plethora* of players to the Pro Bowl? When we are offered a *plethora* of baked goods or a *plethora* of choices, should we rejoice at having so many or worry that it's too much?

Wreckless writers can avoid this unintentional irony and potential ambiguity by using *abundance, a lot, many, a wealth, array,* or *multitude* when that is the intended meaning and reserving *plethora* for when the context implies excess, much more than needed: "With the *plethora* of conflicting information out there, it's no wonder people find the issue maddening" (wowowow.com); "Every day, the sun rises on Wall Street, and a *plethora* of professional analysts wake to issue new opinions on stocks" (msnbc.com).

And by the way, there is no *aura* in *plethora*. The word is properly pronounced with the stress on the first syllable: PLETH-uh-ruh.

ACCIDENT 285
Don't write *neither one*
"Neither one of these teams can really afford to lose," writes Fred Bierman in the college sports blog of *The New York Times*. Make that *Neither of these teams can afford to lose*. In the original sentence, *really* is adverbiage (see "When You See an Adverb, Kill It" on page 33) and *one* is superfluous, as it invariably is when coupled with *neither:* "Neither ~~one~~ of these women shed a tear during their intros" (*Staten Island Advance*); "Neither ~~one~~ of them noticed the car following them or the lady in the black wig and large glasses driving

it" (Maria Paige, *In Plain Sight*). The same is true for *either one*, which can usually do without *one:* "I don't like your chances if either ~~one~~ of you tries to force this new romance to work" (*Sacramento Bee*).

ACCIDENT 286
Take care to distinguish *torturous* and *tortuous*

Torturous, with an *r* in the middle, means "causing or involving torture or great suffering; extremely painful." *Tortuous*, without the *r* in the middle, means "winding, circuitous, full of twists and turns." Driving at night in the fog along a *tortuous* (winding) road can be a *torturous* (painful) experience. The *tortuous* path to economic recovery can be *torturous* for those at the bottom of the wage-earning barrel. And a book replete with *tortuous* language can be *torturous* to read.

Writers frequently misuse the "winding" word for the "painful" word: "This was a case of years of tortuous [*torturous*] abuse" (SouthCoastToday.com); "Going 0-12 last season was tortuous [*torturous*] for everyone" (*Seattle Times*); "University of the Philippines law professor Harry Roque blamed the 'tortuous conditions' [*torturous conditions*] of Philippine prisons for the decision to transfer Larrañaga" (inquirer.net); "So if your cucumbers and tomatoes and squash have muddled through the tortuous [*torturous*] late days of summer, you can enjoy them with dill, lettuce and peppery mustards" (*Winston-Salem Journal*).

These examples illustrate correct usage: "Dr. Zats is no stranger to the sometimes *torturous* footwear high fashion can ask of working women" (Reuters); "They were seated at adjoining tables in a hotel banquet room following their *tortuous* trek from San Francisco to Las Vegas to Indianapolis to St. Louis" (*The San Diego Union-Tribune*).

ACCIDENT 287
It's *if worse comes to worst,* not *if worse comes to worse*

The *Oxford English Dictionary* shows that the traditional form of this pessimistic idiom, dating from the sixteenth century, is *if the worst come(s) to the worst,* meaning "if things fall out as badly as possible or conceivable." But the "more modern and more logical idiom," says Garner's *Modern American Usage*, is *if worse comes to worst;* "with its progression from comparative to superlative . . . [it] is the better choice."

This expression is frequently misrendered as *if worse comes to worse*, the least logical arrangement of all: "Also, you would have to make sure you would be able to afford the payments on it if worse comes to worse [*worst*]" (Motley Fool: caps.fool.com).

ACCIDENT 288

Tedious overuse of *critical* to mean "highly important, essential"

Why, when the English language has so many ways of saying that something is important—including *essential, urgent, crucial, vital, indispensable, fundamental, imperative,* and *paramount*—do writers so often turn up their noses at this synonymic bounty and reach instead for the overworked word *critical?* Laziness is one plausible answer. Another is that the path of least resistance often tempts us to use the words we most often read and hear, even when we know they're hackneyed or imprecise.

The *Baltimore Sun* writes of "three issues *critical* to Maryland citizens"; the *East Oregonian* tells us that "it is *critical* that more parents become active partners in the process"; and West Virginia senator Jay Rockefeller insists that "we must protect our *critical* infrastructure at all costs." Why *critical* in all these contexts? Why not *extremely important* or *crucial* in the first instance, *essential* or *imperative* in the second, and *vital* or *indispensable* in the third?

And why is a need always *critical?* Will someone die if it isn't satisfied? If you said, "I have a critical need to go to the bathroom," people are likely to burst out laughing. Yet in a hyperbolic world where a crisis must be a *serious crisis* to merit any attention, we fear that a need will be ignored unless we call it a *critical need.*

Critical is the pet word of the literary couch potato, who is content to stuff whatever junk food is at hand into a sentence rather than take the trouble to concoct something more nourishing. The next time it seems important to be earnest about something's importance, ask yourself if there's a *critical need* to use *critical.*

ACCIDENT 289
Don't write *just recently*

Because *just* and *recently* both refer to something that has happened within a brief preceding time, it's poor style to pair these words as a set phrase. Use one or the other instead: "He now serves on numerous company boards and has just recently [*just* or *recently*] released his first documentary film" (Reuters). At the beginning of a sentence, use *recently* alone or *just* with a specific date: "Just recently [*Recently* or *Just last week, month,* etc.], a similar trial in children began in the UK following the success of earlier trials in adults" (*New Scientist*).

ACCIDENT 290
Don't *make a decision* when you can *decide*

If the syntax of a sentence allows you to shorten *make a decision* to *decide*, by all means do so to make the sentence leaner and cleaner. Sometimes you can't do it, as in this example: "You find yourself having to make a decision that could lead to stress eating if you aren't careful" (*Huffington Post*). But many times you can, as in these examples: "The Fed is far more likely than Congress or the White House to make a decision [*decide*] on the merits rather than on the politics" (*The New York Times*); "Coach Pete Carroll, however, reiterated that he had no fixed timeline to make a decision [*decide*] about who will start Saturday's Pacific 10 Conference opener" (*Los Angeles Times*).

ACCIDENT 291
It's *a homage*–not *an homage* or *an hommage*

The problem with how certain people write *homage* begins with how they pronounce it. *Homage* came into English from Old French in the thirteenth century, and since the eighteenth century pronouncing the *h* has been de rigueur. In other words, for more than two hundred years the preferred pronunciation has been HAH-mij. But a frenchified variant without the *h* (AH-mij) persisted among those speakers enamored of their own preciosity. This *h*-less *homage* has achieved enough popularity to persuade some finicky writers and editors that it's better to write *an homage* rather than *a homage*, thus demonstrating one's preference for the presumably upscale AH-mij over the pedestrian HAH-mij: "Indeed, his book is patently an homage to Mr. Schlesinger's" (*The New York Times Book Review*); "Yet the urge to write sequels and prequels is almost always an homage of sorts" (*The New York Times*).

It is nothing but affectation, however, to say AH-mij and write *an homage*, especially if *homage* appears in italics as if it were a foreign word: "an *homage* to a Jasper Johns minimalist 'White Flag' painting" (*The New York Times*). "It is a silly (but quite common) pretension to omit the /h/ sound" in *homage*, says *Garner's Modern American Usage*, and it is equally pretentious to commit that silliness to print with *an homage*.

I wish the story ended there, but it gets worse. For some unfathomable reason, it is becoming fashionable among the literati and other complacent members of the better-educated crowd to pronounce the centuries-old English *homage* as if it were a French loanword still wet behind the ears: oh-MAHZH. This preposterous de-anglicization in speech has spawned a preposterous de-anglicization in print, and we now sometimes see the French *hommage* thrust like a prissy pinkie into an English sentence: "Rakoff's first novel is an *hommage* to Mary McCarthy's 'The Group,' set in the 1990s" (*Los Angeles Times*); "This year, they want to pay *hommage* to the late King of Pop by breaking the Guinness World Record" (*Riverfront Times*, St. Louis).

Fastidiousness in the use of words is laudable except when it descends into mannerism. There will always be a pinkie-in-the-air crowd that loves to fiddle idly with the language. The rest of us hardworking speakers and writers should stick with what is established and preferred. Say HAH-mij and write *a homage*.

ACCIDENT 292
Don't write *sufficient enough*
Sufficient means "good enough, adequate for the purpose, as much as is needed," so adding *enough* after it is pleonastic: "I thought this would serve as a sufficient ~~enough~~ introduction to European travel" (*Brandeis Hoot*); "The district feels that notifying the school board

and assistant superintendent was not sufficient ~~enough~~" (*Lansdale Reporter,* Pennsylvania).

ACCIDENT 293
Use *pleaded,* not *pled*
In American English, *pled* has long been considered inferior to *pleaded* as the past tense of *plead.* Newspaper stylebooks prefer *pleaded,* as do most modern authorities on usage. And although *pled* is common in speech, *pleaded* is far more common in print.

One other thing: When referring to a plea made in a court of law, do not write *pleaded innocent.* The correct form is *pleaded not guilty.*

ACCIDENT 294
Misuse of *incidences,* and proper use of *incident, instance, incidence*
If you've been reading this book from the beginning, or if you've been dipping into it frequently to correct your recklessness or confirm your wrecklessness, by now you have probably gathered that accidents of style are surprisingly common *incidents.* They're all over the Internet like cow pies in a pasture, and you can find many *instances* of them even in the most reputable publications. There's no way that I know of to measure how often accidents of style happen, but if there were, we could determine the *incidence* of accidental style.

An *incident* is something that happens, an occurrence, minor event or episode: *an embarrassing incident.* An *instance* is a case, example: *an isolated instance of poor judgment. Incidence* is the rate of occurrence; it refers to how often or to what extent something happens: *the incidence of traffic jams during rush hour; the incidence of swine flu in California.*

The *incidence* (rate) of something might be determined by how many *incidents* (occurrences) of it there are: *There have been more incidents of road rage, so the incidence of road rage has increased.* And any of those *incidents* of road rage could be held up as an *instance* of road rage, a case or example of it.

No doubt because *incidences* sounds so much like the plurals *incidents* and *instances*, it is frequently misused for those words: "Police issue license suspensions in two drinking and driving incidences [*incidents*]" (*Blue Mountains Courier-Herald*, Canada); "Police have not revealed a supposed motive for the crime, which they have referred to as an incidence [*instance*] of 'workplace violence'" (*Christian Science Monitor*).

If *incidences* is interchangeable with *incidents* or *instances*, it's wrong. In the following sentence, either *incidents* or *instances* would work depending on whether you mean "occurrences" or "cases": "Since 2000, only six incidences [*incidents* or *instances*] of rabid animals have been recorded in the state's most heavily populated county" (*Charleston Gazette*, West Virginia).

The plural *incidences* is acceptable only when referring to the rate of occurrence of several different things at once: "The overall *incidences* of kidney, bladder, pelvis, and ureter cancers in Denmark increased in both sexes from 1944 to 2003" (*Renal and Urology News*). When used correctly, *incidences* is interchangeable with *rates*: "Higher education is also statistically correlated with improved lifestyle behaviors, including reduced incidences [*rates*] of absenteeism, alcohol abuse, criminal behavior, welfare dependence and unemployment" (*Houston Chronicle*). But even when used properly, *incidences* is inferior to the far more familiar *rates*, which is the better choice for nontechnical writing.

Finally, don't be ridiculously redundant and use *incidence* and *rate* together. The writer of this sentence was asleep at the wheel: "Teton County had *an incidence rate* of more than 204 per 100,000" (*Jackson Hole Daily*, Wyoming).

ACCIDENT 295
Misuse of *liable* for *likely*
Use *likely* for any specific action or event that will probably happen: *It's likely that we'll go; It's likely to rain.* Use *liable* of any unfortunate result that will probably happen: *If it rains hard, we're liable to get soaked; You're liable to lose money gambling in Las Vegas.* Writers frequently use *liable* when no unfortunate result is implied: "Even

at five in the morning on a Tuesday, it's liable [*likely*] to be more lively than your average main street or shopping mall" (*Esquire*).

To avoid this accident of style, remember that whatever follows *liable* cannot be good. Or memorize this sentence from Patricia T. O'Conner's *Woe Is I*: "*If Madeline goes skating, she's **liable** to fall, and not **likely** to try it again.*"

ACCIDENT 296
Misuse of *simplistic* for *simple*
A *simple* explanation is plain, clear, and concise. A *simplistic* explanation is oversimplified, shallow, superficial. Style guides often urge you to keep it *simple*. But the writers on Madison Avenue, who don't want you to think too hard about what they're selling, strive to make their advertising messages *simplistic*.

Writers who are tempted to use a longer word where a shorter one will do tend to reach for *simplistic* instead of *simple*: "In Japan, the most hard-core aficionados pass over the fatty cuts of bluefin, considering them too simplistic [*simple*] a pleasure" (*Christian Science Monitor*).

Also avoid the phrases *too simplistic* and *overly simplistic*, which are redundant because *simplistic* already suggests making something *too* or *overly* simple: "Such historical analogies are ~~overly~~ simplistic and fatally flawed, if only because each presidency is distinct in its own way" (*The New York Times*). The writer of that sentence could have made it even cleaner and more balanced by deleting *fatally* too, avoiding an overworked phrase (*fatally flawed*) and eliminating a supererogatory adverb with a single stroke of the mouse.

ACCIDENT 297
Misuse of *infinitesimal*
Infinitesimal means "immeasurably small, incalculably minute." One drop of rain is an infinitesimal amount of rain, and a dime is an infinitesimal amount of money in a trillion-dollar budget. Lured by the length and heft of this six-syllable word, and misled by the presence in it of *infinite*, writers sometimes misuse *infinitesimal* to mean "infinite, boundless, limitless," or "unfathomable, incomprehensible."

"The *Dictionary* indeed is a work of art, encapsulating an almost infinitesimal belief in the magic of poetry and prose," writes Andrew O'Hagan in *The New York Review of Books*. The dictionary referred to is Samuel Johnson's landmark lexicon of 1755, and it is not likely that Dr. Johnson, one of the most literate writers who ever lived, had an immeasurably small belief in the magic of poetry and prose. Another example: "They embarked on the pursuit of the precise, devoting their lives to erecting strict systems of thought that sought to explain life in all of its infinitesimal [*infinite*] detail" (*Tablet Magazine*).

Misuse of *unequivocably* for *unequivocally*

Unequivocal means "plain, clear, not ambiguous"; the corresponding adverb is *unequivocally*. Those are the unequivocal and indisputable facts. However, if you happen to own any Merriam-Webster's Collegiate dictionary published since the 1970s, you will find the word *unequivocably* listed followed by the usage label *nonstand* (an abbreviation of *nonstandard*), which, in the dictionary's front matter, the editors say they use "a few words or senses that are disapproved by many but that have some currency in reputable contexts." Don't believe a word of that nonsense; it's a stylistic speed trap.

There is nothing reputable about *unequivocably*. It's an erroneous word, born of a mispronunciation, and a misspelling spread by sloppy typing and proofreading. Usage experts are unanimously opposed to it and other dictionaries do not recognize it. If you spell or say *unequivocally* with *vocably* instead of *vocally* at the end, you will surely be cited by the language police.

Here are some examples of disreputable usage: "But instead it comes off as unequivocably [*unequivocally*] Disney" (*The San Diego Union-Tribune*); "I'm not going to predict unequivocably [*unequivocally*] that another team will be joining Marquette in those state finals" (*Gary Post-Tribune*); "Not the greatest recording artist of all time, not the greatest rock singer or break dancer of all time, but, simply and unequivocably [*unequivocally*], the greatest artist" (Lewis Lapham, *Imperial Masquerade*).

The proper word, *unequivocally*, is pronounced uhn-i-KWIV-uh-kuh-lee. Remember to get *vocal* with *unequivocal* and *unequivocally*.

ACCIDENT 299

Watch out for *if and when* and *when and if*

Let's begin with *if and when*—for which I retrieved more than twenty-seven hundred hits on Google News. This popular coupling has been denounced by authorities on usage for decades. It's justifiable, perhaps, if you're being contentious and you want to assert that you'll do something only when some condition is met: *We will agree to pay if and when you agree to our terms*. But even in that context *if* or *when* alone can do the job without sounding lawyerly and pompous.

In nonlitigious usage, writers typically use *if and when* when they want the reader to know that something may or may not happen. But *if* already expresses both those possibilities and is invariably the better choice: "If ~~and when~~ 'Law & Order' does come to a conclusion, Wolf said he isn't planning a grand finale" (*Los Angeles Times*); "Isaac Perlmutter, for instance, would receive roughly $34.1 million . . . for his options if ~~and when~~ the deal closes" (*Los Angeles Times*).

If you want to emphasize that something will happen only if something else happens first, dispense with the wordy *if and when* and use *when* or *only when* instead: *We'll go on that cruise ~~if and~~ when you get that raise. I'll apologize ~~if and~~ when he does.*

Now let's discuss the inverted phrase *when and if*. This is my advice: don't use it. It's illogical. The word *when* preceding *if* is like *after* preceding *before*. You can predict *when* something may happen *if* you know that it will happen, but you can't say *when* it will happen if you don't know *if* it will happen. As with *if and when*, either *if* or *when* is the better choice: "It's anyone's guess where she will settle when and if [*when* or *if*] the condo she's owned since 1995 is sold" (*Houston Chronicle*).

ACCIDENT 300

Misuse of *adverse* for *averse*

Averse and *adverse*, which differ in spelling by one letter, are both
words of opposition. *Averse* means "opposed because of a strong feeling of dislike or repugnance; unwilling, disinclined." *Adverse* may
mean "opposed in a contrary or hostile manner" (*adverse criticism*);
"opposed to one's interests" (*an adverse outcome*); "unfavorable" (*adverse weather*); or "causing harm" (*adverse effects, adverse reaction*).

The similarity in spelling and the shared sense of opposition are
no doubt why some writers use *adverse* when they mean *averse*:
"Still, he wasn't adverse [*averse*] to taking chances" (*The New York
Times*); "Facebook . . . isn't adverse [*averse*] to making big purchases"
(*ComputerWorld*); "The company would not be adverse [*averse*] to
buying another real estate investment trust" (Reuters). It may help
to remember that *averse* is invariably followed by the preposition *to*
while *adverse* is usually followed by a noun.

ACCIDENT 301

Don't confuse *flounder* and *founder*

To *flounder* means "to struggle awkwardly, stumble or plunge about
as if stuck in mud." *Flounder* may be used either literally—for example,
of a fish out of water—or figuratively: "As Julie *flounders*, feeling lost,
her one solace is cooking and food" (*Observer Online*); "But with the
economy souring, and Republicans *floundering*, his cool competence
and steady message won the day" (FOXNews.com).

To *founder* means "to fall down, collapse, or sink." *Founder* may
also be used literally—of a sinking ship, for instance—or figuratively:
"By then, Kelly's marriage had *foundered* and he was living apart
from his three young daughters" (*Washington Post*); "Only a year
ago, Morgan Stanley nearly *foundered* like Lehman Brothers" (*The
New York Times*).

The choice between *flounder* and *founder* can sometimes be tricky
because, when used figuratively, both words connote failure. But
flounder suggests awkward or desperate struggling against a failure
that may be avoidable, while *founder* suggests a failure that is already
accomplished or inevitable. If the economy *flounders*, it struggles to

recover from a recession. If the economy *founders*, it collapses into a depression.

Sometimes *founder* is misused to suggest awkward struggling: "Jim Tracy took over the Colorado Rockies when they were foundering [*floundering*] in last place" (*Philadelphia Inquirer*). If the Rockies are in last place, they can't *founder* (sink, collapse) any further. But they can *flounder* (struggle awkwardly) there indefinitely.

More often, though, it's *flounder* (struggle) that is misused for *founder* (sink): "But after his tax increase proposal floundered [*foundered*] last summer, the governor cut state-supported drug treatment programs by tens of millions of dollars" (WLS-TV, Chicago); "It looked like his career was floundering [*foundering*] and he was just hanging around until Social Security kicked in" (*The Trentonian*). Proposals and careers can't stumble or plunge about (*flounder*), but they can fail or collapse (*founder*).

ACCIDENT 302
Don't confuse *on behalf of* with *in behalf of*

What a difference a tiny preposition makes.

If you do something *on behalf of*, you do it as an agent or representative, acting in place of another or others: "Experian said in its lawsuit that LifeLock doesn't have the legal authority to request fraud alerts *on behalf of* consumers" (*Dallas Morning News*). Lawyers always speak *on behalf of* their clients.

If you do something *in behalf of*, you do it to help or benefit something or someone else: "The United States could find itself fighting a resurgent Taliban *in behalf of* a government with diminished popular support" (*Salt Lake Tribune*). Philanthropists donate money *in behalf of* worthy causes.

On behalf of is typically misused for *in behalf of*: "Most of the fraud perpetrated on behalf of Mr. Karzai, officials said, took place in the Pashtun-dominated areas of the east and south" (*The New York Times*). The fraud was perpetrated for the benefit of Mr. Karzai, to help him get reelected, so it was perpetrated *in his behalf*.

ACCIDENT 303

It's your *forte*, not *forté*

The word *forte*, meaning "strong point, something at which one ex-
cels," comes from the French *fort* and is traditionally pronounced in
one syllable, like the English *fort*. Because of confusion with the
Italian musical direction *forte*, which is pronounced in two syllables,
FOR-tay, with the stress on the first syllable, the "strong point" *forte*
came to be pronounced FOR-tay as well. For better or for worse,
this is now the dominant pronunciation in American speech.

In recent years, however, a new variant pronunciation has sprung
up: for-TAY, with the stress on the second syllable. And this affected, faux-French pronunciation has spawned an affected, faux-
French spelling with an accent over the *e: forté*. As accidents of style
go, this one is like hanging fuzzy dice from the rearview mirror of
your Porsche.

Don't put on the low-rent dog. Spell it *forte*, without a silly accent, and pronounce it FORT or FOR-tay.

ACCIDENT 304

Don't use *molest* for *molestation*

"Bermuda leader's son pleads not guilty to molest" (Associated Press).
"Tennis teacher to get prison time in molest case" (*San Francisco
Chronicle*). "Boy made up molest story" (*San Jose Mercury News*). "New
York rabbi sentenced to 30 years for child molest" (*Newsday*).

All these headlines—and I could cite more—misuse the verb to
molest for the noun *molestation*. Though I sympathize with the
headline writer who must truncate copy to say what needs to be
said in a circumscribed space, arbitrarily lopping off the tail ends of
words goes beyond the pale. Unless you're some sort of avant-garde
writer, it is not permissible to single-handedly initiate functional
shift—the term linguists use for the conversion of a word from one
part of speech to another without any change in form—in this case
the use of a verb, *molest*, as a noun.

Let me be clear: I do not object to functional shift. That would
be ludicrous, like objecting to language itself. The English language
would be an impoverished and inadequate creature if we could not

make its words serve different purposes to suit our needs. I celebrate a language supple enough to allow us to *suspect* a *suspect*, *handle* a *handle*, *present* a *present*, and *resolve* to have *resolve*. And I am more broad-minded than many language commentators when it comes to embracing functional shift brought about by sweeping social or technological change.

Today, if we want to *contact* people we can *telephone*, *fax*, *e-mail*, *text*, *RSVP*, and even *Google* or *Twitter* them. We can *host* a party, *access* a file, and *chair* a meeting. We can *premiere* a play or movie and publish a *debut* novel. We can dump the daily *commute* and *transition* to working at home while *parenting* our kids. And, because it's prudent to avoid using brand names as verbs, instead of *Xeroxing* a document we *photocopy* it, and instead of *FedExing* a package we *overnight* it.

No reasonable person would dispute that these are useful conversions that enhance communication. The trouble with functional shift, however, begins when a verbal innovation is trying to fill a hole in the language that is already full. What, for example, is gained by using *author* to mean *write*? How is *gift* an improvement on *give* or *donate*? And would someone please explain why the clumsy, pretentious *impact* became the trendy way of saying *affect* or *influence*?

Functional shift that smacks of jargon muscling its way into the mainstream can also be objectionable. *To mainstream*, *to office*, and *to dialogue* (or *dialog* as it is often annoyingly spelled) are current examples of jargony noun-to-verb conversions that seem strained or pompous. *Molest* as a substitute for *molestation* is an example from the verb-to-noun category.

This clipped noun, says the evidence of my eyes and ears, first became popular in the argot of social service workers dealing with child abuse cases, who shortened *child molestation* to *child molest* and finally to *molest*. From there it spread to the criminal justice system, where it was picked up by journalists and transmitted, like a virus, to headline writers, who found it an irresistible shortcut.

But it is not a desirable shortcut. We already have a well-established noun, *molestation*, so the conversion is superfluous. And, unlike *quote* used informally for *quotation*, there is no colloquial advantage to be had from using *molest* for *molestation*. In fact, doing so can be downright strange. Doesn't a *priest molest case* sound as weird as an *infest of lice* or an *invest adviser?*

ACCIDENT 305
Don't use quotation marks after *so-called*

"A word or phrase preceded by *so-called* should not be enclosed in quotation marks," says the fifteenth edition of *The Chicago Manual of Style*. "The expression itself indicates irony or doubt." The editors might have added that using quotation marks with *so-called* is overkill, as in this example: "The only question remaining about this so-called 'controversy' is this" (letter to *The San Diego Union-Tribune*). If you feel you cannot do without the ironic quotation marks, delete *so-called*. That strategy would have worked well in this example from The Associated Press: "Since April, when newly released memos revealed the Bush administration had sanctioned certain ~~so-called~~ 'enhanced interrogation' tactics . . ."

ACCIDENT 306
How and when to capitalize "kinship names"

The Chicago Manual of Style lays out the basic rule: "Kinship names are lowercased unless they immediately precede a personal name or are used alone, in place of a personal name." To that I would add this somewhat more complicated qualification: Capitalize kinship names for preceding generations in direct address. But lowercase them in apposition or after a pronoun such as *my, her, his, our, your,* and *their*. Kinship names for the same or succeeding generations are lowercased except when used as nicknames. And pet names—such as *honey* and *dear*—are always lowercased.

Let me try to clarify that with some examples.

I told my mother that my father was on the phone. I could have said, "Excuse me, Mother, but Father is on the phone," but instead I said, "Mom, Dad's on the phone."

My dad talked to my mom for a while and then my mom said,

"Your grandmother Kate and grandfather Joe want to talk to you." I chatted with them for a while and then said, "I love you, Grandpa Joe. I love you, Grandma Kate."

Then my aunt Marge and my uncle Bob got on the phone, and after talking with them I said, "Mom, do you want to talk to Aunt Marge and Uncle Bob?"

My mother said, "I'd love to talk to them and to your cousins too. Are Cousin George and Cousin Sally there?"

"Yes, everybody's there," I said. "All the cousins and nieces and nephews and sons and daughters and grandsons and granddaughters. Even the neighbors' children—the Brobdingnagian brothers and Lilliputian sisters—are there."

"Thank you, darling," said Mom. "You're my sweetie."

ACCIDENT 307
Proper use of *alternate* and *alternative*

To the discriminating writer, the adjectives *alternate* and *alternative* are not interchangeable. I was gently taught this lesson many years ago by the syndicated columnist James J. Kilpatrick, a usage connoisseur of the first order, when he read the manuscript of my first book and saw that I had continually used the phrase *alternate pronunciation* rather than *alternative pronunciation*. Kilpatrick helped me understand that I wasn't referring to a pronunciation that could take the place of another, perhaps in an emergency (an *alternate* one), but to a pronunciation that you might decide to use instead of another (an *alternative* one). It was a subtle difference, I realized, between substitution and choice.

In the sense we are concerned with here, the adjective *alternate* refers to a secondary thing that substitutes or stands in for a primary thing, a replacement: "The Aztec City Commission appointed a new *alternate* municipal court judge on Aug. 25" (*Farmington Daily Times*, New Mexico). By contrast, the adjective *alternative* means "available in place of another" and refers to anything you might choose over something else: "An *alternative* idea was to temporarily widen the road while resurfacing work took place" (*Guernsey Press and Star*, UK).

An *alternate route* is a backup route, the one you take when you can't take your regular route. An *alternative route* is a route you choose to take because there's less traffic, it's more scenic, or you're bored with the usual route. An *alternate plan* is the plan you adopt when the original one fails. An *alternative plan* is an additional plan that you consider or that you choose because you don't like the original plan.

Sometimes it's hard to tell which word is properly called for because the context seems to imply both substitution and choice: "An *alternate* title for the book might be 'Idiots'" (*The New York Times Book Review*). Are we talking about a title that might stand in for the original (an *alternate*) or a title that might be as good as or better than the original (an *alternative*)? I vote for *alternative* because the writer is proposing a title that might be chosen over the original rather than a replacement for one that didn't work out.

Here's another challenging example: "Mesa teachers plan to have an *alternative* assignment for those children whose parents want them to skip the lesson" (KPHO-TV, Phoenix). Are the teachers offering a choice of assignment (*alternative*) or a replacement assignment (*alternate*)? Here I vote for *alternate*. The children have no choice; they must skip the lesson and do the assignment the teachers will provide as a substitute.

As you might imagine, *alternate* (substitution) is misused for *alternative* (choice) far more often than the other way around: "The Village at Wolf Creek developer is considering an alternate [*alternative*] plan" (*Valley Courier*, Colorado); "The film sets up Howard as being Mary's alternate [*alternative*] love interest" (*Seattle Post-Intelligencer*).

A final word on *alternative*, the noun. Over the years some purists have insisted that it must refer to a choice between two things, never more. This contention, says *Garner's Modern American Usage*, has been called a fetish and "has little or no support among . . . stylistic experts or in actual usage." In *American Usage and Style: The Consensus* (1980), Roy H. Copperud writes that "the idea that *alternative* may apply to a choice between two and no more is a pedantry discountenanced by no fewer than nine authorities."

ACCIDENT 308

Avoid *as yet* and *as of yet*

Using *as yet* and *as of yet* is not an error; it's poor style. *Garner's Modern American Usage* says the phrases "are both invariably inferior to *yet* alone, *still, thus far,* or some other equivalent."

Some examples with revisions: "We don't know as yet how this will play out" (*Huffington Post*); make that *We don't know yet.* "As yet, Rio has received no formal notification of its employees' purported offences" (*Business Standard*); make that *Rio has not yet* [or *still has not*] *received formal notification.* "They say that the necessary permit for burial has not been applied for as of yet" (*Buffalo News*); make that *not yet been applied for* or *not been applied for yet.* "It's no surprise that the rest of the teams in the WAC would want similar success, but as of yet, few have found it" (ESPN); make that *but so far* [or *thus far*] *few have found it.*

ACCIDENT 309

Avoid the cutesy *well*

"*Rather, very, little, pretty*—these are the leeches that infest the pond of prose, sucking the blood of words," writes E. B. White in "An Approach to Style," the final chapter in *The Elements of Style.* To that list of leeches I would add *well,* which in the pond of contemporary prose has become a mannerism embraced by all manner of writers.

If you don't know what I'm talking about, *well,* I suppose I'll have to explain. And I hope you don't think that by denouncing this unwell use of *well* I'm just, *well,* an obnoxious denunciator. I just want to point out how inserting *well* into a sentence is a cutesy way of trying to draw attention to how clever you are without actually being, *well,* cute or clever. (Delete those self-conciously cute and clever *well*s and you have three respectable sentences.)

Here's Ethan Smith writing in *The Wall Street Journal* and being, *well,* a little cutesy: "The centerpiece of the ticketing company's anti-scalping strategy is eliminating, *well,* the tickets." Here's Kevin Maney writing in *The Atlantic* and being, *well,* rather clever: "But the ratings game still faces, *well,* a few challenges." And here's Mignon Fogarty (aka Grammar Girl) being, *well,* pretty perky:

"'Popcorn for the brain.' That's what an O *Magazine* writer said when recommending my audiobook *Grammar Girl's Quick and Dirty Tips for Better Writing* in the July 2009 issue with, *well,* Ms. Winfrey on the cover!" You could say all these uses of *well* are <u>very</u> tiresome, but instead let's just say they're tiresome.

Rather, very, little, pretty—these are, *well,* the leeches that infest the pond of prose. Wreckless writers are advised not to get *well* soon.

ACCIDENT 310
When to drop *a, an,* or *the* in a title
If the title of a literary, musical, or artistic work begins with *a, an,* or *the,* you may omit the article if it doesn't suit the structure of a sentence. This typically happens for three reasons.

1. When an adjective precedes the title:

    The comprehensive *Chicago Manual of Style*
    An incomparable *Magic Flute*
    T. S. Eliot's epochal *Waste Land*

2. When a possessive precedes the title:

    Charles Dickens's *Tale of Two Cities*
    Mark Twain's *Adventures of Huckleberry Finn*
    The University of Chicago Press's *Chicago Manual of Style*

3. When another article precedes the title:

    A *Chicago Manual of Style* rule
    An *Adventures of Huckleberry Finn* scholar
    The *Midsummer Night's Dream* fairies

ACCIDENT 311
Avoid the hackneyed construction *It's not about* x, *it's about* y
"It's not about how many times you get knocked down. It's about how many times you get back up," writes Todd Zolecki at MLB .com, echoing my sentiments about *it's not about . . . it's about.*

No matter how many times this worn-out figure of speech gets taken to the mat by some writer who thinks he's a champion stylist, it always scrambles to its feet and asks for more abuse. Isn't it about time we gave this battered and bloodied construction a well-deserved rest?

Elsewhere in this book I remarked that the conscientious prose stylist is always skeptical of any words, expressions, or figures of speech whose popularity stems from what H. W. Fowler called "the herd instinct and lack of individuality." If you want to establish a voice, meaning a style of writing that is recognizably your own, the first thing you must do is jettison whatever lots of other writers are doing. They are only copying each other because it's easier to be superficially appealing than to do the hard work of finding fresh ways to say what you mean.

The hack regurgitates *It's not about where you're from, it's about where you're going* and revels in his brilliant parallelism, never pausing to wonder whether the meaning of *it* might be crying out for elucidation. The stylist recasts the concept stripped of its verbosity and banality: *Where you're from doesn't matter. Where you're going does.*

Even first-rate writers sometimes get sucked into the vortex of this trite rhetorical tandem. At the close of one of his columns in *The New York Times*, Paul Krugman, like all good opinion writers, tried to orchestrate his words into a hortatory crescendo. But instead of striking chords that were original and pure, he played the lame warhorse *it's not about . . . it's about* and the conclusion fell flat: "We need to do this for the sake of our future. For this isn't about looking backward, it's about looking forward—because it's about reclaiming America's soul."

The passage lacks balance, its rhythms are clunky, and it's ungracefully repetitive (the word *about* occurs three times, as does the sound of *for*). Putting a few more drops of sweat into these words, and using anaphora and alliteration rather than resorting to cliché, could have made the peroration pitch-perfect: "We need to do this for the sake of our future. We need to stop looking backward and start looking forward—toward reclaiming America's soul."

ACCIDENT 312

Take care where you put *only*

Reckless writers toss *only* into a sentence with little regard for how it can subtly affect meaning. Wreckless writers use *only* the way a driver uses a turn signal: to show the reader where they're going. And they do that by putting *only* as close as possible to the word or phrase it's meant to modify.

Only she saw him means that she was the only person to see him. *She only saw him* means that she saw him but didn't hear, feel, smell, or taste him. *She saw only him* means she saw but one person—him. In each case, *only* modifies what immediately follows it, and where it is placed affects how we interpret the sentence.

Consider this example: "He only writes about beverages that are available in South Carolina and Georgia" (islandpacket.com). The literal meaning here—that he only *writes* about these beverages but doesn't do anything else, such as speak—is surely not what the writer intended. The writer meant that this man writes about these beverages and no other ones, so *only* should have been placed after the verb *writes*.

Probably in imitation of speech, the amateur writer and the pro alike routinely place *only* before a verb rather than after it, where it would be closer to what it's supposed to modify. But if "a simple repositioning" puts *only* where it belongs "without creating a distraction, there is no reason not to do it," says *Bryson's Dictionary of Troublesome Words*. Consider how these sentences are improved by repositioning *only* so it's next to what it modifies: "The Sun Devils have ~~only~~ played *only* two games so far" (*Atlanta Journal-Constitution*); "Phelps ~~only~~ goes *only* where he gets attention (*Yeshiva World News*); "Health officials are asking people to ~~only~~ use the ER *only* if they have severe symptoms" (KECI-TV, Montana); "It should ~~only~~ be ingested *only* when in a heavily diluted, homeopathic form" (*The New York Times*); "It ~~only~~ works *only* because the actors . . . are a match made in TV heaven" (*Minneapolis Star Tribune*).

Writers are also tempted to insert *only* into verb phrases when, once again, its proper position is after the verbs and next to what it modifies: "Insurgencies can ~~only~~ be defeated [*only*] when local communities and military forces work together" (*The New York Times*); "Iran revealed the existence of the plant to the UN watchdog on Monday, saying it was not yet operational and would ~~only~~ be used *only* for nuclear energy" (BBC News); "That policy, set in November 1961, would ~~only~~ be reversed, to tragic ends, *only* after his death" (*The New York Times*).

The inattentive writer gives no second thought to writing *they only went once, it only works for so long,* and *it only goes back so far.* The circumspect writer, wary of the hazards involved in placing *only* before a verb, will change those phrases to *they went only once, it works for only so long,* and *it goes back only so far.*

Of course, you can take the quest for clarity and precision only so far before it becomes persnickety. So with the placement of *only* some exceptions must be made for idiom. For example, only a prig would change the position of *only* in such expressions as *it can only get worse* (or *better*), *this will only take a second, it only goes to show, it only makes sense, you only live once, we can only hope,* and *I only have eyes for you.*

ACCIDENT 313
It's spelled *ophthalmology*, not *opthalmology* or *opthamology*

These misspellings of *ophthalmology* are undoubtedly caused by the common mispronunciation ahp-thuh-MAH-luh-jee. Pronounce this word correctly, with the *ph* like *f* and an audible *l* in the second syllable, and you will never misspell it: ahf-thul-MAH-luh-jee.

ACCIDENT 314
Misuse of *exceptionable* for *exceptional*

If there's a choice between two words that sound alike, one a common word and the other an unusual one, the second-rate writer will always choose the unusual one. Unusual words are more impressive, right? Not if you misuse them. Then they're screeching accidents of style.

Exceptionable is an unusual word, a rarely used synonym of *objectionable*. You take exception, object, to that which is *exceptionable*. The common word *exceptional* means "outstanding, superior, extraordinary." When the unusual *exceptionable* does appear, it's almost always mistakenly used for *exceptional:* "While the taste and texture of these fries were decent (if not all that *exceptionable*), the serving size is much more filling" (examiner.com). I'd take decent fries over exceptionable ones any day, wouldn't you? "Orlando's downtown and adjoining districts make for an *exceptionable* time, whether it is a family vacation or a romantic weekend for two" (eGruve.com). I've had some exceptionable vacations and romantic weekends in my day, and I don't want to repeat them, especially in Orlando.

In formal situations, misusing *exceptionable* for *exceptional* can be embarrassing and damaging to your credibility. "We congratulate Julius Genachowski on his confirmation as chairman of the FCC," wrote Brian Roberts, chairman and CEO of Comcast, in a statement released to the media. "He has an exceptionable [*exceptional*] combination of public service and real-world business experience which are vital at this exciting time in communications and technology."

ACCIDENT 315
Don't use *hoi polloi* to mean "the elite"

There are three potential accidents of style lurking in the compound noun *hoi polloi*. The first is minor, punishable by a slap on the wrist and a small fine. The second is a debatable infraction, decried by some authorities but countenanced by others. The third is serious, a smashup that traffic reporters like to call an "injury accident," the injured party in this case being the English language.

The following sentence, from an article by Christian Brose at ForeignPolicy.com, willfully and wantonly commits all three accidents: "Apparently Rothkopf was one of the many members of the foreign policy hoi-polloi that went into intellectual hibernation in 2004 and only awoke this January." Did you spot the three offenses?

The minor violation is writing *hoi-polloi*. A hyphen in *hoi polloi* is nonstandard, so pay $200 and do not pass Go. The second breach of convention is less clear-cut. *Hoi polloi* is Greek for "the many," and in precise English usage it means "the common people, the masses." The Greek *hoi* means "the," so purists have long insisted that anyone who refers to *the hoi polloi* is guilty of redundancy because it means "the the masses." Many authorities on usage, including *Bryson's Dictionary of Troublesome Words* and *The New York Times Manual of Style and Usage*, are unequivocally opposed to pairing *the* with *hoi polloi*. But in a 2002 survey, 78 percent of *The American Heritage Dictionary*'s usage panel admitted using this redundant *the*, and *Garner's Modern American Usage* says it "ought to be accepted."

I'm not sure I'm ready to accept that recommendation and cast my lot with all those loosey-goosey usage panelists. For the same reason that I would write *the Sahara* instead of *the Sahara desert* because I know that *Sahara* is Arabic for "desert," I still refrain from putting *the* in front of *hoi polloi*. But the practice is now so widespread that I think I can agree to classify it as a legalized cacoëthes*— like smoking (a former vice of mine)—and politely avert my gaze.

The final accident, the serious smashup, is misinterpreting *hoi polloi* as meaning "the elite, upper crust, or privileged few," the opposite of its proper meaning. This is doubtless the result of a mistaken assumption that *hoi polloi* must have something to do with *hoity-toity* because of their similarity in sound and spelling. And because *hoity-toity* means "haughty, snobbish," adjectives often applied to the upper crust and privileged few, unwary writers began using *hoi polloi* of any group regarded as an elite.

Although the dictionaries haven't caved in yet, this disastrous blunder is steadily infecting educated speech and writing: "Word of Frenchy's Dipped Sandwich spreads through the L.A. police force and criminal underworld and on to the Jazz-Age hedonists of the Hollywood hoi polloi" (TheStranger.com); "As an expert on Ger-

---

*A *cacoëthes* (kak-oh-EE-theez), from the Greek *kakos*, "bad," and *ethos*, "habit," is a bad habit, incurable itch, insatiable urge or desire.

man cinema he could go to a Third Reich film shindig and be able to mix it up with the hoi polloi" (Quentin Tarantino, the filmmaker, quoted at birminghampost.net).

But examples of the correct use of *hoi polloi* to mean "the masses" are still plentiful (albeit usually preceded by *the*): "It will let passengers board the plane first, thus exempting them from the stress of checking in early and standing in line with the hoi polloi" (*Baltimore Sun*); "The concept of one health care scenario for privileged lawmakers and another for the hoi polloi is untenable" (*Atlanta Journal-Constitution*). Incidentally, in both those sentences *the* before *hoi polloi* could have been deleted without causing any harm.

Concise conclusion: Don't hyphenate *hoi polloi*, use it to mean "the common people, the masses," and try to resist the cacoëthes of *the* hoi polloi.

ACCIDENT 316

It's *diphtheria* and *diphthong*—with *diph*, not *dip*

Diphtheria and *diphthong* are often misspelled *diptheria* and *dipthong* (without that first *h*) because they are often mispronounced with *dip* in the first syllable instead of *diph* (dif). But if you pronounce these words correctly—dif-THEER-ee-uh and DIF-thong—it's unlikely that you'll ever misspell them.

ACCIDENT 317

Use *instinctive,* not *instinctual*

Some writers use *instinctual* and *instinctive* interchangeably, perhaps because they think two words are always better than one, while others favor the less-common *instinctual*, perhaps because it sounds more erudite. But using words interchangeably, as if they were cogs in a machine, is never an effective style choice, and using a word because you think it makes you sound intelligent is not likely to impress any readers.

When two similarly formed words seem interchangeable, try to determine if there is any subtle distinction between them; if it appears that there isn't, use the word that is more common or less pretentious. If you follow that rule of thumb, you should have no trouble choosing *submission* over *submittal, investigative* over *investigatory, orient* over *orientate,* and *instinctive* over *instinctual.* And, like Indiana Jones, you will have chosen wisely, for in each case the second word is merely a needless variant of the first.

    Instinctive came into the language in the mid-seventeenth century. *Instinctual* was born in the 1920s, apparently the offspring of psychology. It "is not often found outside learned monographs," wrote the lexicographer Robert W. Burchfield in 1996. I wish that observation were true today. Judging from Google News, the upstart *instinctual* now appears in all manner of journalistic writing, from articles on health to popular music to sports: "Her very *instinctual* play leads to some impressive passing and some threaded looks that pick apart defenses" (ESPN.com). Even so, *instinctual* has a clinical aroma that *instinctive* does not, which perhaps explains why *instinctive* is still about five times more common. Careful writers will do their part to keep it that way.

ACCIDENT 318
Do not write *the reason . . . is* (or *was*) *because*

I learned not to write *the reason . . . is because* the way most professional writers do: the hard way. In my first book, which was about pronunciation,* I wrote this infelicitous sentence: "The reason *data* is pronounced DAY-tuh is because it was taken into English from Latin and follows the rules for the so-called English pronunciation of Latin." My *reason . . . is because* somehow got by the copyeditor and the proofreader—and by me, of course, again in galleys—and the book went through four printings with that hideous *lapsus calami* before I was informed, in no uncertain terms by various alert readers, that I was guilty of one of the Great Redundancies of Our Time. Chastened and edified, I emended the offending sentence for the fifth and subsequent printings. It now reads, "*Data* is pronounced DAY-tuh because . . ."

---

*There Is No Zoo in Zoology (1988), later superseded by *The Big Book of Beastly Mispronunciations* (1999, 2005).

" 'The *reason* is *because*' is a notorious little waste of words, no purpose being served by using both *reason* and *because* to explain oneself," writes Barbara Wallraff in *Word Court*. As Patricia T. O'Conner points out in *Woe Is I*, "*because* means 'for the reason that,' " so if you write *the reason is because* you are writing that *the reason is for the reason that*.

This "notorious little waste of words" is apparently one of the usage world's best-kept secrets because it appears not only in flawed first books by upstart language mavens but also in the edited prose of respected publications and in books by well-known writers: "Pinker sensibly points out that thinking precedes writing and that *the reason* we sound smarter when writing *is because* we deliberately set out to be clear and precise" (*The New York Times Book Review*); "Yet he has been so good for so long that I suspect *the only reason* he has not produced a signature masterwork *is because* he stubbornly refuses to do so" (*The New York Times Book Review*); "*The reason* we see so much chronic disease in the West *is because* these are illnesses that appear relatively late in life" (Michael Pollan, *In Defense of Food*).

To correct this redundant construction, most usage guides recommend rewording the sentence using either *reason . . . is that* or *because*. In other words, to fix *The reason I like the Beatles is because they remind me of Chuck Berry*, you would change it to read either *The reason I like the Beatles is that they remind me of Chuck Berry* or *I like the Beatles because they remind me of Chuck Berry*.

Though the first rewording is acceptable, the second is far superior. As *Bryson's Dictionary of Troublesome Words* observes, the overriding fault with these *reason . . . is because* sentences "lies at the front end. Remove *the reason* and its attendant verb *is* and in most cases a crisper, more focused sentence emerges."

Without a ponderous *reason . . . is*, the faulty sentences quoted above emerge from the dungeon of redundancy into the crisp, focused light of day: "Pinker sensibly points out that thinking precedes writing and that we sound smarter when writing *because* we deliberately set out to be clear and precise"; "Yet he has been so good for so long that I suspect he has not produced a signature masterwork *only because* he stubbornly refuses to do so"; "We see so much chronic disease in the West *because* these are illnesses that appear relatively late in life."

ACCIDENT 319
Don't use the plural *bacteria* as a singular noun

In scientific writing and in careful usage, *bacteria* is a plural noun that takes a plural verb: *These bacteria cause disease.* The singular is *bacterium*, which takes a singular verb: *the bacterium that causes anthrax.*

The plural *bacteria* should not be used for the singular *bacterium.* This fatal accident of style appears with numbing frequency in journalism, especially headlines: "Deadly Bacteria [*Bacterium*] Begins to Infiltrate Fresh Fruit Juices and Produce" (*The New York Times*). Reuters news service tripped up in successive sentences: "They found that in 53 percent of the cases the infection came from the bacteria [*bacterium*] that causes cat scratch fever. In the remaining 47 percent the trench fever bacteria [*bacterium*] was responsible." The error is so virulent that it sometimes appears in scientific publications: "A specific protein on the surface of a common bacterial pathogen allows the bacteria [*bacterium*] to leave the bloodstream and enter the brain" (ScienceDaily.com). Occasionally the mistake mutates and you see a correct plural *bacteria* incorrectly paired with a singular verb: "Janis George boiled water to wash dishes in her Milford home after coliform bacteria was [*were*] found in the town's water supply" (*Boston Globe*).

The writer of an article in *The San Diego Union-Tribune* got it right in this sentence: "If the enzyme is absent or its activity is suppressed, the bacterium dies." But alas, whoever composed the caption for the photo accompanying the article got it wrong: "Methicillin-resistant *Staphylococcus aureus* bacteria [*bacterium*] is commonly known as MRSA and is a major source of infections in hospitals."

The phrase *strain of bacteria* takes a singular verb because the noun *strain* is singular: "Scientists have created *a strain of bacteria* that *stimulates* insulin production in the stomach of diabetic mice" (*Popular Science*).

One last caveat. Avoid, at all costs, the nonstandard anglicized plural *bacterias*, which is suicidally semiliterate: "At issue are cheeses such as *queso fresco* [etc.] . . . which may be made with unpasteurized milk that could contain harmful bacterias [*bacteria*]" (*Los Angeles Times*).

ACCIDENT 320
Put your adverb in the middle of a compound verb

There seems to be a cherished superstition among newspaper writers and editors that the proper place for an adverb is before rather than between the parts of a compound verb such as *have been* or *will be*. They insist on writing *currently have been* and *eventually will be* rather than *have currently been* and *will eventually be*. Perhaps, as some usage arbiters have speculated, they equate splitting a verb phrase with splitting an infinitive, which H. W. Fowler exposed as a cherished superstition way back in 1926 in his classic *Modern English Usage*. Whatever the reason, the practice is unidiomatic, and it has long been denounced—not *it long has been denounced*—by authorities on usage.

"In fluid writing," says *The New York Times Manual of Style and Usage*, "an adverb used with a compound verb should normally be placed between parts of the verb"—just the way *normally* is in that directive. Unfortunately, this straightforward point is usually lost (*not* usually is lost) on many writers, especially journalists.

In the following examples, the adverb is improperly positioned before rather than between the parts of the verb phrase: "As a saner, slower traveler, you ~~easily~~ could *easily* cover five in a weekend" (*Seattle Times*); "Golf carts ~~soon~~ will *soon* be humming along neighborhood streets" (*Daytona Beach News-Journal*); "Murnane said those kinds of discussions ~~already~~ have *already* cropped up" (*Northwest Herald*, Illinois); "Obama did what many people ~~long~~ have *long* urged him to do" (*Washington Post*); "John Boehner was introduced as the majority leader who ~~never~~ has *never* sponsored an earmark" (Robert D. Novak). The benefit of placing the adverb within the verb phrase is that the stress then falls squarely on the adverb and gives the sentence a more natural rhythm.

An exception to this rule of placement can sometimes be made with *probably*, depending on where the writer wants the stress to fall in the sentence. Here it naturally and properly splits the verb phrase: "Sotomayor would probably be a reliably liberal vote on a court split into conservative and liberal blocs on many major issues" (*Washington Post*). But in the following sentence *probably* could either split the verb phrase or precede it, and the writer chose the latter option: "Your daughter probably would love a father figure" (*Boston Globe*). (Perhaps the writer was responding to the tacit question *Would she?* with *She probably would.*) And in this sentence placing *probably* before the verb phrase gives the adverb the additional stress the writer needed: "Souter told The Atlantic's Marc Ambinder that he 'probably' would have retired no matter who was elected president" (*Washington Post*).

ACCIDENT 321
Don't use a singular verb after *group of* + [plural noun] + *who/that*

If *group* is used by itself, the verb that follows is singular: *a group that **makes** up nearly half the state's 5.2 million registered voters*; *a group that **raises** campaign contributions from special-interest factions*. But if *group* is followed by *of* and a plural noun, the verb must be plural to match the plural noun: *a group of friends that **are** like family*; *a group of people who **demonstrate** in support of the troops.*

I do voice work as a sideline to writing, and I once had a gig where the script contained these two definitions: "*government:* the group of people that rules a community, state, or nation"; and "*orchestra:* a group of musicians that plays different kinds of music and performs together." The director insisted the wording was correct, but it wasn't. She refused to believe that it was the plural nouns *people* and *musicians* that governed the verb in the sentence, not the word *group.* Preferring to avoid a ruckus and collect my fee, I read the script as it was written. But it should have been *the group of people that* (or *who*) ***rule** a community*, and *a group of musicians that* (or *who*) ***play*** . . . *and **perform** together.*

ACCIDENT 322
How not to use A.D.

The *Oxford English Dictionary* "represents more than a century of effort on the part of hundreds of learned scholars who have compiled an inventory of all the English words that have been in substantial use since 1150 A.D." (*The New York Times Magazine*). Can you tell what's wrong with that sentence?

The abbreviation A.D. stands for *anno Domini*, which is Latin for "in the year of the Lord," usually rendered in speech as "in the year of our Lord." Unlike its temporal partner B.C., A.D. properly goes before the year noted, not after. Thus: *Claudius I, the Roman emperor, lived from 10 B.C. to A.D. 54.* In the sentence above from the *Times Magazine*, it should have been A.D. 1150, not 1150 A.D.

With centuries, you may write *the fourth century A.D.* or *the fourth century*, as you please. The *New York Times* style manual favors the former; The Associated Press style manual favors the latter.

ACCIDENT 323
It's *militate against*, not *mitigate against*

To *mitigate* means "to lessen in intensity, make less severe, ease, allay, assuage": "Twitter has taken some steps to *mitigate* the spike in traffic and ensure that the site is not knocked offline again" (*PC World*). *Militate* means "to operate, weigh, or work" and is invariably paired with *against*: "Almost everything in modern society *militates against* our falling in love hard or long," writes Christina Nehring in *The Atlantic*. "It *militates against* love as risk, love as sacrifice, love as heroism."

Writers who mean *militate against* ("weigh or work against") frequently misrender the phrase as *mitigate against*: "But he is small, not blazingly fast, and 19 years old—all factors that mitigate against [*militate against*] making an instant impact in the NHL" (*Vancouver Sun*). They also frequently miswrite *mitigate against* when they mean *mitigate* ("make less severe"): "The Blacksmith Institute is working in seven countries to mitigate against lead pollution from improper recycling" (isria.com).

CHARLES HARRINGTON ELSTER

ACCIDENT 324

Colons and semicolons always go outside parentheses and quotation marks

Some examples (wholly fabricated for the occasion): *Did you just see that colon following a closing parenthesis?* Here's a colon following a closing quotation mark: *He recited the last line of Keats's sonnet "Bright Star": "And so live ever, or else swoon to death."* Here's a semicolon following a closing parenthesis: *He said it was a sonnet (by Keats, I think); he recites it beautifully.* And here's a semicolon following a closing quotation mark: *He said, "My favorite sonnet is by Keats"; then he recited it.*

ACCIDENT 325

Use a singular verb after *one in* [a number] or *one out of* [a number]

These constructions must always take a singular verb. It should be *One in four Americans has high blood pressure* not *One in four Americans have high blood pressure*. *Bryson's Dictionary of Troublesome Words* suggests inverting the sentence so you'll see the proper noun-verb agreement. Thus: *Out of every four Americans, one has high blood pressure.*

An erroneous plural verb after *one in* or *one out of* often appears in edited writing: "And one in five call [*calls*] the Bible 'an ancient book of fables, legends, history and moral precepts recorded by man'" (*USA Today*). Even if *one in* or *one out of* appears more than once in a sentence, the verb should still be singular: "Moreover, statistics show that one out of three Americans and one out of five Koreans have [*has*] trouble sleeping" (*JoongAng Daily*). Here inversion again helps clarify things: "Out of every three Americans and every five Koreans, one *has* trouble sleeping."

A plural verb is permissible only when the subject of the sentence is plural and the *one in* or *one out of* is parenthetical: "Already, an estimated 10.2 million seniors—one out of five in America—have enrolled in Medicare Advantage" (*The Wall Street Journal*).

Sometimes the choice of a plural pronoun causes a writer to use a plural verb: "One out of every four West Virginia students *say they've* feared going to school because *they'd* be bullied" (*West Virginia MetroNews*). The writer thought that using *they* would be the best way around having to use the exclusionary *he* or the awkward *he or she* required by a singular verb: "One out of every four West Virginia students *says he or she has* feared going to school because *he or she'd* be bullied." But the sentence can be revised more deftly to avoid both pitfalls: "One out of every four West Virginia students *fears* going to school because of bullying."

ACCIDENT 326
Improper use of *bring* for *take*
Any reliable usage guide will tell you that *bring* implies movement toward the writer or speaker while *take* implies movement away from the writer or speaker. As Richard Lederer and Richard Dowis write in *Sleeping Dogs Don't Lay,* "We bring in the newspaper, but we take out the trash." And when you go to a restaurant they *bring* the food to your table and *take* your money when you're done.

Simple enough, right? Not so fast. Consider this one-sentence summary of the book *A Lion Called Christian:* "Two men buy a pet lion cub in London and bring him to Africa when he is grown." If *bring* implies movement toward the writer or speaker, we must infer that the two men come from Africa or that the sentence appeared in an African publication. But the two men are not African and the sentence appeared in the bestseller list of *The New York Times Book Review.* So *bring* in this context is, if not wrong, then at least peculiar.

Here's another example: "Galvin said he had signed and sealed the certificate of appointment, and given it to Kirk to bring to Washington." Any reader of that sentence would be justified in assuming that it was written for a Washington-based publication because the movement described is toward Washington. But the sentence was published in the *Dover-Sherborn Press,* a newspaper in Massachusetts, where the event it relates took place.

This problem of ambiguous location is all too common with *bring* and *take.* Here's another example, from a photo caption: "The Torah he's unfurling . . . came from a town in Czechoslovakia, where it was hidden during the Holocaust and then brought to Israel." If that had appeared in an Israeli publication, *brought* would be correct. But the Torah in question now belongs to a synagogue in San Diego, and the caption appeared in *The San Diego Union-Tribune.*

So what's to be done here? Wreckless writers should follow the advice of *The New York Times Manual of Style and Usage,* which says that *take* should be used for "any movement that is not toward the speaker or writer. So the Canadian prime minister cannot be *bringing* a group of industrialists to a conference in Detroit, except in an article written from Detroit." That's why the headline *Simon Cowell to bring "X Factor" to U.S.* is appropriate for a publication in the United States, but for a publication in the United Kingdom it should be *Simon Cowell to take 'X Factor' to U.S.*

To the *Times* manual's directive I would add this elaboration: If the writer or speaker's location is unknown or irrelevant, use *bring* only for movement toward what is being discussed, and *take* for any other kind of movement: *He ordered a sandwich, and when they brought it to him he ate it greedily. Every Sunday after church she took her elderly mother to their favorite restaurant for lunch.*

In the following examples *bring* is incorrect because the writer's location is unknown or irrelevant and the movement is not toward what is being discussed: "Surely someone would see her sitting there alone at the top of the visitors' section and bring [*take*] her home" (Richard Russo, *Empire Falls*); "On November 14, 2003, at Abu Ghraib prison, on the outskirts of Baghdad, six hooded Iraqi prisoners . . . were brought [*taken*] to the Military Intelligence cellblock and handed over to . . . the military police officer in charge of the night shift" (*The New Yorker*).

In many instances, idiom governs the choice between *bring* and *take.* For example, in the headline "Obama set to bring nonproliferation case to U.N." *bring* is wrong because—although we may *bring* a case *against* someone and *bring* a case *to* trial—idiom requires that we *take* a case *to* a court or public forum. But *bring* is established in expressions like *bring to light, bring to justice,* and *bring to the table,* perhaps because there's a figurative implication that the writer or speaker is in the light, at the seat of justice, or at the table.

ACCIDENT 327

Improper use of *beg the question*

"From the Bible on the seat to the spiffy wax job to the college parking sticker on the front windshield, the automobile begged the question: Why would the gainfully employed, college-educated, devout,
outwardly normal Oscar Castillo turn a church into a bloody shooting range, then kill himself?" (*The San Diego Union-Tribune*). Leaving
aside the question of how automobiles can beg questions, or even ask
them, let us turn our attention to the proper and improper use of the
expression *beg the question*.

Consider this sentence: "The increasing influx of drugs into this
country *begs the question* as to what we can do about it" (Lesley Stahl
on *60 Minutes*). Here, as in the talking automobile citation, it seems to
mean "to raise or invite an obvious question." Now consider this sentence: "*Begging the question* involves talking around the issue without
addressing it" (Dianna Booher, *E-Writing*). Here the writer is telling us
that it means "to evade or ignore a question or issue."

If you use *beg the question* in either of these senses, you will have
plenty of company and even the sanction of some dictionaries. But
you will show yourself to be a writer who follows the unthinking
herd rather than one who chooses words with care.

To beg the question is a venerable idiom that comes to us through
law from the ancient art of rhetoric. It is a type of logical fallacy,
known formally by its Latin name: *petitio principii*. In logic, *to beg the
question* means "to assume as true what needs to be proved" or, as
Garner's Modern American Usage puts it, "to base a conclusion on an
assumption that is as much in need of proof or demonstration as the
conclusion itself." When the lawyer asks the defendant, "Do you still
have extramarital affairs?" before it has been proved that he ever
committed adultery, *that* is begging the question. And the statement
Reasonable people are people who reason intelligently begs the question
What is intelligent reasoning?

Using *beg the question* to mean "raise the question" or "evade the
issue" is the result of a restless desire for elegant variation. The consequence of this ignorant usage is that a vague, superfluous phrase

is supplanting a precise idiom that we still sorely need. For if we stop using *beg the question* in its traditional sense, we will no longer have a succinct way to describe the presumptuous logic of the young man in a public speaking class who, hoping to persuade his audience that the arts should be dropped from his high school curriculum, began by saying, "Since I know we all agree that taking music and art does nothing to prepare you for college, a career, or life, I'll start there."

Jacques Barzun, one of the great sages of English usage, demonstrates the difference between begging and raising questions in this passage from *A Word or Two Before You Go:* "The scientific students of language, who inveigh with so much unscientific passion against normative grammar and ideals of correctness, assert that all one can ask of a speaker or writer is that he be 'effective'—specious counsel which begs the question ["What is effective?"] and raises another: How to be effective when conventions break down? One might as well expect motorists to drive 'effectively' without lights or traffic rules, scrambling to their destination anyhow."

ACCIDENT 328
Never use *Let me see* or *Let's see* as an opener

It has been postulated that an infinite number of monkeys tapping on an infinite number of keyboards would eventually reproduce all the works of Shakespeare. To my knowledge, no one has yet tried to guess what the first intelligible words those monkeys would manage to type after producing Lord knows how much gibberish. I'd bet good money that those first simian words would be *Let me see.*

The writer who broaches a topic with *Let me see* and expects the reader to follow along obediently is like the vagabond who, unsummoned, approaches your car at a stoplight, wipes half your windshield with a filthy rag, and demands a handout. This lamest of rhetorical devices is invariably a setup, a con, the prelude to a haughty diatribe in which the writer displays his superior reasoning and confirms the stupidity of others by demolishing a straw man, usually with a lethal dose of sarcasm. One example, from a master of the technique: "Let me see, preventing politicians from communicating with their own constituents? That sounds just like the sort of transparency that Democrats promised to bring to Washington" (Sean Hannity, FOXNews.com).

Often the writer will extend the phrase to *Let me see if I have this right, Let me see if I've got this straight,* or *Let me see if I understand,* perhaps in the belief that the feigned modesty of that preamble will ensnare the gullible reader. But the sagacious reader, mindful of the trap being laid, will either step with care or turn around and run.

Let me see at the opening of an argument is not the bell at the beginning of a boxing match; it's the horn that says a truck runneth over. If you want to be an honorable polemicist, come out with your dukes up and leave the sucker punches to the blowhards.

ACCIDENT 329
Don't use *enormity* to mean *enormousness*

"Isn't it just like Americans," writes Barbara Wallraff in *Word Court,* "to want to trade in one of very few words we have to denote real, unmitigated atrocity for yet another word that means large size?" Ms. Wallraff is referring to our lazy use of *enormity,* which properly refers to something monstrously wicked or outrageously evil, in place of *enormousness* and other words denoting something very big. "If we are moral people," she concludes, "we should strive to retain *enormity* as one of few words adequate to decry historic events on the scale of the Serbian slaughter of Albanians in Kosovo in 1999, the mid-1990s genocide in Rwanda, and Hitler's Holocaust."

I'm with Ms. Wallraff all the way, and so are almost all other modern authorities on usage. *Immense* may make *immensity,* but *enormous* makes *enormousness,* not *enormity:* "They get up every morning knowing the *enormousness* of the task ahead of them, carrying on despite the gnawing feeling that whatever they attempt will always be a drop in the ocean" (*Sarasota Herald-Tribune*).

The fourth edition of *The American Heritage Dictionary* says that writers who ignore the distinction between *enormity* ("monstrous evil") and *enormousness* ("hugeness, vastness") "may find that their words have cast unintended aspersions or evoked unexpected laughter." Examples of these literary mishaps are easily found. Here *enormity* casts an unintended aspersion: "During the past several days we have seen close up yet another measure of the enormity of Ted Kennedy's presence in the life of this community" (*Boston Herald*). Senator Kennedy wasn't *that* bad, was he? And here it evokes laughter at the writer's ineptitude: "To me, the enormity of their love and patience has been humbling beyond description" (*Naperville Sun*, Illinois). Often a writer's choice of *enormity* only muddles things and makes the intended meaning ambiguous: "Opinions about the bill's substance would benefit 'The Courant' readership more than a dismissive reaction to those fearful of its provisions and enormity" (*Hartford Courant*). Is the bill evil or just very large and complicated?

Although *enormity* is best used, as Ms. Wallraff notes, of events that are monstrously wicked or evil, such as the terrorist attacks of 9/11, the word may also apply to outrageously evil, violent, or immoral actions on a smaller scale: "Neighbors were still trying to grasp the enormity of the shootings Friday" (WGCL-TV, Atlanta). Once in a while a writer manages the neat trick of using *enormity* to convey the notion of vastness without straying from the word's traditional sense of great wickedness: "The SEC investigated Madoff around the edges over the years, even shutting down a feeder fund in the early 1990s, but the agency never grasped the enormity of his fraud" (*Washington Post*). But as they say on TV, unless you're a pro, don't try this at home.

Moral: Use *enormousness*—or *bigness, hugeness, vastness, massiveness, immensity,* and *prodigiousness*—when referring to something very large, and reserve *enormity* for evil, wickedness, and crimes of great magnitude.

USE THE RIGHT WORD, NOT ITS SECOND COUSIN

"The fried eggs add extra unctuousness to a clever carbonara."

—Bon Appétit

I don't know about you, but I wouldn't want even a drop of unctuousness in my spaghetti carbonara. *Unctuous,* from the Latin *ungĕre,* "to anoint," means "like an ointment or unguent; oily, soapy, or greasy." Figuratively, *unctuous* means "too suave or oily in speech or manner" (*Webster's New World College Dictionary,* 4th ed.).

If those fried eggs are unctuous, somebody didn't cook them right. The writer was probably thinking of *smoothness* or *silkiness* but wanted to impress the reader with a more upscale word. But sometimes it's better not to go shopping for a flamboyant outfit when you look fine in the clothes you already own.

ACCIDENT 330

Don't use *disinterested* to mean *uninterested*

Those who were never taught the distinction between *disinterested* and *uninterested* often assume the words are interchangeable, and they tend to choose *disinterested* when they mean "not interested" because it sounds more elegant or literary. This mistake has become so common that dictionaries now include the meaning "not interested, indifferent" for *disinterested,* which has only encouraged confusion.

Today, when a writer means "not interested" you are more likely to read *disinterested* than *uninterested,* as in these erroneous examples: "Voters who are too lazy or *disinterested* to vote, shouldn't" (*Winnipeg Free Press*); "*Disinterested* in her work, she decided to help the poor" (AssociatedContent.com); "The latest Eurobarometer survey suggests 53% of EU citizens are 'somewhat' or 'very' *disinterested* in the elections" (BBC News); "His team has been *disinterested* about half the time in the playoffs" (FOXSports.com). In all those sentences *uninterested* is the proper word.

We are witnessing the gradual eradication of an eminently useful distinction, and I exhort you not to abet this atrocity. *Disinterested* properly means "impartial, unbiased, not having any selfish interest." When you are *disinterested* you have nothing to gain or lose, so you can judge fairly. When you are *uninterested*, you simply lack interest. *Bryson's Dictionary of Troublesome Words* expresses it nicely: "A disinterested person is one who has no stake in the outcome of an event; an uninterested person is one who doesn't care."

ACCIDENT 331
How not to use a colon

Don't use a colon after *namely*. Use a comma or no punctuation: "A special hot seat has been reserved, however, for those seen as directly responsible for causing the economic crisis—namely, bankers" (*San Francisco Chronicle*); "By the mid-1960s, the property was in the hands of the King and Pacheco families, namely Joe King and Richard M. Pacheco, both now deceased" (*Arizona Star*). It's all right to use a colon before *namely* to introduce something you want to emphasize: "Fortunately we have a thousand years of experience with neutral adjudication: namely, courtroom trials" (*Jurist*). A colon may also take the place of *namely*, as in *I need only three tools to cook: a knife, a pan, and tongs.*

Don't use a colon with *for example* if that phrase introduces elements that belong in the body of a sentence: *He was enamored of many glamorous actresses, for example, Penélope Cruz and Scarlett Johansson.* However, you may use a colon after *for example* if you are introducing something that can stand by itself as a sentence. *Consider this sentence, for example:* is an acceptable way to introduce a separate sentence that serves as an example.

"Never use a colon after a sentence fragment," cautions Mignon Fogarty in *Grammar Girl's Quick and Dirty Tips for Better Writing.* That is poorly worded advice. You're well within your rights if you use a colon after a single word or a phrase as long as it introduces one or more stand-alone examples—meaning a complete sentence or sentences. I have done that throughout this book with *Thus, Remember, One other thing, A postscript to this discussion,* and other introductory words and phrases.

What Fogarty probably meant is that you should never interrupt a sentence by putting a colon after a verb or preposition because it creates an awkward sentence fragment before the colon. In other words, as Edward D. Johnson writes in *The Handbook of Good English,* "Do not use a colon to introduce words that fit properly into the grammar of the sentence without the colon."

For example, don't write *The menu includes: soup, salad, entrée, and dessert* because the colon after the verb interrupts the flow of the sentence. For the same reason, don't break the flow of a sentence with a colon after a preposition, as in *Smoking is not allowed in: the stairwells, elevators, and restrooms* and *She had serial affairs with: Manny, Moe, and Jack.* But it's fine to use a complete sentence followed by a colon to introduce a list: *The menu includes the following: soup, salad, entrée, and dessert. She had serial affairs with three men: Manny, Moe, and Jack.*

Don't use a colon after *like* to introduce an example: *People ask me interesting questions about language like: "Is there a word for when inanimate objects conspire against you?"** The colon in that sentence is intrusive, as it is in this real-life example: "Lévy is better when tracing these filiations and complexities than when making idealist generalizations like: 'the double crown of freedom and equality'" (Christopher Hitchens in *The New York Times Book Review*). Again, there is no reason to toss in a distracting colon when the grammar of the sentence flows smoothly without it.

There is also no reason to toss in a colon because you think it looks serious or clever, as David Brooks of *The New York Times* did in this sentence: "Experienced leaders can certainly blunder if their minds have rigidified (see: Rumsfeld, Donald)." An ostentatious colon like that is: weird.

---

*Yes, there is: *resistentialism.* To learn more, go to http://members.authorsguild .net/chelster.

Although it's permissible to use a colon to introduce a quotation, take care not to do it indiscriminately. *The Chicago Manual of Style* says, "Such perfunctory phrases as 'Jacqueline Jones writes:' or 'The defendant stated:' are often awkward, and sensitive writers avoid them." That's why I didn't introduce that quotation from *The Chicago Manual of Style* with a colon after *says*. "The colon is a strong mark of punctuation," says *The Handbook of Good English*, "and it holds the reader up more than the comma does." After verbs that introduce quotations, use a colon only when you have good reason to hold the reader up and draw attention to what follows. Otherwise, it's smoother, and always acceptable, to introduce a quotation with a comma after the verb.

ACCIDENT 332

Confusion between *precipitous* and *precipitate*

Precipitous (pruh-SIP-i-tus) means "steep, like a cliff or precipice." *Precipitate* (pruh-SIP-i-tit) means "sudden, abrupt," or "rash, impetuous." *Precipitous* is properly used of physical things or characteristics, while *precipitate* applies, says *Garner's Modern American Usage*, to "actions, movements, or demands."

Writers frequently misuse *precipitous* for rash or sudden actions, movements, and demands. In the following examples, the proper word is *precipitate*: "For Mr. Burress, 31, it has been a precipitous fall from triumph to trouble" (*The New York Times*); "Leaving Vienna was precipitous, but the only way out" (Selden Edwards, *The Little Book*); "Striking Iran's nuclear program will not be precipitous or poorly thought out" (John Bolton in *The Wall Street Journal*).

In journalism and business writing, *precipitous* is often paired with the words *drop* and *decline*. If the intended meaning is clearly "steep," this is acceptable: "Since the recession began, there has been a *precipitous* decline in trust" (*Business Day*). But often the intended meaning is "sudden, abrupt," so *precipitous* is incorrect: "This follows a precipitous [*precipitate*] decline on Wednesday morning, when it fell 4.5% in under an hour" (*Asia Times* online).

Occasionally you will come across a sentence where the writer has no idea what *precipitous* means. Here, for example, the writer seems to be confusing *precipitous* with *crucial* or *pivotal:* "Washington Mutual's failure last September marked a *precipitous* moment of this recession" (*Information Week*). As Mark Twain might have said, don't reach for a fancy word if you can't misuse it properly.

ACCIDENT 333
It's spelled *rarefied,* not *rarified*

Even in edited prose, this word is misspelled perhaps as often as it's spelled right. Far too many writers and editors are unsure whether to use *rarefy* or *rarify*—and no wonder, since four of the six major American dictionaries list *rarify* as a standard alternative spelling. And if you look up *rarefy* in the great *Oxford English Dictionary*—which, by the way, may be available to you free online through your local public library—you will find examples of the spelling *rarify* dating back to the year 1500 (the earliest citation for the word is 1398). Does that make *rarify* acceptable today?

No. *Rarefy* with an *e* has the etymological pedigree (Latin *rārēfăcĕre*, "to make less solid"), and it has long been the preferred form. Though writers persist in using the eccentric *rarify* and dictionaries continue to record it, I have yet to find a reputable arbiter of usage who considers it correct.

ACCIDENT 334
Don't use *diffuse* to mean *defuse*

In dispensing advice on how to handle a mother with advanced Alzheimer's who makes inappropriate remarks (such as "You are extremely fat"), Philip Galanes, the "Social Q's" columnist for *The New York Times*, says it's probably best to say something simple like "'I'm sorry for my mother. She isn't well.' That should diffuse the situation." Good advice, perhaps. But he should have written *defuse*.

This mistake is increasingly common, perhaps because the pronunciation of *diffuse* and *defuse* is often identical (di-FYOOZ). Their meanings, however, are far apart. To *diffuse* is to spread or distribute widely, disperse or disseminate. To *defuse* is to remove the fuse from, and so to ease or mollify; make less harmful, dangerous, or difficult.

If your intended meaning is "to spread out, scatter, or disseminate," use *diffuse*. Lamps *diffuse* light. The sun *diffuses* fog. And kindergarten teachers *diffuse* rudimentary knowledge while their sniffling, sneezing pupils *diffuse* germs.

If your intended meaning is "to make something less harmful or troublesome," use *defuse*. You can *defuse* a bomb, render it harmless, or *defuse* a ticklish or potentially explosive situation.

Diffuse is sometimes misused for *defuse* when referring to bombs: "Oeth said by using the robot to diffuse or detonate bombs, he hopes it will significantly decrease the risk to officers" (*Princeton Daily Clarion*). But most often *diffuse*, to spread or distribute, is mistakenly applied to troublesome situations.

In the following examples *defuse*, not *diffuse*, is the proper word: "Legalization would also help diffuse the violence in Mexico" (*Salt Lake Tribune*); "Woods had a chance to diffuse any hint of a problem last week" (*Golf Digest*); "The reported shootings occurred before talks with international monitors Thursday on efforts to diffuse tensions in the region" (Associated Press).

A C C I D E N T   3 3 5
Do not use *who* to refer to a thing

The relative pronoun *who* has traditionally applied only to human beings, as in the title of Oliver Sacks's book *The Man Who Mistook His Wife for a Hat*. But in recent years there has been a growing trend to use *who* for things, especially companies and other large institutions that are decidedly nonhuman.

This trend began, as such changes often do, in speech. To cite but two examples from some years ago, I heard Colin Powell, when he was secretary of state, say, "We're looking at those terrorist organizations *who* have the capacity," and Noah Adams on NPR's *All Things Considered* say, "This should affect the companies *who* do a lot of borrowing."

Today this "corporate *who*" seems to be everywhere, and you don't have to look hard to find it in edited writing: "Companies *who* stand to win or lose big from the proposed legislation are shelling out hefty bucks for Washington lobbyists" (*Baltimore Sun*); "But complaints, particularly from schools *who* issued potential layoff notices to 14,000 teachers in the spring" (*The San Diego Union-Tribune*); "The companies trying to commercialize the technology are, in a way, irrelevant. (Why not just back the one *who* promises to be less hostile?)" (*The New York Times Magazine*).

In the preceding examples, *who* is erroneously used for *that*, the relative pronoun that properly refers to things, as in *things that go bump in the night*. *Who* is also often misused for *which*, another relative pronoun that applies to things: "Today it was the nation's hospitals, who [*which*] agreed to pony up some 150 billion dollars" (Robert Siegel on NPR's *All Things Considered*); "You wouldn't think so, however, if you consulted the Census Bureau and the National Endowment for the Arts, who [*which*], since 1982, have asked thousands of Americans questions about reading" (Caleb Crain in *The New Yorker*).

If Rite Aid can now be "the only drugstore *who*," you have to wonder what bizarre thing we will choose to pseudohumanize next. Robots? Machines? Don't laugh, because the unthinkable is already happening: "Devastator—the new villain made out of seven individual robots who [*that*] hide in the form of construction equipment" (*USA Today*); "You begin your journey as the sole living robot in a teeming city of thousands of machines who [*that*] have laid dormant for millennia" (escapistmagazine.com). After skidding out of control with the oxymoronic *living robot*, that abominable sentence hits the guardrail with *machines who*, then flips over and bursts into flames with *have laid*, which means "have put," not "have been at rest." It should have been *machines **that** have **lain** dormant*. (See Accident 13.)

The widespread misuse of *who* to refer to businesses, organizations, and goodness knows what else flouts a cherished convention of English usage and blurs a useful distinction. I urge you to take special care to avoid this grave accident of style.

MAINTAIN
TOP
SAFE
SPEED

ACCIDENT 336

Don't confuse *sensuous* and *sensual*

Sensuous refers favorably to things experienced through the senses: *sensuous music, sensuous colors, a sensuous massage, the sensuous aroma of fine food*. *Sensual* refers, usually unfavorably, to the gratification of the senses or physical appetites, especially in a self-indulgent or sexual way: *the sensual excesses of the glutton, the sensual and sordid nightlife of the city; the sensual cravings of a drug addict*.

Sensual, which should apply to the gratification of desire, is often misused for *sensuous*, which should apply to the senses or to pleasurable sensations: "A remarkable work of recollection and imagination . . . written with beautiful, sensual [*sensuous*] detail" (*Boston Globe*); "What makes this novel so striking is that it joins both blindness and insight, the sensual [*sensuous*] world and the world of the mind, to tell a story about the unfolding of modern American life" (*Salt Lake Tribune*). Here the headline for a book review uses *sensuous* correctly: " 'Censoring' is sly, playful, *sensuous*—and sensational." But in the book review itself the writer gets it wrong: "The effect . . . is deliriously sensual [*sensuous*] prose" (*Los Angeles Times*).

If you mean "lovely, pleasurable," or "experienced through the senses," use *sensuous*. If you mean "self-gratifying" or "pertaining to physical desires," use *sensual*. *Sensuous* writing is lovely, gorgeous writing; it appeals to your sense of beauty. *Sensual* writing is erotic, sexually arousing.

ACCIDENT 337

Don't confuse *purposely* and *purposefully*

When you do something *purposely*, you do it on purpose, intentionally: *He flirted with her purposely and shamelessly*. When you do something *purposefully*, you do it with determination to accomplish an objective: *With a barrage of flowers, chocolates, and schmaltzy music, he purposefully sought to win her heart*.

Perhaps because *purposefully* is the longer, weightier word, writers often use it when they mean merely "intentionally" rather than "with a specific purpose in mind": "Last year's 'Burn After Reading'

THE ACCIDENTS OF STYLE

was the purposefully [*purposely*] oddball follow-up to their more conventional and commercially successful 'No Country for Old Men'" (*Los Angeles Times*); "A memorial bears his name and the names of the 39 others on slabs of purposefully [*purposely*] unfinished stone" (*San Francisco Chronicle*).

This sentence uses *purposefully* correctly: "Striding ever more purposefully up to the biggest meathead in a dingy bar . . . he would say whatever it took to goad his quarry into dealing with him mano a mano" (guardian.co.uk).

ACCIDENT 338
Misuse of *verdict* and *ruling*

From *The Cleveland Plain Dealer:* "Assistant Cuyahoga County Prosecutor Paul Soucie said he was disappointed by the judge's verdict." From BBC News: "The court presiding over the trial of Burma's detained opposition leader Aung San Suu Kyi will deliver its verdict on Friday, her lawyer has said." Can you tell what's wrong with those two sentences?

Judges, whether acting alone or as a court, render or deliver *rulings*, not *verdicts*. "Only juries can render *verdicts*. Judges never can," explains James J. Kilpatrick in *The Writer's Art*. "Judges can find a defendant guilty, or hold a defendant guilty, or even rule that a defendant is guilty as charged. If the trial is a jury trial, what we get at the end is a *verdict*."

This distinction between *verdict* and *ruling* is tricky to keep straight, for even Mr. Kilpatrick, who is as fine a writer as they come but as human as the rest of us, slipped up once in a column that appeared five years after he published his ruling on these two words: "The case was heard last April before Administrative Law Judge Karl Engeman. In December he returned a verdict [*ruling*] against Mrs. Smith and in favor of the unwed couple."

Another accident of style that writers often get into with *verdict* and *ruling* is switching blithely back and forth between them, as if the words were interchangeable. In a story about a British libel case where the judge ruled against a Holocaust-denying historian, a reporter for the *Chicago Tribune* did this egregiously: "International Jewish groups applauded the unsparing British court *verdict* against Irving. . . . The *verdict* shredded Irving's reputation. . . . Professor Deborah Lipstadt of Emory University . . . hailed the *ruling*. . . . The *ruling* also was a victory for Penguin Books, her British publisher. . . . [Irving] said he had two words to describe the *ruling*. . . . Irving may appeal the *verdict*."

In every instance in that story, *verdict* should have been *ruling*. But the reporter was no doubt suffering from a bad case of *monologophobia*, a fear of repeating the same word. "A *monologophobe* (you won't find it in the dictionary)," writes Theodore M. Bernstein in *The Careful Writer*, "is a writer who would rather walk naked in front of Saks Fifth Avenue than be caught using the same word more than once in three lines. What he suffers from is *synonymomania* (you won't find that one, either), which is a compulsion to call a spade successively *a garden implement* and an *earth-turning tool*. The affliction besets journalists in general and sports writers in particular."

Instead of flip-flopping between the correct *ruling* and the incorrect *verdict*, the *Chicago Tribune* reporter should have assuaged his monologophobia by here and there tossing in the word *decision*, an unobjectionable substitute for *ruling*.

ACCIDENT 339
Don't use *noisome* to mean "noisy"

Noisome means "offensive, disgusting, especially to the sense of smell." It does not, as many writers think, mean "noisy": "They complain of unruly crowds and noisome [*noisy*] disturbances into the wee hours that keep them awake all night and make them fearful of walking the streets" (*Baltimore Sun*).

Noisome also does not mean "outrageous" or "disgraceful," as the writer of this sentence apparently thought: "We are all familiar with the right to bear arms and the noisome extremes indulged [in] by its zealots" (*New York Times* editorial).

And though *noisome* is etymologically related to *annoy*, using it to mean merely "annoying" or "irritating" waters down the word's potency. *Noisome* should be reserved for that which is extremely unpleasant or offensive, particularly to the sense of smell. In this artful sentence, which is about vehicles that run on diesel fuel, the writer takes pains to make sure the reader knows that *noisome* means "smelly and disgusting" and not "loud": "Imagine trying to market a product that most Americans regard as old and obsolete, that is re-membered—if at all—as low-class and low-tech, noisy and *noisome*, and whose most notable advocates are truck drivers with prominent trouser cleavage" (Dan Neil in the *Los Angeles Times*).

ACCIDENT 340
Misuse of *differing* for *different*
"The difference between the adjective *different* and the participle *differing*," says *Garner's Modern American Usage*, "is the difference between the verb phrases *differ from* and *differ with*." In other words, it's a difference between dissimilar things and dissimilar ways of thinking. If one thing *differs from* another, it varies or is not the same. If one thing *differs with* another, it diverges or dis-agrees.

You can have *differing* opinions, beliefs, ideas, views, notions, ac-counts, perspectives, interpretations, and philosophies. But you have *different* needs, styles, interests, effects, approaches, levels, surfaces, degrees, technologies, and exit strategies—all of which I found *differ-ing* paired with on Google News. The indifferent writer of the fol-lowing sentence managed to misuse *differing* with three *different* things: "There are multiple breakfast, lunch and dinner options for local residents and visitors of differing [*different*] ages, interests and income levels" (*Evening News and Tribune*, Indiana).

Here's a tip: If you're ever stuck in midsentence worrying over this distinction, you'll always be safe using the all-purpose *different*, which can apply either to things that are not the same or to things that are not in agreement.

ACCIDENT 341

Proper use of *altercation*

The traditional meaning of *altercation* is "a vehement or angry dispute; a noisy controversy" (*Oxford English Dictionary*). An altercation is verbal while a fight is physical, Eric Partridge tells us in *Usage and Abusage*. In precise usage, an altercation may develop into a fight: "Witnesses reported the shooting was related to an altercation between the victim and a suspect earlier the same day" (*Chicago Sun-Times*).

I wish we could leave it there, but we can't. Journalists—doubtless mimicking the poor usage of the police, who love inflated words— have used *altercation* so often for violent disputes that the word now invariably appears in place of *fight:* "Tila Tequila Hospitalized After Altercation [*Fight*] with NFL Player Boyfriend" (tvguide.com). In fact, *altercation* and *fight* are so hopelessly confused that writers have started using a kind of retronymic* redundancy, *verbal altercation*, when they want to make clear that the dispute was limited to angry words: "Man shot after verbal altercation" (*Bay City Daily Tribune*). What's wrong with the word *argument*, for Pete's sake? I got more than two hundred hits for the ridiculous *verbal altercation* on Google News, which means it may soon become a cliché.

It's probably too late to rescue *altercation* from the battering it has taken in the media, but careful writers should at least try to rein in this loose usage and stick to this definition: "verbal contention which may or may not be accompanied by blows" (*Webster's New World College Dictionary*). As *Garner's Modern American Usage* observes, "It's wrong to say that someone is killed during an altercation." It's also taking things too far to use *altercation* when the dispute involves lethal weapons or serious injury, as in this headline: "Montgomery man shot, stabbed in altercation" (*Newsday*).

The thing to remember here is if it's a fight, just call it a fight.

---

*"A retronym is an adjective-noun pairing generated by a change in the meaning of the noun, usually because of advances in technology" (Richard Lederer, *Crazy English*). For example, *telephone* was the original term, followed by the retronyms *rotary phone, touch-tone phone, wireless phone,* and *mobile* or *cellular phone.*

USE THE RIGHT WORD, NOT ITS SECOND COUSIN

"O'Connor's highhanded attitude toward Congress, state courts and the American people reached its apotheosis in Bush v. Gore."

—Jeffrey Rosen, *The New York Times Magazine*

Apotheosis means "the act of raising a person to the status of a god"; "the glorification of a person or thing"; or "a glorified ideal" (*Webster's New World College Dictionary*, 4th ed.). A highhanded attitude is not something that gets glorified or becomes a glorified ideal, nor is it a point or stage you reach.

The writer needed a word that meant "highest point" or "utmost expression," and he chose *apotheosis* probably because it sounds a bit like *acme* and *apogee*, both of which, along with *zenith*, are used of highest points. The words *culmination* and *climax* would have worked in this context too, as would the simple and straightforward *peak*, which might be the best choice of the bunch.

Remember: Using a big long word can be a beautiful thing—unless you should have used an everyday word instead.

ACCIDENT 342

Write *used to*, not *use to*, for what you *used to* do or what you're *used to*

Used to can mean "formerly, at one time" (*We used to live there*) or "accustomed to, familiar with" (*She is used to it*). In these senses, just as you would write *accustomed to* and not *accustom to*, always write *used to*, with the *d*, and not *use to*. Because *used to* can sound like *use to* in speech, *use to* is a frequent error in blogs and online postings: "There will be a time when those who use to [*used to*] invest, but turned trader to survive, can put away their tools and rest on their labors" (Motley Fool: caps.fool.com).

Also take care to write *never used to*, not *never use to*, even in transcribed speech: "'We never use to [*used to*] pay attention to the parties. When I was first elected, the people of this county were Democrats,' said Rigby" (*Rexburg Standard Journal*, Idaho).

Now for an exception, of sorts. Many contemporary authorities on usage call for *use to* rather than *used to* after *did* or *didn't*, as in *Did he use to go?* and *He didn't use to go.* The reasoning for this is that *did* is the past tense of *do*, so *use* shouldn't also be in the past tense (*used*); that's why, for instance, we say *Did he have to go?* and *He didn't have to go* instead of *Did he had to go?* and *He didn't had to go.* But as *Garner's Modern American Usage* observes, *used to* is not behaving here like a normal verb; it's a fixed, idiomatic phrase with its own special function.

While the sentence *Did you use to do it?* looks as if it might be missing a *what* at the beginning or a noun after *use* (a knife? a gun?), in the sentence *Did you used to do it?* it's clear that *used to* is a phrase meaning "formerly, in the past." The same goes for sentences like *She didn't used to have such a good job* and *He didn't used to smoke*, where the phrase *used to* is plainly understood to mean "customarily in the past."

Garner and I are in the minority on this point, but there is no denying that in general usage *used to* occurs far more often than *use to* after *did* and *didn't*. Nonetheless, in any kind of dignified writing (other than fictional dialogue) *didn't use(d) to* is at best colloquial, and you'll always be on safer ground with *never used to*.

ACCIDENT 343
Write *as if . . . were*, not *as if . . . was*

When you use *as if* to introduce a statement that is untrue or hypothetical, the verb that follows must be in the subjunctive mood (*were*) and not in the indicative mood (*was*). Why? Because the indicative is used for statements of fact (*that cheese was made from goat's milk*), while the subjunctive is used of what is often called "a condition contrary to fact" (*if the moon were made of cheese*). The counterfactual subjunctive occurs whenever a string quartet makes music from the eighteenth century sound *as if* it *were* written yesterday. And it occurs whenever Hamlet, alone on stage, delivers his soliloquy *as if* no one *were* sitting in the audience listening.

Here's an example of *as if* introducing something untrue: "When the system is placed on the stand, the notebook charges *as if* it *were* plugged into a wall outlet" (*ChannelWeb*). And here's *as if* introducing something hypothetical: "Let's approach the war on terror *as if* it *were* another Cold War" (*Foreign Policy*).

Writers often have trouble with the *as if* construction, improperly following it with the factual *was* instead of the counterfactual *were*—as in this sentence, which begins with the counterfactual and proceeds to the factual: "Peter was dressed as if it was [*were*] a cold day when it was actually in the high 70s" (*Woonsocket Call*, Rhode Island).

Some other examples: " 'Come to the UN,' she said, as if it was [*were*] this magical theme park" (*Kansas City Star*); "She was wearing a purple tank top and a short white skirt that looked as if it was [*were*] about to slide off her slim hips" (*Washington Post*). The writer of this sentence, a well-known linguist, undermined his credibility by using an ungainly *was* for *were*: "No linguist joins a Safire in decrying . . . split infinitives, as if it was [*were*] ungainly that Star Trek opened with 'to boldly go where no man has gone before' " (John McWhorter at Forbes.com).

When an *as if* construction begins with *it was*, what follows is still untrue or hypothetical, so wreckless writers should be careful to stick with the subjunctive *were*. These examples get it right: "It was as if he were testing Don, whose moral makeup he doesn't seem to trust" (Slate.com); "It was as if she were visiting a convention of aunts and grandmas, rather than a foreign country" (*San Francisco Chronicle*). These examples get it wrong: "It was as if she was [*were*] stating a fact about the weather" (Selden Edwards, *The Little Book*); "It was as if she was [*were*] suddenly sitting there naked" (Richard Russo, *Empire Falls*).

Finally, *as if that weren't enough* is often miswritten *as if that wasn't enough*. The construction should have the subjunctive *were* because it implies a condition contrary to fact; it says, "That was plenty, but we're proceeding *as if it were not* and going over the top." In this passage, Bob Fischbach of the *Omaha World-Herald* uses the construction elegantly: "Here is a villain so black he would murder his brothers and young nephews, besmirch the reputation of his mother and lop off the heads of those loyal to him, all in his quest to hold the throne of England. *As if that weren't enough* to make him repulsive, he has a humpback, a shriveled arm and a bad leg, which might at least partly explain his deformed and diabolical mind."

ACCIDENT 344

Be careful how you use *not only . . . but also*

There are three pitfalls to look out for when using the construction *not only . . . but also*. First, you must make sure that the wording is parallel, meaning that what follows each element should be syntactically the same, as in these examples: "Massachusetts is not only liberal but also traditional" (*Washington Post*); "It hopes to tap not only local donors large and small but also successful Brooklynites" (*The New York Times*); "He looks like the sort of man who could not only own a Ferrari but also know how to drive one" (*BusinessWeek*). In the first sentence the elements frame two adjectives; in the second they frame two plural noun phrases; and in the third they frame two verb phrases.

When the syntax isn't grammatically parallel after each element, the sentence gets out of whack: "These buildings should not only be utilitarian but also appealing" (*Canton Daily Ledger*, Illinois). In that sentence the verb *be* is out of place; it should precede *not only* so that a single adjective follows both *not only* and *but also*.

See if you can detect the unparallel syntax in the following two examples: "The Pirates are not only a franchise committed to winning but also are doing every practical thing they can to win" (Bud Selig, commissioner of Major League Baseball, quoted in the *Pittsburgh Post-Gazette*); "Unemployment insurance is designed . . . with the goal of not only providing relief to the unemployed, but also to provide a countercyclical stimulus to the economy during periods of high unemployment" (MarketWatch.com).

To make the syntax parallel in the first sentence, *not only* needs to move forward: "The Pirates are a franchise committed not only to winning but also to doing every practical thing they can to win."

The second sentence, which suffers from wordiness as well as faulty parallelism, needs some pruning and reshaping to make things correspond: "Unemployment insurance is designed . . . not only to provide relief to the unemployed but also to provide . . ."

The second pitfall with *not only . . . but also* is inserting an unnecessary comma between the two elements. Here the comma before *but also* is like a pothole in the road: "In Prose's hands, Anne emerges as a writer not only by circumstance, but also by sensibility" (*Jewish Daily Forward*). And some comma-happy writers think that if a comma precedes *but also* there ought to be one before *not only* as well: "He said that he wants to 'bend' the cost curve, not only for government expenditures, but also for private-sector expenditures" (FOXNews.com). Both commas in that sentence are superfluous.

Finally, don't precede *not only . . . but also* with a redundant *but* or *also*. The following sentences are made clunky by this repetition: "But not only has the weird, small stuff hung around . . . but it also continues to be found by its audience" (*The New York Times Magazine*); "The further honoring of St. Louis' roots as an Olympic host, Viverito says, also would bolster not only its regional business connections but also perhaps its international opportunities" (*St. Louis Post-Dispatch*). In the first example, the opening *but* should be deleted. In the second, the *also* before *would bolster* should be cut.

ACCIDENT 345
Misuse of the verb *loathe* for the adjective *loath*

I'm generally a nice guy, but I'm not *loath* to say that I *loathe* the misuse of *loathe* for *loath*. Do you know the difference between these words?

The adjective *loath* (no *e* at the end) is a strong synonym of *reluctant*. When you are loath to do or say something, you are reluctant, unwilling, disinclined almost to the point of aversion or disgust. The verb to *loathe* (with an *e* at the end) means "to hate, despise, abhor." When you loathe something, you find it disgusting or despicable.

Loath and *loathe* are distinguished not only in spelling and meaning but also in pronunciation. The *th* in these words has a different sound. *Loathe* has the "voiced" *th* of *bathe* and *breathe* and rhymes with *clothe*. *Loath* has the "voiceless" *th* of *thin* and rhymes with *both* and *growth*.

I have heard some of the most prominent broadcasters on radio and TV use *loathe* when they mean *loath*, and the mistake often appears in print, even in the most prestigious publications: "Today, we are loathe [*loath*] to condemn anyone or anything for fear of being labeled ourselves as judgmental or politically incorrect" (Michiko Kakutani in *The New York Times Magazine*); "Talking at the debate about how she would 'positively affect the impacts' of the climate change for which she's loathe [*loath*] to acknowledge human culpability, [Sarah Palin] did a dizzying verbal loop-de-loop" (Maureen Dowd in *The New York Times*).

It's not hard to avoid this unfortunate accident of style and keep these two words straight if you remember these three things: (1) *loath* rhymes with *both* and *loathe* rhymes with *clothe;* (2) *loath* is followed by *to* while *loathe* should not be followed by *to;* and (3) when you *loathe* you hate, detest, so you must loathe *something*, but when you are *loath* you are reluctant, so you must be loath *to do something*.

ACCIDENT 346

Do not write *would have liked to have*

The wordy and grammatically contorted construction *would have liked to have* is a common blunder in speech that should not find its way into any kind of careful writing. What follows *would have liked* should be an infinitive, not another *have*.

"Some residents said they would have liked to have heard pros and cons of downsizing" (*Buffalo News*). Make that *would have liked to hear* or *wish they had heard* instead. "They would have liked to have served on the same ship, but the Navy would have none of that" (Cincinnati.com). That should have been *would have liked to serve* or *wish they had served*. "Yet he [Gordon Brown] gave the impression yesterday that he would have liked to have sat anywhere else in the Commons but for that front bench just near Tony Blair" (dailymail.co.uk). The headline for the article in which that last sentence appeared got it right: "Gordon *would have liked to sit* anywhere but near Tony." Rewording the offending sentence with *he would rather sit* would also have worked.

And here's one more—from the celebrated writer Gore Vidal, no less, as quoted in the online edition of *The New York Times*: "I would have liked to have been president, but I never had the money." Vidal should have said *I would have liked to be president* or *I wish I had been* (or *could have been*) *president*.

Don't use *nemesis* to mean "formidable rival or adversary"

"A nemesis," says *Bryson's Dictionary of Troublesome Words*, "is not merely a rival or traditional adversary . . . but one who exacts retributive justice or is utterly unvanquishable." In Greek mythology, explains the *Century Dictionary* (1914), Nemesis was "a goddess personifying allotment, or the divine distribution to every man of his precise share of fortune, good and bad. It was her especial function to see that the proper proportion of individual prosperity was preserved, and that any one who became too prosperous or was too much uplifted by his prosperity should be reduced or punished; she thus came to be regarded as the goddess of divine retribution."

Sportswriters are particularly enamored of using *nemesis* to mean "rival, adversary," often in the hackneyed phrase *old nemesis*: "Berlin Legion Facing Old Nemesis Manchester" (*Hartford Courant*); "The Mets rose up to batter their old nemesis, the Braves, 9–4" (*Star-Ledger*, New Jersey). Other writers pull *nemesis* out of their wordbag for any sort of enemy or antagonist: "That, and the fact that Mickey's gone missing, brings an old nemesis, LAPD Detective Bigfoot Bjornsen, down on Doc like a ton of bricks" (*Akron Beacon Journal*); "But that doesn't necessarily mean Iran will only be looking inward despite . . . a revival of attacks on old nemesis Britain and other European nations" (Associated Press).

Don't be an enemy of language who uses *nemesis* for any old rival or enemy. Be a wreckless writer who reserves this word for that which metes out retributive justice or that is impossible to overcome.

ACCIDENT 348

Misuse of the singular *minutia* for the plural *minutiae*

We often see the word *minutia* used to mean "minute details," as in *the gruesome minutia of a murder trial*, or "insignificant details," as in *try not to get sidetracked by minutia*. But such uses are tire-screeching accidents of style. The proper word for these senses is *minutiae*, differing by only one letter, a final *e*.

Minutia is a singular noun and *minutiae* is the plural: *this minutia is; these minutiae are*. Most contexts require the plural, but writers invariably get it wrong. In fact, when I checked the first fifty hits for *minutia* on Google News, the word was improperly used as a plural in every one. Some examples: "Why anybody would feel compelled to share the excruciatingly tedious minutia [*minutiae*] of their life is bewildering" (*Fort Worth Star-Telegram*); "Instead, Nutt is most interested in what many others would consider minutia [*minutiae*]" (*Jackson Clarion-Ledger*); "If you get caught up in the minutia of details [*in the minutiae*], it's a signal that you need to get away from things" (syndicated horoscope column by Holiday Mathis). In this last example, *minutia of details* is both a grammatical blunder and a redundancy.

It's next to impossible to find an example of the proper use of *minutia* as a singular noun. There was only one on Google News, and it was disappointingly tautological: "Each tiny piece of minutia [*Each minutia*] is chronicled in an encyclopedia of carefully constructed details" (newsinfilm.com). But examples of the plural *minutiae* used correctly are plentiful: "Their letters and diaries are full of the *minutiae* that make history vivid" (guardian.co.uk); "The Obama Administration is shifting its pitch for health care reform away from the *minutiae* of costs and insurance regulation" (npr.org).

A final note, on pronunciation: *minutia*, the singular, is pronounced mi-N[Y]OO-shuh or mi-N[Y]OO-shee-uh; *minutiae*, the plural, is pronounced mi-N[Y]OO-shee-ee.

ACCIDENT 349

There's a difference between *compared to* and *compared with*

"The guy who put a lit firecracker between his buttocks is a piker compared to the Russian soldiers who took a smoke break in an ammunition warehouse—the explosions went on for a week," writes Colette Bancroft in the *St. Petersburg Times* (Florida).

That's a funny sentence, but it misuses *compared to* for *compared with*.

There's a subtle and useful distinction between the two constructions that, sadly, is increasingly ignored, even by highly experienced wordslingers. In *The Careful Writer*, Theodore M. Bernstein explains the difference: "When the purpose is to liken two things or to put them in the same category, use *to*. When the purpose is to place one thing side by side with another, to examine their differences or their similarities, use *with*."

When you compare something *to* something else, you point out how the two things are alike in certain important respects: "Shall I compare thee *to* a summer's day?"; "Alexander Pope compared Homer's poetic talent *to* the river Nile overflowing its banks"; "You can't compare apples *to* oranges."

When you compare something *with* something else, you note how the two things stack up against each other: "Fourth-quarter earnings are down compared *with* the same quarter last year"; "Compared *with* the 1930s, today's economy seems robust"; "Obama has raised more than $450 million, compared *with* about $205 million for McCain."

The following examples all use the wrong preposition: "Obama's mortgage-assistance program is tiny compared to [*with*] the bank bailouts" (*The New Yorker*). "But it's almost nothing compared to [*with*] what we miss" (*San Jose Mercury News*); "The DIA's shortfalls are unusually large compared to [*with*] other major museums" (*Detroit Free Press*); "He had eight TDs after three games last year, compared to [*with*] five this season" (*Dallas Morning News*); "European economic leaders . . . were quick to highlight their banks' and insurers' relatively strong position compared to [*with*] their Wall Street peers" (*International Herald Tribune*).

Allison Aubrey got it right when she wrote on npr.org that "adults with the highest levels of BPA in their urine were more than twice as likely to report having diabetes or heart disease—compared *with* adults with the lowest levels of the chemical in their urine."

Richard Russo got it wrong when he opened his Pulitzer Prize–winning novel *Empire Falls* with this sentence: "Compared *to* the Whiting mansion in town, the house Charles Beaumont Whiting built a decade after his return to Maine was modest."

And though Michael Powell, writing in *The New York Times*, used *compared to* correctly in the following sentence, he took his eyes off the road and made a bush-league mistake: "Our autumn of disintegrating stock markets, disappearing credit and depressing unemployment numbers can not reasonably be compared to 1929 and its aftermath." Did you spot the boo-boo? *Can not* should have been *cannot*.

A search on Google News turned up 141,740 hits for *compared to*—compared with (not *to*) only 109,380 hits for *compared with*. It should be the other way around. Why? Because *compare to* is usually figurative and often literary ("Reading that book is perhaps best compared *to* wading through sludge"), while *compare with* is literal, indicating an ordinary side-by-side comparison ("The study compared organic produce *with* conventional produce"). Thus, says Bernstein, "the uses calling for *with* far outnumber those calling for *to*."

Unfortunately, most writers are indifferent to this fine distinction. Only one of the first forty Google News hits I got for *compared to* used the phrase correctly—a headline that read, "Wind damage compared to tornado."

A postscript to this discussion: Though *in comparison to* and *in comparison with* are historically interchangeable, the better choice is *in comparison with* because the phrase always refers to comparing one thing *with* another: "Elizabeth Edwards's memoir shows that the pain of infidelity pales in comparison to [*with*] the loss of a child" (*The Atlantic*). An even better choice is to use *compared with* instead of the wordier *in comparison with*.

ACCIDENT 350
Who and *whom*

Most of us probably wish that the pesky *whom* would just go away, as it has been trying to do for a long time with little success. I grew up in the 1960s and 1970s, when instruction in pseudoscientific "language arts" replaced the teaching of composition and grammar; consequently, I've never felt entirely comfortable with *whom*. Because of that unease and because in less than a second *whom* can make any sentence sound ten degrees stuffier, I try to avoid it. Even William Safire, who wrote the "On Language" column in *The New York Times Magazine* for thirty years, was uneasy about *whom*, so he came up with a rule for writers afflicted with *who/whom* anxiety: "When *whom* is correct, use some other formulation." More on that crafty suggestion in a moment.

Everyone is comfortable with the use of *whom* in well-worn phrases like *to whom it may concern* and *for whom the bell tolls*. And most of us can tell that it's not only stilted but also a mistake to sound like a hypercorrect British butler and say *Whom shall I say is calling?* because without that parenthetical *shall I say* it's obviously wrong to say *Whom is calling?* But beyond that, for many of us the gray grammatical fog starts to come on little cat feet and obscure our ability to distinguish these pronouns.

In traditional grammar, *whom* has two main functions. It can be the object of a verb: **Whom** *did you* **tell?** *The man* **whom** *the police* **arrested** *was released*. Or it can be the object of a preposition: *the person* **to whom** *they delivered the letter; the woman* **with whom** *I dined last night*.

Many usage guides recommend a simple substitution trick to help you tell whether *who* or *whom* is correct. If *he, she*, or *they* can take the place of the pronoun, it should be *who*. If *him, her*, or *them* can take the place of the pronoun, it should be *whom*. So if we ask *for whom the bell tolls* we know it has to toll for *him* (or *her* or *them*) and not for *he* (or *she* or *they*), so *whom* is correct. And *This is the candidate whom we like better* is also correct because we would say we like *him* or *her* better, not *he* or *she*. But *They hired a contractor whom they knew would do good work* is not right because we wouldn't say we knew *him* or *her* would do good work, so it should be *who*. With that sentence, and others like it, you can also remove any parenthetical words—in this case *they knew*—to strip things down to their bare grammatical bones: *They hired a contractor **who** would do good work.*

This trick won't save you in every instance with *who* and *whom*, but it should spare you error and embarrassment in most of your' writing. If the context is more complicated and you're unsure which word to use, you can follow Safire's rule and recast the sentence. For example, if you can't decide whether to write *the person who we spoke to* or *the person whom we spoke to* (it's *whom* because we spoke to *him* or *her*), you can always write *the person that we spoke to*. And if you're concerned about using *that* for a person (which you shouldn't be),* you can write *the person we spoke to*, which is tighter and smoother without any pronoun at all. So if you're waffling between *the oppressors who we struggle against* and *the oppressors whom we struggle against* (it's *whom* again because we struggle against *them*), just use *that* or no pronoun at all: *the oppressors [that] we struggle against.*

Now let's switch gears and look at where and when it's acceptable to use *who* instead of *whom*. A full-page ad for Barnes & Noble in *The Wall Street Journal* asks, "Who's Kidding Who?" Should that be *Who's Kidding Whom?* The cover of *Newsweek* asks, "Black Like Who?" Did they make a mistake? And the headline on the front page of *The New York Times Book Review* asks, "Who Do You Love?" Is that *who* wrong? Traditional grammar says yes, in all three cases it should be *whom*. But the practical, real-world answers to those questions, respectively, are yes, not really, and not anymore.

In the English language, idiom often trumps grammar. In other words, sometimes what feels right is preferable to what is right. It

---

*No matter what some may say, it has long been acceptable to use *that* with people (as in Mark Twain's 1899 story "The Man That Corrupted Hadleyburg"). The choice between *who* and *that* is merely a preference based on what a writer thinks works best in context. To quote just one of many authorities that (not *who*) sanction *that* for people as well as for things: "*That* for *who* is sometimes objected to, but the objection has no basis" (Roy H. Copperud, *American Usage and Style: The Consensus*).

should be *who's kidding whom* because in this case proper grammar—*who* is doing something to *whom*—is also the established idiom: "Look who's calling whom a liar now" (Associated Press); "Obama and Big Health: Who's Co-opting Whom?" (npr.org). But *Black Like Whom?*—in which *whom* is the object of the preposition *like*—is so painfully stilted that *Newsweek*'s editors decided to use the more natural and unpretentious wording instead. Finally, the editors at *The New York Times Book Review* chose to print the headline *Who Do You Love?* instead of *Whom Do You Love?* because 99.9 percent of us don't say it that way. We haven't used *whom* at the beginning of a question for a long time. We say *Who's that from? Who are you talking to? Who did you go with?* and *Who am I kidding?* We have also jettisoned *whom* when it's the object of a verb in constructions like *Do you know who I saw at the party? She doesn't care who you tell,* and *It's not what you know, it's who you know.*

So, don't be afraid to use *who* when it comes naturally to you and *whom* seems unidiomatic. But also be mindful that *whom* still plays a role in the language that should be respected.

Are You Roadworthy?

Just as every would-be driver must pass a road test before being allowed behind the wheel, so should anyone who aspires to write be required to demonstrate basic verbal competence before being licensed to cruise the highway of words.

Below are 125 quotations from newspapers, magazines, books, and sources on Google News. Each contains one, and occasionally more than one, accident of style discussed in this book. Try to (not *try and*) identify what's wrong in each quotation, then compare your work with (not *to*) the answers that follow the test. To be considered competent, you must score at least 90. A score of 115 or higher is wreckless.

1. Whose vision of patriotism is closest to your own, Obama's or McCain's?
2. This . . . will give the public their first chance to ask questions of the candidates.
3. The Bahamian lawyer accused of trying to blackmail John Travolta was caught on tape saying she felt badly about shaking down the actor so soon after his son's death.
4. And the general concensus is if an ABC soap is to go, it should be *All My Children*.
5. My band of right-wingers is reknown for its empathy.
6. Does your bank pay you back when you use another banks ATM?
7. To be safe we need to go back at least a couple generations.
8. Wait a minute—isn't "Whole Grain White Bread" a contradiction in terms? Evidently not any more.

9. Welch said many homeless people fall between the cracks and don't get some of those simple services.
10. But there's an old adage, often attributed to Mark Twain, that advises against picking fights with people who buy ink by the barrel.
11. Excellent renumeration package with great bonus earnings for right candidate.
12. The Welsh singer has scratched a number of dates due to strained vocal chords.
13. In 1999, ten years after the fall of the Wall, a survey found that East and West Germans were drifting farther and farther apart.
14. Multiple chemical sensitivity (MCS) affects men, women, and children irregardless of gender, race, and economic status.
15. The university's theater department had a culture of permissiveness in regards to teacher-student relationships.
16. When Southwest first announced it would fly from Boston to Baltimore for $49 each way, JetBlue added a route there too.
17. There is a handful of titles that are considered the movie masterpieces you must see.
18. Souter was one of those old-line Yankee Republicans, a man who had the temerity to exhibit an independent streak and not simply tow the line.
19. Bill authored by Yee may give cops more money to fight human trafficking.
20. Rep. Bob Filner . . . said he expects San Diegans will have a chance to see "some of the polarization that this process has affected."
21. Chipotle Mexican Grill is testing a kid's menu in its twenty-one Sacramento-area restaurants, starting on October 12.
22. Subscribers to both the print and online editions would get it for free.
23. I would just as soon avoid him all together.
24. The large playing fields will be covered with artificial turf and completely surrounded by a sixteen-foot-high chain-link fence.
25. A man is fighting for his life after being shot Sunday night outside of his home.

26. Saudi Arabia cut its production last year in order to prop up world oil prices.

27. Canadian Pacific says no final decision has been made to permanently shelve the expansion into the coal-producing region.

28. Space is limited, so attendance will be on a first-come, first-serve basis.

29. Despite some dissent . . . they continued on for six hundred miles.

30. And that is also the main reason why the stock is where it is at now.

31. Lowe is accused of robbing jewelry with a retail value of about $1 million.

32. Buying votes is not a new phenomena in Lebanon.

33. At some point in time, Republicans are going to have to do something other than just vote no.

34. Their home is still in the process of being renovated after Hurricane Katrina.

35. Each branch has also been open one fewer hour Monday through Thursday and two fewer hours on Saturdays.

36. Have a complaint about your broker? You better have proof.

37. Historians are certainly within their rights in trying to supplement the historic facts with some guesses about the influences of the time and the place.

38. Let's get the pronounciation of your name correct. I've heard it in many ways.

39. The note was discovered in a safety deposit box shortly after [Damon Runyon] died in December 1946.

40. He has overcome these kind of odds before.

41. If I am fortunate enough to share a stage with this president and debate him, one of the first things I'll tell him is there's a defining issue between he and I.

42. My younger sister, kid brother, and myself were assigned rooms that were unremarkable.

43. Dr. Hansen of the ASPCA advises against applying flea powders and sprays in addition to a spot-on treatment because chemicals in different products could interact with each other.

44. The Bush-era policy . . . remains for all intensive purposes in effect.
45. The Center for Biological Diversity said that it would poll its members as to whether it should replace Verizon as its cellphone carrier.
46. But on Saturday, the leading man snuck away from the set so the trio could stroll along the Charles River and play at a nearby park.
47. There were probably leagues set up just for boys like himself.
48. Having said that, there will be a natural decline in new-vehicle sales for the rest of the year.
49. It reminds of the Anglo-French attack on Suez in 1956.
50. Those alternatives are far more preferable than risking disrupting or distracting those who are in synagogues to pray for the coming year.
51. Maine yielded just three hits and struck out five prior to leaving.
52. Wherever one goes in America, the people one meets are probably kin, if you look back far enough.
53. Mr. Yoo is one of those who wrote memos laying out the legal parameters for aggressive interrogation of al Qaeda captives.
54. George parodies politicians who say they are personally opposed to abortion but support women's legal right to choose.
55. I cannot support her nomination because I'm not persuaded that she has the right judicial philosophy for the Supreme Court.
56. Beachwater pollution comes from a variety of different sources.
57. In June, Neil Patrick Harris emceed the Tony Awards for CBS, earning good reviews while boosting the audience tuning in to these theater kudos.
58. Then I flipped to MSNBC, and lo! . . . they had the exact same two clips.
59. She is an alumni of Notre Dame.
60. She waved her arms to try and save herself, but she was too far off-balance and had to jump off.
61. Neither Williams nor Earley were prepared to reveal exactly what was said to the lineswoman.

62. The reported shootings occurred before talks with international monitors Thursday on efforts to diffuse tensions in the region.

63. It will reoccur every two years, with the next one scheduled in 2011.

64. Thrift has always been a morally charged category, used to define a vision of the good life and to separate out the upright and righteous from the prodigal and wayward.

65. But there is still the usual mountain of work to do at home—homework, laundry, dinner, dishes and etc.

66. When children get sick with the flu they tend to spread it quickly because they congregate together.

67. David Douglass wore the sweater to help him emulate Hemingway's look in a *Life* magazine cover from 1957.

68. Photo booths are enjoying a healthy revival at events such as parties and weddings, where they provide a fun picture-taking experience for guests.

69. Panicked Muslims clamor up the gangplank to a ferry, lugging whatever possessions they can manage.

70. Keeping the faith is one thing, paying for a ticket is something else entirely.

71. Not speaking until age six, his world is filled with numbers and colors.

72. There should be more to a cabin than simply an inexpensive motel room built in close proximity to lots of trees.

73. A sitting parent, for example, might earn one point per each child.

74. The team also removed a few elements that didn't jive with this year's theme.

75. Countering the Republicans, Pelosi convenes Democrats to talk faith.

76. Each and every one of you are my heroes.

77. In a bid to infuse the story with continual drama, Conroy aggregates tragedies to an implausible degree.

78. Worse, he woke that morning almost nauseous with the understanding that the night before he'd actually eaten a snail.

79. Neither video is particularly convincing as a piece of documentary evidence, owing to the fact that you can't really tell who's standing where when they throw the ball.

80. Many influential gay rights groups fear a fight in federal court will ultimately end up before a U.S. Supreme Court comprised of a socially conservative majority that could deal the same-sex marriage campaign a significant setback with an adverse ruling.

81. *Paper Heart* sets the dials on the wayback machine even further, giving us adult characters so childish you want to give them milk and cookies.

82. I did this in one of the worst economic crisises of our century, and I was able to get financing for this project because of their help and their support.

83. Rosie cracked jokes about *The View*, illiciting roars of laughter from the audience.

84. Traffic officers will go after drivers who flaunt the state's hands-free cellphone law.

85. Ensure all promises made verbally are included, in writing, in the contract.

86. Both of the protesters were later released.

87. Corrections officials agreed to stop using race as the sole criteria for assigning bunks in the reception centers.

88. Adam Duritz, the Counting Crows frontman famous for both his dreadlocks and dating record, is back in the spotlight.

89. As far as the claim for Leonard's front door, Guglielmi said the estimate for repairs was high enough that the claim will have to go through the Board of Estimates.

90. She tells parents to lie prone and place their babies on top of them, face-to-face.

91. Lynchburg is presently facing a $500,000 free-speech complaint from a city detective.

92. His campaign is cheapening his greatest strength—and making a mockery of his already dubious claim that he's reticent to talk about his POW experience.

93. The alarm clock is set to give us precisely enough time to . . .

get ready for work and grab some breakfast before hitting the road. We're very economic with our time.

94. Allred filed a lawsuit Monday demanding a guardian be assigned to steward the money generated by the octuplet infants borne to Octomom Nadya Suleman.

95. Suffice to say, it was not exactly ladylike.

96. We can still hear his voice bellowing through the Senate chamber, face reddened, fist pounding the podium.

97. Buying at the rate of fifty books a week has clearly made it impossible for him to read most of his purchases, though he strives at least to peruse each one.

98. The president has been one of the only honest brokers in this entire process.

99. Sennheiser announces a plethora of new headphones.

100. This is one of those rare works that does equal justice to the standards of the academy and to an intelligent reader's desire to be both edified and entertainingly engaged.

101. What it is, is meat pounded thin, coated in egg and bread crumbs and sautéed in butter.

102. I know if we would have been at Acadia on Sunday, there would have been a lot of arguing over how close to get.

103. This was a case of years of tortuous abuse.

104. Also, you would have to make sure you would be able to afford the payments on it if worse comes to worse.

105. He now serves on numerous company boards and has just recently released his first documentary film.

106. The Fed is far more likely than Congress or the White House to make a decision on the merits rather than on the politics.

107. Police have not revealed a supposed motive for the crime, which they have referred to as an incidence of "workplace violence."

108. Even at five in the morning on a Tuesday, it's liable to be more lively than your average main street or shopping mall.

109. Such historical analogies are overly simplistic and fatally flawed, if only because each presidency is distinct in its own way.

110. The company would not be adverse to buying another real estate investment trust.

111. But after his tax increase proposal floundered last summer, the governor cut state-supported drug treatment programs by tens of millions of dollars.

112. The film sets up Howard as being Mary's alternate love interest.

113. He only writes about beverages that are available in South Carolina and Georgia.

114. As an expert on German cinema he could go to a Third Reich film shindig and be able to mix it up with the hoi polloi.

115. The reason we see so much chronic disease in the West is because these are illnesses that appear relatively late in life.

116. But he is small, not blazingly fast, and nineteen years old—all factors that mitigate against making an instant impact in the NHL.

117. During the past several days we have seen close up yet another measure of the enormity of Ted Kennedy's presence in the life of this community.

118. Striking Iran's nuclear program will not be precipitous or poorly thought out.

119. A memorial bears his name and the names of the thirty-nine others on slabs of purposefully unfinished stone.

120. We are all familiar with the right to bear arms and the noisome extremes indulged in by its zealots.

121. There will be a time when those who use to invest . . . can put away their tools and rest on their labors.

122. Peter was dressed as if it was a cold day when it was actually in the high seventies.

123. The Pirates are not only a franchise committed to winning but also are doing every practical thing they can to win.

124. Today, we are loathe to condemn anyone or anything for fear of being labeled ourselves as judgmental or politically incorrect.

125. Compared to the Whiting mansion in town, the house Charles Beaumont Whiting built a decade after his return to Maine was modest.

Answers to "Are You Roadworthy?"

1. *Closest* should be *closer*.
2. *Their* should be *its*.
3. *Badly* should be *bad*.
4. *General consensus* is redundant for *consensus*, and *consensus* is misspelled.
5. *Reknown* should be *renowned*.
6. *Banks* should be *bank's*.
7. *A couple* should be *a couple of*.
8. *Any more* should be *anymore*.
9. *Between the cracks* should be *through the cracks*.
10. *Old adage* is redundant and should be either *adage* or *old saying*.
11. *Renumeration* should be *remuneration*.
12. It should be *vocal cords*.
13. It should be *further and further apart*.
14. *Irregardless* should be *regardless*.
15. *In regards to* should be *regarding* or *concerning*.
16. Delete the redundant *first*.
17. *Is a handful* should be *are a handful*.
18. *Tow the line* should be *toe the line*.
19. *Authored* should be *sponsored*.
20. *Affected* should be *effected*.
21. *Kid's menu* should be *kids' menu*.
22. *Get it for free* should be *get it free*.
23. *All together* should be *altogether*.
24. *Completely surrounded* should be *surrounded*.
25. Delete *of* after *outside*.
26. Delete the superfluous *in order*.
27. Delete *final*.
28. Make it *first-come, first-served*.
29. Change *continued on* to *continued* or *went on*.
30. Delete *at*.
31. *Robbing* should be *stealing*.
32. *Phenomena* should be *phenomenon*.
33. *At some point in time* should be *at some point*.

34. Delete *in the process of.*
35. *One fewer hour* should be *one less hour.* But *two fewer hours* is correct.
36. *You better* should be *you had better.*
37. *Historic facts* should be *historical facts.*
38. *Pronunciation* is misspelled.
39. *Safety deposit box* should be *safe-deposit box.*
40. *These kind* should be *these kinds.*
41. *Between he and I* should be *between him and me.*
42. *Myself* should be *I.*
43. *Interact with each other* should be *interact.*
44. *For all intensive purposes* should be *for all intents and purposes.*
45. *As to* should be *about* or *on.*
46. *Snuck* should be *sneaked.*
47. *Himself* should be *him.*
48. *There will be a natural decline* cannot follow *Having said that* because the introductory modifying phrase needs a personal subject to tie it to the sentence.
49. *It reminds of* should be *It reminds me of* (or *one*).
50. *Far more preferable than* should be *much preferable to.*
51. *Prior to* should be *before.*
52. *You look* should be *one looks,* or *one goes* and *one meets* should be *you go* and *you meet.*
53. *Parameters* is misused here for *guidelines* or *justification.*
54. *Personally* is superfluous and should be deleted.
55. *Persuaded* should be *convinced.*
56. *Variety of different* is redundant. Use *variety* or *different.*
57. *Kudos* is not a proper plural noun, and it is not a synonym of *awards.*
58. *The exact same* should be either *the same* or *exactly the same.*
59. *Alumni* should be *alumna.*
60. *Try and* should be *try to.*
61. Change *were* to *was* because *neither* takes a singular verb.
62. *Diffuse* should be *defuse.*
63. *Reoccur* should be *recur.*
64. Delete *out* after *separate.*

65. Change *and etc.* to *etc.*
66. *Congregate together* is redundant. Use *congregate* alone or some other wording.
67. *Emulate* should be *imitate.*
68. *Fun* as an adjective is loose and juvenile usage.
69. *Clamor* should be *clamber.*
70. Change the comma to a semicolon or period to repair the comma splice.
71. *Not speaking until age six* can't logically modify *his world.* To fix this dangler, change *his world is filled with numbers and colors* to *he lives in a world filled with numbers and colors.*
72. *Close proximity* is redundant; replace it with *near.*
73. *Per each* should be either *per* alone or *for each.*
74. *Jive* should be *jibe.*
75. *Democratics* should be *Democrats.*
76. *Each and every* is redundant; use *each* or *every* alone. Also, *are* should be *is* and *heroes* should be *hero.* Or you can recast the sentence in the plural: *All of you are my heroes.*
77. *Continual* should be *continuous.*
78. *Nauseous* should be *nauseated.*
79. *Owing to the fact that* should be *because.*
80. *Comprised of* should be *composed of.*
81. *Childish* should be *childlike.*
82. *Crisises* should be *crises.*
83. *Illiciting* should be *eliciting.*
84. *Flaunt* should be *flout.*
85. *Verbally* should be *orally.*
86. Delete *of the*, which is often unnecessary after *both.*
87. *Criteria* should be *criterion.*
88. Insert *his* before *dating* so that *both* modifies syntactically parallel elements.
89. Insert *is concerned* after *front door,* so that *as far as* is supported by a verb.
90. *Prone* should be *supine.*
91. *Presently* is superfluous here and should be deleted.
92. *Reticent* should be *reluctant.*

93. *Economic* should be *economical.*

94. *Borne* should be *born.*

95. Insert *it* after *suffice.*

96. *Podium* should be *lectern.*

97. *Peruse* should be *skim* or *browse.*

98. *One of the only* should be *one of the few* or *perhaps the only.*

99. *Plethora* should be *abundance* or *many.*

100. *Does* should be *do* because a plural verb should follow *one of the/those* [plural noun] *that/who . . .*

101. *What it is, is* should be *It is* or *It's.*

102. *Would have been* should be *had been.*

103. *Tortuous* should be *torturous.*

104. It should be *worse comes to worst.*

105. *Just recently* is redundant; use *just* or *recently.*

106. *Make a decision* should be *decide.*

107. *Incidence* should be *instance.*

108. *Liable* should be *likely.*

109. Delete the redundant *overly* in *overly simplistic.*

110. *Adverse* should be *averse.*

111. *Floundered* should be *foundered.*

112. *Alternate* should be *alternative.*

113. *Only writes* should be *writes only.*

114. *Hoi polloi* means "the common people," not "an elite or special group."

115. The sentence needs to be recast to avoid the redundant *the reason . . . is because:* "We see so much chronic disease in the West because these are illnesses that appear relatively late in life."

116. *Mitigate against* should be *militate against.*

117. *Enormity* ("monstrous evil") is misused here to mean "prodigious extent."

118. *Precipitous* should be *precipitate.*

119. *Purposefully* should be *purposely.*

120. *Noisome* ("extremely unpleasant or disgusting") is misused here to mean "outrageous, disgraceful, shocking."

121. *Use to* should be *used to.*

122. The second *was* in the sentence should be the subjunctive *were*.

123. The sentence bungles the *not only . . . but also* construction, which must frame syntactically parallel elements. It should read like this: "The Pirates are a franchise committed *not only* to winning *but also* to doing every practical thing they can to win."

124. *Loathe* should be *loath*.

125. *Compared to* should be *compared with*.

BIBLIOGRAPHY

The American Heritage Dictionary. 2nd college ed. Boston: Houghton Mifflin Company, 1985.

The American Heritage Dictionary of the English Language. 4th ed. Boston: Houghton Mifflin Company, 2000.

The American Heritage Guide to Contemporary Usage and Style. Boston and New York: Houghton Mifflin Company, 2005.

Apostrophe Protection Society. http://www.apostrophe.org.uk.

Barzun, Jacques. *Simple and Direct: A Rhetoric for Writers.* New York: Harper & Row, 1985.

————. *A Word or Two Before You Go.* Middletown, CT: Wesleyan University Press, 1986.

Baugh, L. Sue. *Essentials of English Grammar.* 2nd ed. Lincolnwood, IL: Passport Books, 1993.

Bernstein, Theodore. *The Careful Writer.* New York: Atheneum, 1983.

————. *Dos, Don'ts, and Maybes of English Usage.* New York: Times Books, 1977.

————. *Miss Thistlebottom's Hobgoblins.* New York: Simon & Schuster, 1971.

Brians, Paul. *Common Errors in English.* Wilsonville, OR: William, James & Co., 2003.

Brockenbrough, Martha. *Things That Make Us [Sic].* New York: St. Martin's Press, 2008.

Bryson, Bill. *Bryson's Dictionary of Troublesome Words.* New York: Broadway Books, 2002.

Burchfield, Robert. *The New Fowler's Modern English Usage.* 3rd ed. Oxford: Clarendon Press, 1996.

Casagrande, June. *Grammar Snobs Are Great Big Meanies.* New York: Penguin Books, 2006.

———. *Mortal Syntax.* New York: Penguin Books, 2008.

The Chicago Manual of Style. 15th ed. Chicago and London: University of Chicago Press, 2003.

Claiborne, Robert. *Saying What You Mean.* New York and London: W. W. Norton & Company, 1986.

Cook, Claire Kehrwald. *Line by Line: How to Improve Your Own Writing.* Boston: Houghton Mifflin, 1985.

Copperud, Roy H. *American Usage and Style: The Consensus.* New York: Van Nostrand Reinhold, 1980.

Davidson, Mark. *Right, Wrong, and Risky.* New York: W. W. Norton & Company, 2006.

Davies, Robertson. *The Enthusiams of Robertson Davies.* Ed. Judith Skelton Grant. New York: Penguin Books, 1990.

Elster, Charles Harrington. *The Big Book of Beastly Mispronunciations: The Complete Opinionated Guide for the Careful Speaker.* Boston and New York: Houghton Mifflin Company, 2006.

———. *Verbal Advantage: 10 Easy Steps to a Powerful Vocabulary.* New York: Random House, 2000.

———. *What in the Word? Wordplay, Word Lore, and Answers to Your Peskiest Questions About Language.* New York: Harcourt, 2005.

Evans, Bergen. *Comfortable Words.* New York: Random House, 1959.

Evans, Bergen, and Cornelia Evans. *A Dictionary of Contemporary American Usage.* New York: Random House, 1957.

Ferguson, Don K. *Grammar Gremlins.* Lakewood, CO: Glenbridge Publishing, 1995.

Fine, Edith H., and Judith P. Josephson. *More Nitty-Gritty Grammar.* Berkeley, CA: Ten Speed Press, 2001.

———. *Nitty-Gritty Grammar.* Berkeley, CA: Ten Speed Press, 1998.

Fiske, Robert Hartwell. *The Dimwit's Dictionary.* Oak Park, IL: Marion Street Press, 2002.

Flesch, Rudolf. *The ABC of Style: A Guide to Plain English.* New York: Harper & Row, 1964.

Fogarty, Mignon. *Grammar Girl's Quick and Dirty Tips for Better Writing*. New York: Henry Holt and Company, 2008.

Follett, Wilson. *Modern American Usage*. Rev. Erik Wensberg. New York: Hill and Wang, 1998.

Fowler, H. W. *The King's English*. 3rd ed. Oxford: Oxford University Press, 1931.

———. *Modern English Usage*. Oxford: Clarendon Press, 1926.

Garner, Bryan A. *Garner's Modern American Usage*. Oxford and New York: Oxford University Press, 2003.

Gilman, E. Ward, ed. *Merriam-Webster's Dictionary of English Usage*. Springfield, MA: Merriam-Webster, 1994.

Goldstein, Norm, ed. *The Associated Press Stylebook and Briefing on Media Law*. Cambridge, MA: Perseus Publishing, 2000.

Gowers, Sir Ernest. *The Complete Plain Words*. London: Her Majesty's Stationery Office, 1954.

Hale, Constance. *Sin and Syntax*. New York: Broadway Books, 1999.

Hendrickson, Robert. *The Facts on File Encyclopedia of Word and Phrase Origins*. 3rd ed. New York: Checkmark Books, 2004.

Hook, J. N. *The Appropriate Word*. Reading, MA: Addison-Wesley, 1990.

Johnson, Edward D. *The Handbook of Good English*. New York: Washington Square Press, 1991.

Kilpatrick, James J. *The Writer's Art*. Kansas City and New York: Andrews, McMeel & Parker, 1984.

Lederer, Richard. *Crazy English*. New York: Pocket Books, 1998.

Lederer, Richard, and Richard Dowis. *Sleeping Dogs Don't Lay*. New York: St. Martin's Press, 1999.

———. *The Write Way: The S.P.E.L.L. Guide to Real-Life Writing*. New York: Pocket Books, 1995.

Lovinger, Paul W. *The Penguin Dictionary of American English Usage and Style*. New York: Penguin Reference, 2000.

Merriam-Webster's Collegiate Dictionary. 11th ed. Springfield, MA: Merriam-Webster, 1998.

Morris, William, and Mary Morris. *The Harper Dictionary of Contemporary Usage*. 2nd ed. New York: Harper & Row, 1985.

Morton, Mark. *Cupboard Love: A Dictionary of Culinary Curiosities*. Winnipeg, Canada: Bain & Cox, 1996.

The New Oxford American Dictionary. New York and Oxford: Oxford University Press, 2001.

O'Conner, Patricia T. *Woe Is I*. New York: Riverhead Books, 2003.

The Oxford English Dictionary. 2nd ed. Oxford: Clarendon Press (Oxford University Press), 1989.

Partridge, Eric. *Usage and Abusage*. New York and London: W. W. Norton & Company, 1997.

Quinion, Michael. http://www.worldwidewords.org.

Random House Webster's College Dictionary. New York: Random House, 2001.

Safire, William. *Coming to Terms*. New York: Doubleday, 1991.

———. *On Language*. New York: Avon Books, 1980.

Shaw, Harry. *Dictionary of Problem Words and Expressions*. New York: McGraw-Hill Book Company, 1975.

Siegal, Allan M., and William G. Connolly. *The New York Times Manual of Style and Usage*. New York: Times Books, 1999.

Stimpson, George. *A Book About a Thousand Things*. New York and London: Harper & Brothers Publishers, 1946.

Strunk, William, Jr., and E. B. White. *The Elements of Style*. 4th ed. Boston: Allyn and Bacon, 2000.

Tarshis, Barry. *Grammar for Smart People*. New York: Pocket Books, 1992.

Wallraff, Barbara. *Word Court*. New York: Harcourt, 2000.

Walsh, Bill. *The Elephants of Style*. New York: McGraw-Hill, 2004.

———. *Lapsing Into a Comma*. New York: McGraw-Hill, 2000.

Webster's New International Dictionary. 2nd ed. Springfield, MA: G. & C. Merriam, 1941.

Webster's New World College Dictionary. 4th ed. New York: Macmillan, 1999.

Whitney, William Dwight, and Benjamin E. Smith, eds. *The Century Dictionary: An Encyclopedic Lexicon of the English Language*. New York: Century, 1914.

Witherspoon, Alexander M. *Common Errors in English and How to Avoid Them*. Totowa, NJ: Rowman & Allanheld, 1982.

a, an, the, in a title, 211
A.D., misuse of, 223
ABC News, 49, 84
ABC of Style, The (Flesch), 85, 91, 157
abridgment
    misspelling of, 34
absolutely, avoid using, 96–97
accidentally
    misspelling of, 16–17
accommodate
    misspelling of, 78
according to Webster, 122
AceShowbix.com, 74
acknowledgment
    misspelling of, 34
ad nauseam/ad nauseum, 77, 115
adage, using "old" with, 50–51
adjective, 33
    misusing superlative, 51–52
admission/admittance, 184
adverb/compound verb, 221–22
adverbiage, 33
adverbs, 33–34
adverse/averse, 203
affect/effect, 30–31
again, *repeat* used with, 168–69
all right/alright, 24
All Things Considered (NPR), 43, 97, 236

all-time record
    as phrase to avoid, 79
allegedly, misuse of, 135
Allentown Morning Call (PA), 188
Allentown Morning Call, 102
almost instead of *most*, 79
alot/a lot, 15
altercation, proper use of, 242
alternate/alternative, 208–9
altogether/all together, 73–74
alum/alumni, 140
ambiguity/ambivalence, 63
American Conservative
    website, 133
American Dictionary of the English Language, An (Webster), 122
American Heritage Book of English Usage, 182
American Heritage Dictionary, 43, 96, 119, 124, 151, 152, 182, 183, 216, 229–30
American Heritage Guide to Contemporary Usage and Style, 41–42, 182
American Journal of Preventive Medicine, 110
American Spectator, 145
American Thinker, 145

American Usage and Style: The Consensus (Copperud), 182, 209, 254n
amid/amidst, 90
among/amongst, 90
among/between, 111–12
amount, misuse of, 28–29
and/or, avoid using, 69–70
and etc., 144–45
and so on and so forth, 77
anniversary, misuse of, 89
anticipate/expect, 191–92
anxious/eager, 143–44
any more/anymore, 58–59
any time/anytime, 2, 132
anyway/any way/anyways, 15–16
Apostrophe Protection Society, 60
apostrophes, 60–63
apotheosis, 243
Appropriate Word, The (Hook), 181
arctic/artic, 44–45
  capitalization, 45
Arizona Daily Star, 66
Arizona Daily Wildcat, 26
Arizona Republic, 83
Arizona Silver Belt, 28
Arizona Star, 232
Arkansas Times, 162
Arlington Times (WA), 108
Armstrong, Louis, 28
artdaily.org, 126
as best/as best as, 110
as far as, 173
as if . . . were/as if . . . was, 244–46
Asheville Citizen-Times, 65
Asia Times online, 234
Associated Press, 14, 72, 88, 89, 91, 103, 122, 132, 161, 170, 182, 207, 236, 249

Associated Press Stylebook, 133, 192
AssociatedContent.com, 26, 49
assure/insure/ensure, 102–3
at. See redundant *at*
at this [particular] point in time, 87
Atlanta Journal-Constitution, 55–56, 151, 168, 213, 217
Atlantic magazine, 132, 210, 223, 252
  online, 23, 129, 165
ATM machine, 179–80
au jus/with au jus, 43–44
Aubrey, Allison, 252
Austin American-Statesman, 144–45
Austin Daily Herald, 188
author as verb, 68
averse/adverse, 203
awesome, avoiding, 53–54

babychums.com, 144
bacteria, 220–21
bad/badly, 54–55
Baltimore Sun, 14, 53, 72, 79, 159, 173, 186, 195, 217, 240
Bancroft, Colette, 251
Barzun, Jacques, 33–34, 228
Basketball Basics, How to Play Like the Pros (Triano), 36
bated breath/baited breath, 125
Bay City Daily Tribune, 242
BBC News, 71, 76, 102, 109, 214, 231, 239
before, 121–22
beg the question, 227–28
begin
  use instead of *commence*, 76–77
Beginner's Greek (Collins), 110
Belfast Telegraph, 78
Bergman, Gregory, 19

Bernstein, Theodore M., 101, 117,
    121, 138, 139, 154, 170–71,
    240, 251, 252
bestsyndication.news, 23
between/among, 111–12
between (for, to) you and me/
    between (for, to) you and I,
    104–5
between this and that/between
    this to that, 147
beyond the pale/beyond the pail,
    113–14
bi- (as prefix), 119–20
Biden, Joe, 39
Bierman, Fred, 193
birminghampost.net, 216–17
BizzWords (Bergman), 19
black-eyed/black-eye/blackeye, 43
BlackBook Magazine, 191
Blogosphere Blowhardese, 62
Blue Mountain Courier-Herald
    (Canada), 199
Bolton, John, 234
Bon Appétit, 152, 231
Booher, Dianna, 227
Book About a Thousand Things, A
    (Stimpson), 65
Booklist, 175
bored with/bored by/bored of, 79
borne/born, 181
Boston Globe, 14, 28, 41, 69, 90,
    98, 100, 112, 122, 152, 155,
    165, 179, 220, 222, 230, 238
Boston Herald, 21
both, 170–71
Bowling Green Daily News, 89
BoxingScene.com, 171
Bradenton Herald (FL), 113
Bradford, Jim, 178
Brandeis Hoot, 197

Bricker, Charles, 1
BroadbandReports, 21
Brockenbrough, Martha, 66
Brooks, David, 233
Brose, Christian, 215
Bryson's Dictionary of Troublesome
    Words, 24, 32, 85, 123, 152,
    156, 169, 169–70, 170, 182,
    191, 213, 216, 219, 224, 232,
    249
Buffalo News, 123, 170, 210, 248
Burchfield, Robert W., 218
buses/busses, 26–27
Business Day, 154, 234
Business Standard, 210
BusinessWeek, 16, 113, 175, 246
but hey, 49–50
by accident/on accident, 27

cacoëthes, 216, 216n
can and may, 85–86
Canton Daily Ledger (IL), 246
Cape Cod Times, 130
capitolweekly.net, 103
careerandjobsUK.com, 62
Careful Writer, The (Bernstein),
    101, 121, 138, 139, 170–71,
    240, 251
Casagrande, June, 59
catachresis, 1n
cave in to/cave to, 77
CBS News, 55, 97, 175
CBSNews.com, 161
CBSSports.com, 32
Century Dictionary, 117n, 249
chaise longue, 52
champing/chomping, 118
ChannelWeb, 245
Charleston Gazette (WV), 145, 199
Chesterton Tribune (IN), 172

Chicago Daily Herald, 27, 173
Chicago Manual of Style, The, 62,
  207, 211, 234
Chicago Sun-Times, 169, 242
  online, 24
Chicago Tribune, 17, 31, 32, 89, 109,
  126, 130, 167, 184, 190, 240
childish/childlike, 161–62
ChipleyBugle.com, 156
Chomsky, Noam, 136
Christian Science Monitor, 27, 111,
  199, 200
Claiborne, Robert, 117
clamor/clamber, 148–49
Cleveland Plain Dealer, 35, 56, 239
cliché, using old with, 50–51
close proximity, 151–52
CNNMoney.com, 48, 83
coincidentally
  misspelling of, 16–17
Collins, James, 110
colon
  how not to use, 232–34
colons and semicolons
  parentheses and quotation
    marks and, 224
Colorado Springs Independent, 169
Colorado Valley Courier, 209
Combs, Britt, 124
Comfortable Words (Evans), 130
comic/comical, 93
commas, 135–39
  quotation marks and, 40
commence
  use begin instead, 76–77
  use start instead, 76–77
compare/contrast, 109–10
compared to/compared with,
  251–52
comprise/make up, 160

ComputerWorld, 176, 203
concise alternatives to verbose
  phrases, 145–47
congregate together/congregate in
  groups, 147
consensus/concensus, 56
consensus of opinion
  as phrase to avoid, 56–57
ConsumerAffairs.com, 42, 48
continue on
  as phrase to avoid, 83–84
continuous/continual, 156–57
converse/conversate, 60
convince/persuade, 99–100
Cook, Claire Kehrwald, 138, 139
Copperud, Roy H., 182, 209,
  254n
Copyediting newsletter, 172
Corpus Christi Caller-Times, 89
Cothern, Andrew, 19
could have/could of, 34–35
could not care less/could care less,
  108–9
Council on Foreign Relations, 165
Cowan, Alison Leigh, 99
Cox Newspapers, 147
Crafts, K., 188
Crazy English (Lederer), 242n
crises as plural of crisis, 165–66
criteria/criterion, 169
critical, overuse of, 195
couple of/couple, 59
Culver, Chet, 103
Cupboard Love: A Dictionary
  of Culinary Curiosities
  (Morton), 82
cut-and-dried/cut-and-dry, 88

Daily Nonpareil, 103
Daily Mail (UK), 161–62, 171

dailymail.co.uk, 248–49
Dallas Morning News, 28, 50, 55,
71, 91, 121, 129, 204, 251
dangling participles, 149–51
Davidson, Mark, 14, 23, 76,
98–99, 110, 133, 139, 159,
160, 170, 181
daylight saving time/daylight
savings time, 133
Dayton Daily News, 139
Daytona Beach News-Journal, 221
decide/make a decision, 196
delve into/dwell into, 97
demise, 176
Democratic Party/Democrat
Party, 152–53
Denver Business Journal, 29
Denver Post, 66
Dershowitz, Alan M., 138
Des Moines Register, 90
DesMoinesRegister.com, 19
Detroit Free Press, 24, 27, 251
Dickens, Charles, 108
differing/different, 241
diffuse/defuse, 235–36
dire straits, 129–30
disinterested/uninterested, 231–32
doctoral/doctorial, 100–101
doctorate/doctorate degree,
100–101
Dos, Don'ts, and Maybes of English
Usage (Bernstein), 154
Dover-Sherborn Press, 225
Dowd, Maureen, 174, 182, 248
Dowis, Richard, 186, 225
due to the fact that, 158

E-Writing (Booher), 227
each, 155–56
eager/anxious, 143–44

Eagle Valley Daily Enterprise, 117
East Oregonian, 195
Eastern Arizona Courier, 78
economic/economical, 178
Economic Times, 149
ecstasy/ecstacy, 21
Editor and Publisher magazine, 109
Edwards, Selden, 73–74, 234, 245
effect, 47
eGruve.com, 215
Elements of Style, The (White,
E. B.), 31, 130, 179, 210
elicit/illicit, 166
embarrass
misspelling of, 62
emigrate/immigrate, 175
eminent/imminent, 121
emissive, 39, 39n
Empire Falls (Russo), 107, 159,
226, 245, 252
Emporia Gazette (KS), 188
emulate/imitate, 144
enervate/energize, 164–65
English words vs. non-English
words, 153
enormity/enormousness, 229–30
ensure/assure/insure, 102–3
Entertainment Weekly, 14, 56, 177
website, 121
ESPN/ESPN.com, 32, 127, 167,
210, 218
ESPNOutdoors.com, 74
espresso, misspelling of, 22
Esquire magazine, 200
Evans, Bergen, 130
every, 155–56
every day/everyday, 1–2, 13
evolutionnews.org, 141–42
Examiner.com, 69, 215
exceptionable/exceptional, 214–15

exceptional/unique, 95–96
expect/anticipate, 191–92
expensive price
    as phrase to avoid, 88

*Facts on File Encyclopedia of Word
    and Phrase Origins, The*
    (Hendrickson), 70–71, 120
fall through the cracks/fall
    between the cracks, 55
Farmington Daily Times (NM), 207
farther/further, 45–46
fatally flawed, 200
Fayetteville Observer, 76
feet/foot, 52–53
fewer/less, 40–43
figuratively, literally for, 48
Filkins, Dexter, 79
fill the bill/fit the bill, 120
final decision
    as phrase to avoid, 73
Fine, Edith H., 149–50
Firefox News, 19
first of all, second of all, 69
Fischbach, Bob, 245–46
Fiske, Robert Hartwell, 181
Five Towns Jewish Times, 70
flaunt/flout, 162
Flesch, Rudolf, 85, 91, 157
Florida Times-Union, 87
flounder/founder, 203–4
fluorescent/flourescent, 78
focus in on, 159
Focus News, 97
Fogarty, Mignon, 120, 148,
    210–11, 232
folderol, 82
for a while/for awhile, 28
for all intents and purposes/for all
    intensive purposes, 115–16

for free
    as phrase to avoid, 72
Foreign Policy, 112, 171, 245
ForeignPolicy.com, 215
Fort Worth Star-Telegram, 130,
    250
forte/forté, 205
fortuitous/fortunate, 183
forward/foreword, 36–37
Fowler, H. W., 101, 161, 191, 212,
    221
FOXNews/FOXNews.com, 14,
    82, 103, 166, 203, 229, 247
FOXSports.com, 231
full complement/full
    compliment, 151
fun, as an adjective, 147–48
functional shift, 205

Galanes, Philip, 235
Garner, Bryan A., 167
Garner's Modern American Usage,
    14, 17, 52, 90, 91, 96, 99, 112,
    133, 141, 148, 159, 181, 182,
    189, 194–95, 197, 209, 210,
    216, 227, 234, 241, 242, 244
Garvin, Glenn, 190
Gary Post-Tribune, 201
gasses/gases, 17
Geek.com, 103
general consensus
    as phrase to avoid, 56–57
Georgetown News Democrat (OH),
    14
Gladstone, William, 150
Glasgow Evening Times, 14
Globe and Mail (Canada), 36
Goldsmith, Oliver, 184
Golf Digest, 236
good/well, 104

Google News, 14, 15, 24, 26, 28,
44, 51, 73, 78, 81, 109, 112,
115, 117, 118, 119, 120, 125,
127, 133, 141, 155, 162, 169,
172, 175, 176, 193, 202, 218,
241, 250, 252
Google Web, 30, 65, 78, 81, 109,
115, 162–63
gourmet.com, 66
graduate/graduated from/was
graduated from, 117–18
*Grammar Girl's Quick and Dirty
Tips for Better Writing* (Fogarty),
120, 148, 210–11, 232
Grand Junction Daily Sentinel, 186
Grapes of Wrath, The (Steinbeck),
138
group of and singular verb, 222
grow, 35
guardian.co.uk, 92, 239, 250
Guernsey Press and Star (UK), 207
gut-wrenching, 176
Gutierrez, Israel, 162

hackneyed phrases and worn-out
words, 74–75
had better, 89–90
Hale, Constance, 16
half/half of, 48
Hamlet (Shakespeare), 178
Hammett, Dashiell, 59
Handbook of Good English, The
(Johnson), 62, 233, 234
hang/hunged, 53
hanged/hung, 5
Hannity, Sean, 229
harebrained
misspelling of, 65
hark back/hearken back/harken
back, 184–85

*Harper Dictionary of
Contemporary Usage*, 182
Harper's magazine, 116
Hartford Courant, 18, 29, 36, 76,
123, 153, 173, 185, 230, 249
Harvard Law School News, 124
Hauther, B., 188
have drunk/have drank, 26
have gone/have went, 25–26
have run/have ran, 25–26, 109
having said that, 177–78
heartrending/heartwrenching/
heartrending, 175–76
Hendrickson, Robert, 70–71,
120
Henry VI, Part One
(Shakespeare), 113
herself/her, 107
himself/him, 107
historian, *a* or *an*, 94
historic/historical, 93–94
Hitchens, Christopher, 233
HIV virus, 179–80
hoi polloi, 215–17
Holden, Stephen, 190
homage/an homage/an hommage,
196
home/house, 142–43
home in/hone in, 99
Honey, I Shrunk the Kids (film), 37
Hook, J. N., 181
Hornaday, Ann, 53
hot water heater/water heater,
78–79
Houma Courier (LA), 149
Houston Chronicle, 199, 202
how come/why, 76
Hudson Reporter, 127
Huffington Post, 21, 24, 46, 91,
115, 126, 129, 138, 196, 210

Huntsville Item (TX), 106
hyphens and words beginning
  with *non*, 140–41

I Am Charlotte Simmons (Wolfe), 45
i.e. and *e.g.*, 77–78
Ibrahim, Azeem, 161
Idaho *Spokesman-Review*, 54
if and when, 202
if I would have . . . I would have,
  188–89
if worse comes to worst/if worse
  comes to worse, 194–95
illicit/elicit, 166
imitate/emulate, 144
immigrate/emigrate, 175
imminent/eminent, 121
impact, overuse of, 46–48
Imperial Ambitions (Chomsky), 136
Imperial Masquerade (Lapham),
  201
imply/infer, 21
in advance of/before, 121–22
in behalf of/on behalf of, 204
In Cheap We Trust (Weber), 141
In Defense of Food (Pollan), 58–59,
  59, 129, 161, 219
In Memoriam (Tennyson), 113
in memoriam/in memorium, 97
in my humble opinion
  as phrase to avoid, 62
in order to/in order for, 73
In Plain Sight (Paige), 194
in regards to/with regards to, 66–67
in the first place, 128
in the process of
  as phrase to avoid, 88–89
incidence, 198–99
incidences, misuse of, 198–99
incident, 198–99

incidentally
  misspelling of, 16–17
incidents/incidences, 2, 198–99
included with it, 163
incomparable, 96
incredible, 40
  misuse of, 38–39
incredulous, 40
Independent (UK), 126
Indianapolis Star, 154–55
individual, use of, 91–92
infer/imply, 21
infinitesimal, misuse of, 200–201
influence, 47
Informationweek.com, 18–19
inimitable, 96
inquirer.net, 194
instance, 198–99
instinctive/instinctual, 217–18
insure/assure/ensure, 102–3
intact/in tack, 24–25
International Herald Tribune, 94,
  251
invitation/invite, 64
Irish Times, 191
irregardless, avoid using, 65–66,
  175
is it just me, or, 178–79
islandpacket.com, 213
isria.com, 223
issues/problems, 157–58
it's/its, 16
it's not about "x," it's about "y,"
  211–12

Jackson Clarion-Ledger, 250
Jackson Hole Daily, 199
Jamestown Post Journal, 92
Jewish Advocate, 72
Jewish Daily Forward, 247

jibe with/jive with gibe with,
154–55
Jimenez, Nick, 189
Johannesburg *Times*, 173
Johnson, Edward D., 62, 233
Johnson, Samuel, 201
JoongAng Daily, 224
Josephson, Judith P., 149–50
judgment
misspelling of, 34
Jurist, 232
just recently, 196

Kansas City Star, 56, 178, 245
KECI-YV (MT), 213
Kennedy, Edward M., 106, 230
Kent State Athletic
Communications, 38
Kerry, John, 104–5
Kilpatrick, James J., 155, 180–81,
208, 239
kinship names, how and when to
capitalize, 207–8
KPHO-TV (Phoenix), 84, 209
KRDO-TV (CO), 83
Krugman, Paul, 212
kudos/kudo, 130–31
KWQC-TV (IA), 189

language/verbiage, 49
Lansdale Reporter (PA), 198
Lapham, Lewis, 201
Lapsing Into a Comma (Walsh),
99, 111–12
Las Vegas Business Press, 189
Las Vegas Review-Journal, 142
Latin *per*
avoid with English words, 153
Lau, Angela, 27
lay/lie, 19–20, 109

Lazarus, David, 32
lectern/podium, 182
Lederer, Richard, 164, 186, 225,
242n
less/fewer, 40–43
Let me see/Let's see, 228–29
Lévy, Bernard-Henri, 126
Lexington Herald-Leader, 77
liable/likely, 199–200
Line by Line (Cook), 138, 139
linking verbs, 54–55
literally/figuratively, 48
little, 211
Little Book, The (Edwards), 73–74,
234, 245
loathe/loath, 247–48
long words and phrases
shorter alternatives for, 92
longer, jargony words
shorter alternatives for, 93
loose/lose, 29–30
Los Angles Times, 16, 32, 42, 80,
89, 106, 107, 131, 156, 169,
170, 183, 186, 188, 196, 197,
202, 221, 238, 238–39, 241
blogs, 24
Lynchburg News & Advance
(VA), 174

McCurry, Mike, 44
McDowell News, 124
Madoff, Bernard, 55, 230
major, 163–64
make a decision/decide, 196
make up/comprise, 160
Making Your Case (Scalia/Garner),
167
Maney, Kevin, 210
manner born/manor born, 178
Marin Independent Journal, 115

Maryland *Herald-Mail*, 70
Massachusetts *Republican*, 126
matchless, 96
Mathis, Holiday, 250
maxim, using *old* with, 50–51
may and *can*, 85–86
may/might, 46
Melon Media, 172
memento/momento, 91
Merchant of Venice (Shakespeare),
    125
*Merriam-Webster's Collegiate
    Dictionary*, 66, 200
*Merriam-Webster's Dictionary of
    English Usage*, 113, 117, 190
MetroWest Daily News (MA),
    174
Miami Herald, 162, 190
Mid-South Horse Review, 139
might/may, 46
militate against/mitigate against,
    223
millennium/millenium, 172
Mills College course catalog, 168
Milwaukee Journal, 157
Minneapolis Star Tribune, 128, 213
Minnesota Public Radio, 186
minuscule
    misspelling of, 123–24
minutia/minutiae, 250
Missoulian (MT), 107
misspelled words, 172
MLB.com, 168, 211
Modern English Usage (Fowler),
    161, 191, 221
molest/molestation, 205–7
momentarily, misuse of, 64
mondegreen, 116
monologophobia, 240
Montgomery Advertiser (AL), 108

Moores, John, 106, 187
moot point/mute point, 87–88
more preferable
    as phrase to avoid, 72
More Nitty-Gritty Grammar
    (Fine/Josephson), 149–50
Mormon Times, 108
Mortal Syntax (Casagrande), 59
Morton, Mark, 82
most, use *almost* or *nearly*, 79
Motley Fool: caps.fool.com, 84,
    125, 195, 243
msnbc.com, 14, 193
mumpsimus, 117, 117n
myself, misuse of, 105–7

NanaimoBulletin.com, 55
Nation, 92, 110
    online, 44
National Geographic News, 17
National Law Journal, 114
National Park Service flier, 21
National Public Radio (NPR),
    175
    All Things Considered, 43, 97,
        236
    npr.org, 118, 185, 250, 252
nauseous/nauseated, 159
nearly instead of *most*, 79
necessary, don't qualify, 51
needless to say
    as phrase to avoid, 76
Nehring, Christina, 223
Neil, Dan, 241
neither one, 193–94
neither, misuse of, 123
nemesis, misuse of, 249–50
nerve-racking/nerve-wracking,
    169–70
New Jersey *Post Chronicle*, 26

New Jersey *Star-Ledger*, 38, 90, 91, 161, 249
New Mexico *Daily News*, 123
New Mexico Independent, 70
New Oxford American Dictionary, 22
New York Daily News, 28, 80, 99, 118, 155, 169, 173, 192
New York Post, 69, 80
New Scientist, 196
New York Times, 14, 19, 31, 41, 44, 50, 72, 73, 80, 91, 92, 95, 97, 99, 118, 129, 130, 134, 152, 153, 154, 159, 160, 165, 167, 170, 174, 182, 188, 190, 192, 193, 196, 197, 200, 203, 204, 212, 213–14, 220, 223, 233, 234, 235, 240, 248, 249, 252
New York Times Book Review, 79, 94, 106, 138, 191, 197, 201, 209, 219, 233, 254, 255
New York Times Magazine, 2, 13, 106, 114, 117, 132, 148, 223, 243, 247, 248, 253
New York Times Manual of Style and Usage, 45, 133–34, 152, 173, 216, 221, 226
New Yorker magazine, 68, 226, 251
New Zealand Herald, 16
New Zealand *Waikato Times*, 24
Newsday, 147, 205, 242
NewsOK.com, 44
Newsweek magazine, 71, 254, 255
Nichols, Don, 63
no one/noone, 15
noisome/noisy, 240–41
North Carolina *Daily Dispatch*, 76
Northwest Herald (IL), 221
not only . . . but also, 246–47
Novak, Robert D., 221

number, amount as misuse for, 28–29
number/volume, 160
number, the/number, a/and the verb, 134

O Magazine, 211
O'Conner, Patricia T., 45, 46, 104, 159, 180–81, 200, 219
O'Hagan, Andrew, 201
Obama, Barack, 21, 26, 52, 84, 97, 123, 126, 127, 165, 175–76, 182, 221, 226, 250, 251, 255, 257
objective pronoun
  misused as subject, 22
octopuses/octopi, 119
off/off of, 23
oftentimes
  as word to avoid, 60
old, use of, 50–51
old saying, 50–51
Omaha World-Herald, 245–46
on screen/on-screen/onscreen, 53
on behalf of/in behalf of, 204
one
  use consistently, 124
one in/one out of
  and singular verbs, 224–25
one less/one fewer, 67–68, 68
one of the/one of those, 187–89
one of the few/one of the only, 186
only, 213–14
ophthalmology mispelling of, 214
opinionati, 178n
oral/verbal, 166–67
Orange County Register, 166
orient/orientate, 131
ourself/ourselves, 108

outside of, 82–83
overexaggerate, 96
owing to the fact that, 158
Oxford English Dictionary, 100, 118, 129, 176, 194, 223, 235, 242

Paige, Maria, 194
pair, as a plural, 35
Parade magazine, 52
parameter(s), 125–26
parentheses and periods, 157
Pasadena Star-News, 154
Patterson, Christina, 126
PC World, 163, 223
peerless, 96
Penguin Dictionary of American English Usage and Style, 41
penultimate, 191
periods
  and parentheses, 157
  quotations marks and, 40
persuade/convince, 99–100
peruse, 185
phenomena/phenomenon, 86–87
Philadelphia Daily News, 60, 77, 100
Philadelphia Inquirer, 121, 151, 204
phrases and words
  shorter alternatives for, 92
PIN number, 179–80
Pittsburgh Post-Gazette, 163, 246
pizzeria, 63–64
pleaded/pled, 198
please be advised that
  as phrase to avoid, 23
pleonasm, 28n
plethora, 192–93
podium/lectern, 182
politico.com, 142
Pollan, Michael, 58–59, 59, 129, 161, 219

Pope, Alexander, 251
Popular Science, 220
pore/pour, 101–2
pour/pore, 101–2
Powell, Michael, 252
precaution/precautionary
  measure, 96
precipitous/precipitate, 234–35
preposition
  ending sentence with, 101
presently, 173–74
pretty, 211
preventive/preventative, 110
previous to
  use before instead, 121–22
Princeton Daily Clarion, 236
Princeton Review website, 109
principle/principal, 102
prior to/before, 121–22
problems/issues, 157–58
proceed on
  as phrase to avoid, 83–84
prone/supine, 1, 171–72
pronunciation, mispronunciation, 98
proverb, using *old* with, 50–51
Providence Journal, 166
public as collective noun, 54
Publishers Weekly, 155
Purcell, Tom, 39
purposely/purposefully, 238–39

quaint, 183
question mark and quotation
  marks, 94–95
Quinion, Michael, 65, 125
quotations marks
  commas and periods and, 40
quotations within quotations, 67

rack/wrack, 169–70
Random House Webster's College Dictionary, 88, 122, 142
Rapp, Daniela, 36
rarefied/rarified, 235
rarely ever/rarely if ever, 134–35
rather, 211
RealClearPolitics.com, 32
re-, words beginning with, 168–69
reason . . . is (or was) because, 218–20
reckless/wreckless, 14
recur/reoccur, 139
redundancy, 57–58
redundant *at*, avoid, 84
reek/wreak, 80
reminds me of/reminds one of/reminds of, 121
remuneration/renumeration, 62–63
Renal and Urology News, 199
RenewableEnergyWorld.com, 167
renowned/renown, 55–56
resistentialism, 233n
restaurateur, mispelling of, 109
reticent/reluctant, 174
retronym, 242n
Reuters, 79, 132, 144, 155, 158, 194, 196
Rexburg Standard Journal (ID), 244
Richmond Times-Dispatch, 19, 126
Right, Wrong, and Risky (Davidson), 14, 23, 76, 98–99, 110, 133, 139, 159, 160, 170, 181
Rinella, Heidi Knapp, 189
Rockefeller, Jay, 195
Rocky Mountain Independent, 184
Rolling Stone, 14
Rosen, Jeffrey, 243

ruling/verdict, 239–40
Russo, Richard, 107, 159, 226, 245, 252

Sacramento Bee, 194
sacrilegious/sacreligious, 162–63
safe-deposit box/safety-deposit box, 99
Safire, William, 117, 253
St. Louis Post-Dispatch, 79, 134, 186, 247
St. Petersburg Times, 15, 251
Salamone, Gina, 99
Salt Lake Tribune, 204, 236, 238
San Antonio Current, 71
San Diego *North County Times*, 173
San Diego Reader, 103
San Diego Unified School District website, 147
San Diego Union-Tribune, 1, 13, 27, 31, 40, 41, 50, 68, 82, 106, 121, 150, 153, 160, 163, 167, 168, 185, 187, 194, 201, 207, 220, 226, 227, 236
San Francisco Chronicle, 28, 142, 205, 232, 239, 245
San Francisco Examiner, 166
San Jose Mercury News, 28, 31, 68, 155, 181, 205, 251
same/exactly the same/the exact same, 132–33
Sarasota Herald-Tribune, 229
Saying What You Mean (Claiborne), 117
Scalia, Antonin, 167
Schmemann, Serge, 94
ScienceDaily.com, 220
Scripps Howard News Service, 92
Seattle Post Globe, 130

Seattle Post-Intelligencer, 32, 38, 68, 140, 184, 209
Seattle Times, 59, 194, 221
self-confessed, 154
Selig, Bud, 246
sensuous/sensual, 238
separate out, 141–42
serve/service, 139
Shakespeare, William, 113, 125, 178
shined/shone, 38
should have/should of, 34–35
shown/showed, 49
shrink/shrank/shrunk, 37
shuttle back and forth, 149
Siegel, Robert, 236
Silence, Language, and Society (Fiske), 181
Simple and Direct (Barzun), 33–34
simplistic/simple, 200
Sin and Syntax (Hale), 16
singular, 96
60 Minutes, 227
Sketches by Boz (Dickens), 108
Sleeping Dogs Don't Lay (Lederer/ Dowis), 186, 225
Smith, Ethan, 210
sneaked/snuck, 119
Snyder, Paul, 21
so-called, avoid quotation marks after, 207
Socialist Worker, 86
Softpedia.com, 163
solecism, 1
sometime/some time, 165
South Florida Sun Sentinel, 90, 171
SouthCoastToday.com, 194
Southwest Virginia Today, 86
special/unique, 95–96
specie/species, 154

spell-checkers, 18, 21, 30, 86, 98, 101, 115, 141, 163
Spellr.us, 172
spoonfuls/spoonsful, 51
Springfield *News-Leader* (MO), 174
Stacey, Phil, 155
Stahl, Lesley, 227
stamping grounds/stomping grounds, 118
start, instead of *commence*, 76–77
Staten Island Advance, 102, 193
Stein, Gertrude, 18
Steinbeck, John, 138
Stimpson, George, 65
straitened, 129–30
straitjacket, 129–30
straitlaced, 129–30
StreetInsider.com, 177
suffice it to say/suffice to say, 179
sufficient enough, 197–98
SunHerald.com, 156
superlative adjectives misusing, 51–52
supersede/supercede, 112
supine/prone, 1, 171–72
supposedly/supposably, 108
supremacist/supremist, 115
surround, 81
Surviving the Undergraduate Jungle (Crafts/Hauther), 188
syncope, 17
synonymomania, 240

Tablet Magazine, 201
Tampa Tribune, 71
Tarantino, Quentin, 216–17
tendinitis, 155
Tennyson, Alfred, Lord, 113
thanking you in advance, 43

that big a problem/that big of
   a problem, 23
the, a, an, in a title, 211
theater/theatre, 98–99
TheBostonChannel.com, 162
thehill.com, 76
theirself/theirselves, 108
there/their/they're, 18–19
there's/they are, 19
these kinds/these kind, 103
TheStranger.com, 216
TheStreet.com, 121
they'll/there will, 44
Thin Man, The (Hammett), 59
Things That Make Us [Sic]
   (Brockenbrough), 66
think to yourself, 28
this is to inform you that
   avoiding, 23–24
those kinds/those kind, 103
'Til Death Do Us Part
   (White, Kate), 113
till/'til/'till, 112–13
time immemorial, 97
Time magazine, 73, 177
timeonline.co.uk, 154
tiny hamlet, 126–27
toe the line/tow the line, 70
Toronto Star, 102, 130
torturous/tortuous, 194
toward/towards, 71–72
transpire, 180–81
Trentonian, 204
Triano, Jay, 36
Troy Messenger (Alabama), 87
True Compass (Kennedy), 106
try to/try and, 127–28
Tucson Citizen, 67
Turan, Kenneth, 183
tvguide.com, 242

Twain, Mark, 33, 126, 211, 235,
   254n, 258
Twelve, The (Gladstone), 150
typographical error, 13

unctuous, 231
unequivocably/unequivocally,
   200–201
uninterested/disinterested,
   231–32
unique, misuse of, 95–96
United Press International, 56
University of British Columbia
   science website, 139
unless and until, 151
unparalleled, 96
unrivaled, 96
until/'til/'till, 112–13
until/up till/up until, 113
until and unless, 151
unusual/unique, 95–96
Updike, John, 68
U.S. News & World Report, 32, 73,
   122, 128, 155
USA Today, 59, 122, 127, 185, 224
use/utilize, 168
used to/use to, 243–44
Utne Reader online, 162

vaildaily.com, 36
Vancouver Sun, 223
variety of different, as phrase to
   avoid, 128–29
Variety, 131
verbal/oral, 166–67
verbiage/verbage, 49
verbose phrases
   concise alternatives to, 145–47
verbs, linking, 54–55
verdict/ruling, 239–40

very, 31, 211
Vidal, Gore, 249
vocal cords/vocal chords, 65
volume/number, 160

WALA-TV (AL), 147
Wall Street Journal, 46, 66, 76, 89,
    100, 101, 112, 114, 121–22,
    126, 127, 128, 135–36, 165,
    168, 210, 224, 234, 254
Wallraff, Barbara, 138, 143, 219,
    229
Walsh, Bill, 99, 111–12
Ward, Randy, 187
Waseca County News (MN), 49
Washington City Paper, 22
Washington Independent, 126
Washington Post, 28, 69, 133, 203,
    221, 222, 230, 245, 246
  blog, 158
Washington Times, 36, 84
water heater/hot water heater,
    78–79
Waterloo Record (Canada), 77
way/ways, 98
WCBG-TV (SC), 31
WCTV-TV (FL), 38
WDBO Radio (FL), 142
Weber, Lauren, 141
Webster, Noah, 122
Webster's Dictionary, citing, 122
*Webster's New International
    Dictionary*, 2nd ed., 53, 63,
    231
*Webster's New World College
    Dictionary*, 128, 130, 242
well
  "cutesy," to be avoided, 210–11
well/good, 104
Welsh rabbit/Welsh rarebit, 82

West Virginia MetroNews, 225
WGCL-TV (Atlanta), 230
what it is, is, 189–91
when and if, 202
whence/from whence, 70
whether/as to whether, 118
while/whilst, 90
White, E. B., 130, 210
White, Kate, 113
who
  referring to a thing, 236–37
  and *that*, 254n
  and *whom*, 253–55
whose/who's, 27
WHSV-TV (VA), 46
why/how come, 76
WikiAnswers.com, 153, 165
Winchester, Simon, 101
Winnipeg Free Press, 231
Winston-Salem Journal, 194
with each other/with one
    another, 114
without further ado/without
    further adieu, 156
WLS-TV (Chicago), 144, 204
WLTX-TV (Columbia, SC), 86
Woe Is I (O'Conner), 45, 46, 104,
    159, 180–81, 200, 219
Wolfe, Tom, 45
Woonsocket Call (RI), 245
Wooten, Jim, 55–56
Worcester Telegram, 170
Word Court (Wallraff), 138, 143,
    219, 229
Word or Two Before You Go, A
    (Barzun), 228
wording/verbiage, 49
words
  long words and phrases, shorter
      alternatives for, 92

longer, jargony words, shorter alternatives for, 93
worldwidewords.org, 125
worn-out words and hackneyed phrases, 74–75
Wortham, Jenna, 154
would have liked to have, 248–49
would have/would of, 34–35
wrack/rack, 169–70
wreak/reek, 80
wreaked havoc/wrought havoc/ wrecked havoc, 80–81
wreckless/reckless, 14
Wright, Sylvia, 116

Writer's Art, The (Kilpatrick), 180–81, 239
WRTV (IN), 148
WSMV-TV (TN), 54
WTVY-TV (AL), 186
WVNS-TV (WV), 14

Yale Alumni Magazine, 134
Yeats, W. B., 181
Yeshiva World News, 213
your/you're, 17–18
yourself/you, 107

Zolecki, Todd, 211